On Becoming a Psychologist

On Becoming a Psychologist explores the professional identity construction of psychology students, examining their entry into the psychology profession from a socio-cultural perspective.

The book brings together socio-cultural approaches and Dialogical Self Theory to gain a comprehensive insight into the developmental processes behind the formation of professional identity. It conceptualises the process of becoming a psychologist as an intrapersonally and interpersonally unique semiotic process of self-regulation that unfolds through dialogical relations with the individual's socio-cultural surroundings. Building on empirical research, the book outlines the results of a longitudinal study of a cohort of psychology students throughout their studies and following their graduation. The study sheds light on how professional role expectations are negotiated between the different aspects of the self, with a particular focus on how the self is positioned throughout the course of professional education.

Offering a unique perspective on the socio-cultural construction of professional identity, this book will be of great interest to scholars, researchers and graduate students in the fields of cultural psychology, applied psychology and social psychology.

Katrin Kullasepp is Associate Professor of General Psychology at Tallinn University, Estonia.

Cultural Dynamics of Social Representation
Series Editor: Jaan Valsiner
Centre of Cultural Psychology, Aalborg University, Denmark

The series is dedicated to bringing the scholarly reader new ways of representing human lives in the contemporary social sciences. It is a part of a new direction—cultural psychology—that has emerged at the intersection of developmental, dynamic, and social psychologies, anthropology, education, and sociology. It aims to provide cutting-edge examinations of global social processes, which for every country are becoming increasingly multi-cultural; the world is becoming one "global village," with the corresponding need to know how different parts of that "village" function. Therefore, social sciences need new ways of considering how to study human lives in their globalizing contexts. The focus of this series is the social representation of people, communities, and—last but not the least—the social sciences themselves.

Books in this series

Educational Dilemmas
A Cultural Psychological Perspective
Luca Tateo

Experiences and Explanations of ADHD
An Ethnography of Adults Living with a diagnosis
Mikka Nielsen

Semiotic Construction of the Self in Multicultural Societies
A Theory of Proculturation
Vladimer Lado Gamsakhurdia

History, Trauma and Shame
Engaging the Past through Second Generation Dialogue
Edited by Pumla Gobodo-Madikizela

On Becoming a Psychologist
Katrin Kullasepp

For more information about this series, please visit: www.routledge.com/Cultural-Dynamics-of-Social-Representation/book-series/CULTDYNAMIC

On Becoming a Psychologist

Emerging identity in education

Katrin Kullasepp

LONDON AND NEW YORK

First published 2023
by Routledge
4 Park Square, Milton Park, Abingdon, Oxon OX14 4RN

and by Routledge
605 Third Avenue, New York, NY 10158

Routledge is an imprint of the Taylor & Francis Group, an informa business

© 2022 Katrin Kullasepp

The right of Katrin Kullasepp to be identified as author of this work has been asserted in accordance with sections 77 and 78 of the Copyright, Designs and Patents Act 1988.

All rights reserved. No part of this book may be reprinted or reproduced or utilised in any form or by any electronic, mechanical, or other means, now known or hereafter invented, including photocopying and recording, or in any information storage or retrieval system, without permission in writing from the publishers.

Trademark notice: Product or corporate names may be trademarks or registered trademarks, and are used only for identification and explanation without intent to infringe.

British Library Cataloguing-in-Publication Data
A catalogue record for this book is available from the British Library

Library of Congress Cataloguing-in-Publication Data
A catalog record has been requested for this book

ISBN: 978-1-138-69819-2 (hbk)
ISBN: 978-1-032-31324-5 (pbk)
ISBN: 978-1-315-51961-6 (ebk)

DOI: 10.4324/9781315519616

Typeset in Times New Roman
by MPS Limited, Dehradun

Contents

List of Figures xi
List of Tables xiv
Series Editor Preface xv
Acknowledgements xix

PART I
Persons into professions—A unique path into a professional role 1

1 Introduction: Becoming a psychologist—What does that mean? 3
   Outline of the book 3
      The book consists of four parts and a total of seven chapters 3
   What this book is and is not about 5
   Who is a psychologist? 5
   Why explore prospective psychologists' experiences in a bachelor's program? 7
   Why professional identity? 8
   Summary 10

2 Theoretical framework: A socio-cultural approach to professional identity construction 14
   Professional identity through the lens of cultural psychology 14
   Turning socio-cultural meanings into personal meanings: Personal culture in the making 16
   Professional identity as a semiotic process, or "All you need is a sign 18

*Pleromatic and schematic sides of one identity: "Hidden"
    richness and simplifications in processes of identity 19*
*The construction of professional identity: Regulating the
    intra-psychological disaccord and accord 20*
The dialogical self 22
Multiplicity within the self 22
Microgenetic dynamics of ontogenetic trajectories 24
*The regulation of different sub-systems of the self: The
    ontogenetic path under construction 25*
*Non-linear transition: I am a psychologist <> I am not a
    psychologist 26*
Summary 27

**3 Introduction to the methodology of the study: Grasping the
    multilinear and unique developmental process over time**   31
A multiple-case study research strategy 32
*Abductive inference: The generalization of knowledge in
    cultural psychology 32*
Historically Structured Sampling (HSS) 32
Participants 33
Longitudinal research design 34
*Methods: Interviews, questionnaires, essays, and theme
    completion method (DDTC; Double Direction Theme
    Completion) 34*
Interviews and questionnaires 35
Essays 36
Rating scales 36
Double Direction Theme Completion (DDTC) method 37
Two kinds of data from DDTC 39
The coding scheme 40
*The professional perspective (I-position I as a
    psychologist) 40*
The personal approach (I-position I as a person) 40
The fluctuation of perspectives 40
The orientation of tension in solutions across the years 42
Description of the profiles of handling tension 42
Summary 43

Conclusion to Part I   45

PART II
A psychologist as a sign 47

4 Psychologists emerge everywhere: The academic and non-academic voices in the focus 49
From the heterogeneity of microsystems to the multiplicity in the self 49
Non-academic arenas in becoming a psychologist 50
Academic others in the inner dialogue 52
Border under negotiation: psychologists <> non-psychologist 53
Unfolding bordering across years 53
Respondent Snap's transition during studies of psychology 54
Extracts from the interviews with Snap 54
Respondent Hei's transition in the academic and non-academic contexts 55
Respondent Uur's becoming a psychologist through various developmental contexts 57
Summary 59

5 A sign of a psychologist as an organizer 61
"I am different now" 61
Re-negotiation borders between what IS and what SHOULD be 63
Summary 65

Conclusion to Part II 66

PART III
Becoming a psychologist: The multiple life trajectories 69

6 Thirteen pathways to entering the professional role 71
Introduction 71
  Thirteen unique trajectories of becoming a psychologist 72
  The trajectories of coordinating different sub-systems in the self and regulation of tension 72
Self-professionalizing cases 74

Respondent 6a—Vik 74
Solutions to the items from DDTC 75
Summary of case Vik 80
Respondent 6b—Snap 84
Solutions to the items from DDTC 84
Summary of case Snap 90
Respondent 6c—Uur 93
Solutions to items from DDTC 93
Summary of case Uur 98
Respondent 6d—Mes 101
Solutions to the items from DDTC 102
Summary of case Mes 107
Respondent 6e—Hei 110
Solutions to the items from DDTC 111
Summary of case Hei 115
Respondent 6f—Ris 119
Solutions to the items from DDTC 119
Summary of case Ris 124
Respondent 6g—Aet 128
Solutions to the items from DDTC 129
Summary of case Aet 134
Self-personalizing cases 137
Respondent 6h—Gar 137
Solutions to the items from DDTC 137
Summary of case Gar 144
Respondent 6i—Par 147
Solutions to the items from DDTC 148
Summary of case Par 153
Self-maintaining cases 156
Respondent 6j—Ele 156
Solutions to the items from DDTC 156
Summary of case Ele 161
Respondent 6k—Pai 164
Solutions to the items from DDTC 164
Summary of case Pai 169
Respondent 6l—Ain 172
Solutions to the items from DDTC 173
Summary of case Ain 179

Respondent 6m—Eri 182
Solutions to the items from DDTC 182
Summary of case Eri 188
Summary of the general findings 190
    The various reasons behind the emergence of professional trajectory 190
    The main generic developmental directions 192
    Dynamics in applying different approaches to the dilemmas 192
    Utilization of a professional approach in solutions to professional dilemmas 193
    Solutions to dilemmas according to the approach 195
        Specific dilemmas and the application of I-positions 195
    Dynamics in the use of the I-positions in solutions to dilemmas 195
    Handling tensions: Regulating affective relations with the professional role 195
    The dynamics of tension in the specific dilemmas 195
    Regulation of tension among the thirteen cases 196
    Conclusion 197

Conclusion to Part III   199

PART IV
General Implications: Basic principles of the socio-cultural construction of professional identity   201

7   **The construction of professional identity through the lens of cultural psychology**   203
    The general principles of assuming a professional role 204
        Unique non-linear trajectories of entry into the role 204
    Regulation of the discrepancy: Moving toward "what should be" 204
    Role-centered and person-centered ways of being a psychologist 205
    Others in the self 206

Navigating a plurality of meanings 207

Concluding thoughts: The future in construction   209

Appendix   212
Index   213

Figures

2.1	The laminal model of internalization/externalization	17
2.2	Pleromatization and schematization (Modified from Valsiner, 2017, p. 183)	18
2.3	Pleromatization and schematization of professional identity	20
3.1	The timeline for the longitudinal contact points over the study period	34
3.2	The structure of DDTC Space	38
3.3	A generic example of ambivalence profiles	39
6.1	Temporary profiles of coordination of perspectives (i.e., professional, personal, 3rd position) and handling tension (i.e., positive and negative affectivity, neutral) in solutions to nine (9) dilemmas	81
6.2	Trajectories of coordination of different sub-systems (i.e., professional, personal) in the self across the years	82
6.3	Temporary profiles of coordination of perspectives (i.e., professional, personal, 3rd position) and handling tension (i.e., positive and negative affectivity, neutral) in solutions to nine (9) dilemmas	90
6.4	Trajectories of coordination of different sub-systems (i.e., professional, personal) in the self across the years	91
6.5	Temporary profiles of coordination of perspectives (i.e., professional, personal, 3rd position) and handling tension (i.e., positive and negative affectivity, neutral) in solutions to nine (9) dilemmas	99
6.6	Trajectories of coordination of different sub-systems (i.e., professional, personal) in the self across the years	100
6.7	Temporary profiles of coordination of perspectives (i.e., professional, personal, 3rd position) and handling tension (i.e., positive and negative affectivity, neutral) in solutions to nine (9) dilemmas	107

6.8	Trajectories of coordination of different sub-systems (i.e., professional, personal) in the self across the years	108
6.9	Temporary profiles of coordination of perspectives (i.e., professional, personal, 3rd position) and handling tension (i.e., positive and negative affectivity, neutral) in solutions to nine (9) dilemmas	116
6.10	Trajectories of coordination of different sub-systems (i.e., professional, personal) in the self across the years	117
6.11	Temporary profiles of coordination of perspectives (i.e., professional, personal, 3rd position) and handling tension (i.e., positive and negative affectivity, neutral) in solutions to nine (9) dilemmas	125
6.12	Trajectories of coordination of different sub-systems (i.e., professional, personal) in the self across the years	126
6.13	Temporary profiles of coordination of perspectives (i.e., professional, personal, 3rd position) and handling tension (i.e., positive and negative affectivity, neutral) in solutions to nine (9) dilemmas	135
6.14	Trajectories of coordination of different sub-systems (i.e., professional, personal) in the self across the years	136
6.15	Temporary profiles of coordination of perspectives (i.e., professional, personal, 3rd position) and handling tension (i.e., positive and negative affectivity, neutral) in solutions to nine (9) dilemmas	144
6.16	Trajectories of coordination of different sub-systems (i.e., professional, personal) in the self across the years	145
6.17	Temporary profiles of coordination of perspectives (i.e., professional, personal, 3rd position) and handling tension (i.e., positive and negative affectivity, neutral) in solutions to nine (9) dilemmas	153
6.18	Trajectories of coordination of different sub-systems (i.e., professional, personal) in the self across the years	154
6.19	Temporary profiles of coordination of perspectives (i.e., professional, personal, 3rd position) and handling tension (i.e., positive and negative affectivity, neutral) in solutions to nine (9) dilemmas	162
6.20	Trajectories of coordination of different sub-systems (i.e., professional, personal) in the self across the years	163
6.21	Temporary profiles of coordination of perspectives (i.e., professional, personal, 3rd position) and handling tension (i.e., positive and negative affectivity, neutral) in solutions to nine (9) dilemmas	169
6.22	Trajectories of coordination of different sub-systems (i.e., professional, personal) in the self across the years	170

6.23	Temporary profiles of coordination of perspectives (i.e., professional, personal, 3rd position) and handling tension (i.e., positive and negative affectivity, neutral) in solutions to nine (9) dilemmas	179
6.24	Trajectories of coordination of different sub-systems (i.e., professional, personal) in the self across the years	180
6.25	Temporary profiles of coordination of perspectives (i.e., professional, personal, 3rd position) and handling tension (i.e., positive and negative affectivity, neutral) in solutions to nine (9) dilemmas	188
6.26	Trajectories of coordination of different sub-systems (i.e., professional, personal) in the self across the years	189

Tables

6.1 The application of I-positions in solutions to dilemmas from DDTC   194
6.2 The regulation of tension in solutions to dilemmas across the years   196
6.3 Regulation of tension among the thirteen cases across the years   197

Series Editor Preface

The Secret Charms of Becoming (and Being) a Psychologist

Becoming any kind of *a professional* is an act of personal adjustment to the social roles that are demarcated by the social representations that make the given profession legitimate in a society. Some are set up formally—for example the representations that define the professions of lawyer, nurse, medical doctor, or teacher are mapped onto the educational institutions that provide certificates of role competence at the end of study courses. Others are informal—professional pickpockets, street musicians, prostitutes, healers, computer hackers, and many others do not have to study to gain their professional credentials, but obtain these in the practice of their astonishing work. Social representations guide the public understanding of what they are doing and what their professionalism is like. It is not surprising that Serge Moscovici's idea for developing the first (and still the basic) theory of social representation was based on the phenomena of the French society's appropriation of the professional knowhow and practices of psychoanalysis (Moscovici, 1961).

The profession of psychology is within the liminal region between formalized educational frameworks that allow the professional role to emerge, and the informal ways of understanding the human *psyche* that cannot be taught formally but may emerge by experience. Young students entering into university-level training to become psychologists are often confronted with the realization that what they are taught may fit white rats or sophisticated computers but not fellow living human beings. Those social representations that carve out the role of a psychologist in the popular vernacular involve the notions of *help* ("psychologists want to help other people"), *science* ("psychologists help others based on science"), and *clairvoyance* ("psychologists have the capacity of direct mindreading"). Such combination of social representations present in the public domain set up ambivalences and anxieties in the lives of young students who slowly move along their life courses to become psychologists. I have asked my students in all places over the world whether their friends from school times have expressed fears that the newly started psychology students would "see them through" and the answer has been "yes!." Attribution of such extraordinary clairvoyance capabilities to beginning students of psychology makes their lives as emerging psychologists deeply ambivalent. They know they cannot read the mind of anybody—even their own. And they soon find out that their teachers are no better. Students learn what textbooks state are the core of "psychological science" but may find it shallow when needed to make sense of deep psychological issues of life, love, death, and dealing with tax collectors. Yet they do not give up and end up appropriating some version of *being a psychologist* to their personal life credos of living a life they find worthwhile.

The present book—the result of its author's worries and personal struggles for over a decade—is the first systematic investigation into the *process of becoming* a psychologist. It diligently traces the emergence of the professional frame of being in the lives of Estonian psychology students longitudinally—a rare treat in the world of psychology where developmental perspectives are rare and funding for multi-year follow-up of development scarce. Done with great diligence—and without funding—the work reported in this book is a result of deeply personally motivated journey into the realities of students' lives within the higher education systems of today. All over the world such systems are under the attack of institutional interests of administrative control paired with selective privatization of potential knowledge making (Valsiner, Lutsenko & Antoniouk, 2018). The result is mechanization and bureaucratization of the education processes under the currently popular neoliberal slogans of "cost effectiveness" and social utility of the attained knowledge.

University students in our contemporary higher education systems are expected to become knowledgeable consumers of the existing knowledge and its promoters in the society—rather than artisans who build up new knowledge. Yet in the middle of such social processes of making consumers are the young students who—in their youthful enthusiasm—want to create something new in the field of their studies. The detailed analyses of the meaning-making processes of psychology students analysed in this book show where—and how—innovations can come into being in the given field. Importantly that would not be possible in the lecture halls where professors deliver the curriculum that ministries of education require and textbooks support. Instead, innovation becomes possible when the young person—on one's way towards becoming a "professional"—invents new ways of making sense of seemingly well-known phenomena. A young man of 24—violating the instructions of his famous advisors to adapt British IQ tests to schoolchildren in a Paris suburb—brings into the study of children's psychological phenomena the experiences he had in his childhood while collecting and classifying mollusks of the Neuchatel lake. He turned the method—"IQ test"—around and made a profile of qualitative cognitive proves out of it. As a result of such non-professional act of "leaving science behind" in favour of the phenomena he laid the foundation for a powerful science of Genetic Epistemology and became the innovator of developmental psychology over the 20th century. That young rascal was Jean Piaget whose grey-haired and pipe-holding images of his later being as a famous psychologist can be seen in many textbooks. What we no not see are the images of the young man who changed the field.

In the present book, there is a major methodological innovation to psychology that is here described systematically for the first time. This is the extension of a traditional and well-known method of "sentence completion test" into a method that in principle allows the researcher to make explicit the dialogical underpinnings of the phenomena and could—if developed further—be the root for building a dialectical method that observes the processes of psychological synthesis. This is the DDTC (Double Direction Theme Completion) technique—colloquially becoming known as the "Double Blanks Method." The simplicity of the method is astounding—instead of letting a respondent to fill in an open slot for just one answer ("When somebody says X to me I feel _____") which would then be viewed as the answer, the DDTC method adds a dialogically oriented second blank to the sentence. So we get:

"When somebody says X to me I feel _____
but _____ **"**

This very simple addition has deep roots in the theoretical and metatheoretical framework of the Methodology Cycle (Branco & Valsiner, 1997). What is being revealed here is not an attempt by a respondent to give a "true answer" (which can never be verified), but to explicate a process of a dialogue within the person who reports such an experience. The "but" (or its alternatives: "because," "and," "yet," "still" etc) guides the respondent towards creating a contradiction about one's relationship with X. So, we may encounter subjective tensions when we feel somebody giving us an evaluative comment (*"you are a beautiful woman"*→ *"I feel this is **deeply sexist but** respond 'thank you'"* versus *"I feel good but I wonder why he says that"*?)

As a method, the DDTC violates the basic norm—repeated endlessly in psychology's methods textbooks—**never ask leading questions!** The whole idea is based on the basic alternative assumptions that all questions produce a directed context—thus a lead—and the best our methods can do is to make use of these leads. The introduction of the second "blank" carries an explicit direction, hoping to trigger in the respondent the construction of an opposition. In abstract terms this can be expressed:

X→←

This structure (X leading in one direction, "but" leading to a different, possibly opposite, direction) is the minimal starting point for detecting a dialogical tension in the constructive mind of the respondent. It is an example of absolutely minimal Gestalt unit of data that can be—and needs to be—analysed as a single instant with possibilities for generalization. I have recently called for the establishing of *nanopsychology* (Valsiner, 2018)—where, in contrast with the mechanical belief in the "big data"—generalizations are possible from minimal data structures. The DDTC method is a way towards establishing such structures. It presumes that the human affective world operates with opposites that can be triggered by appropriate methods. The use of the Dialogical Self Theory starting from the work of Hubert Hermans is not coincidental in this book. It follows from the general logic of the Methodology Cycle. Similarly the use of the Trajectory Equifinality Approach (Sato, Mori & Valsiner, 2016) is a methodological framework that is crucial for understanding the development of professional identity in human life course.

Taken together, the work presented in this book is systematically focusing on the processes of emergence—both microgenetic and ontogenetic—of professional identities. Each person builds one's uniquely personal version of professional identity on the basis of subjective relating with one's profession. The reader here finds many examples that can lead to further development of process-focused methodology. In this potential, the present book is a basic contribution to the field of the social sciences where the tension between interest in basic processes and existing methods based on the study of outcomes prevails. Overcoming of such tension is simple—develop process-focused methods for process-interested theories. This is done in this book as it leads the field to new directions.

Jaan Valsiner
Aalborg, December 2ß18

References

Branco, A. U., & Valsiner, J. (1997). Changing methodologies: A co-constructivist study of goal orientations in social interactions. *Psychology and Developing Societies, 9*(1), 35–64.

Moscovici, S. (1961). *La psychanalyse: Son image et son public.* Paris: PUF

Sato, T., Mori, N., & Valsiner, J. (Eds.) (2016). *Making of the Future: The Trajectory Equifinality Approach in Cultural Psychology.* Charlotte, NC: Information Age Publishers

Valsiner, J. (2018). Needed in psychology: Theoretical precision. *Europe's Journal of Psychology, 14*(1), 1–6. 10.5964/ejop.v14i1.602

Valsiner, J., Lutsenko, A., & Antoniouk, A. (Eds.) (2018). *Sustainable Futures for Higher Education: The Making of Knowledge Makers.* Cham, CH: Springer.

Acknowledgements

As the central principle of this book states, becoming is the result of interactions, and the completion of this book has been a joint project in many senses. Although I am its sole author, it reflects ideas elaborated in conversations with my colleagues and the friends I have met during this academic endeavor. My ideas and thoughts have evolved through their involvement, for which I am very grateful. I have had the opportunity to get to know many inspiring people, the real treasure in life, who have encouraged me to pursue my goals. Not only their support but also their commitment to what matters to them in their lives has energized my own efforts to achieve what matters to me. I would like to express my sincere appreciation to all of them.

I am deeply indebted to Jaan Valsiner, who has been my mentor since the beginning of my academic journey. Although it has not been easy to keep up with his deep theoretical perspective in conversations, I am glad for the opportunity to find myself constantly in the "zone of proximal development" in these discussions, which has provided a place for negotiating my own development and professional identity.

I owe big thanks to Sergio Salvatore and Tatsuya Sato for their hospitality during my visits to the University of Salento (Italy) and Ritsumeikan University (Japan), respectively. Their scholarly ideas influenced the frame of reference I applied when attempting to capture the complexity of developing phenomena, and they graciously involved me in cooperation with their colleagues. International cooperation has brought me into contact with creative and intellectually stimulating colleagues and opportunities to participate in joint projects with them. I also owe thanks to Giuseppina Marsico, Luca Tateo, and Alicia Español for discussions that have helped to further elaborate my ideas and "re-negotiate the borders."

For making the exchange of ideas in the international community available to me, I am grateful to Angela Branco, Monica Roncancio Moreno, Sandra Liliana Londoño Calero, Mauricio José Cortés Rodríguez, and Tania Zittoun, and to the intellectual atmosphere at the University of Brasilia, at the Pontificia Universidad Javeriana, at Universidad Pontificia Bolivariana, and at the University of Neuchâtel. Back at home, my appreciation goes to my colleagues from Tallinn University for their support. Special thanks go to Äli Leijen and Aivi Toompalu for encouragement and collaboration. I also had the great pleasure of exchanging ideas with Mariann Märtsin and Stefan Cristian Ionescu during my stay at Clark University, and I am very grateful for their continued support in my academic journey.

I had the privilege to discuss the topic of this book at multiple conferences and with the involvement of academics in the international network of Kitchen Seminars. In relation to this, I would like to thank the staff of the Niels Bohr Center at Aalborg University and Clark University.

This project could not have happened without the generous help of the psychology students who found time to be interviewed and fill out questionnaires during the three years of their studies. I would like to express my sincere gratitude to all of them. Special thanks go to the Archimedes Foundation and Tallinn University for financing my international exchange and teaching mobility. I am also grateful to my friends, who were incredibly patient while I composed this book.

Finally, writing this book, as well as my entire academic journey so far, has been not a solo project—the encouragement of my family and their faith in me has been invaluable in enabling me to navigate both its challenges and possibilities.

Part I

Persons into professions—A unique path into a professional role

Chapter 1

Introduction: Becoming a psychologist—What does that mean?

Existence is about becoming. Not only do we ourselves change, but so do our relations with others and the world. This inherent feature of our existence incorporates processes of emergence, and it inspires intellectual debates and provides intriguing challenges in comprehending the whole complexity of the phenomenon of becoming. It is far from being an underdeveloped topic in scientific debates, and interest in it has a long history. This book continues the line of discussions around the topic and provides a glimpse into the socio-cultural process of becoming a psychologist, which is conceptualized in this book as the construction of a professional identity.

According to the postmodern perspective, a person is a hybrid being with many identities that are fluid across time and contexts. Without losing the feeling of sameness over time, our self-perception changes as we interact with different people, transition from one social setting to another, or assume social roles. We can also decide whom we will become—police officers, photographers, teachers, or politicians, or we can hope to flourish as artists or choose eccentric lifestyles. Yet, for various reasons, some human beings prefer to become psychologists, which is one of the numerous ways of being based on the different occupational options available in the modern world. By making the decision to become a psychologist, one faces a task, metaphorically speaking, to find a space for one more identity—the professional identity of a psychologist—among many others. Using the example of psychology students' experiences during the period of their bachelor's studies, a time of systematic educational-institutional intervention in students' development to prepare them for their (professional) future, this book explores how the process of "making a place" for one more identity occurs.

Outline of the book

The book consists of four parts and a total of seven chapters

In Part 1, the discussion begins with an introduction to the conceptual framework of the book. Chapter 1 addresses the concept of professional

DOI: 10.4324/9781315519616-2

identity and deals with becoming a psychologist as a guided process that takes place in environments of heterogeneous representations. The formation of a professional path is linked with the academic-institutional and non-academic development settings. Chapter 2 focuses on the theoretical model of becoming a psychologist. It introduces the concepts of the dialogical self (developed by Hubert Hermans), the laminal model of constructive processes of internalization and externalization (set forth by Jaan Valsiner), hierarchies of signs, and pleromatic and schematic identity.

The process of becoming a psychologist is conceptualized in terms of cultural psychology as an intrapersonally and interpersonally unique semiotic process of self-regulation that unfolds through dialogical relations with the individual's socio-cultural surroundings. To examine this process, a longitudinal study was conducted; its methodology is introduced in Chapter 3. The sample in this study consists of a cohort of psychology students who participated in questionnaires, interviews, and essay-writing and were surveyed periodically through three years of undergraduate studies (a three-year bachelor's degree program) and answered follow-up questions after graduation.

Part 2 is divided into two chapters (4 and 5) in which the emergence of the I-position I as a psychologist is discussed. This exploration of the development of professional identity draws from the findings of the empirical study of psychology students. Based on these results, Part 2 posits that assuming the professional role of a psychologist manifests through an inclination to construe the surrounding world and one's self-understanding in concordance with social and personal representations of psychologists and the individual's knowledge about the field of psychology. The central argument in Chapter 4 holds that social encounters in various systems (as defined by Urie Bronfenbrenner) shape the I-position I as a psychologist. The social others' counterparts in the self—I-positions like "my fellow students," "my family member," "a media figure"—are involved in the negotiation of professional identity. Chapter 5 further analyzes how their image of psychologists organizes the experiences of professionals-to-be as they internalize the professional role.

While Part 2 shows how students make sense of the dynamics in non-professional settings, the focus in Part 3 is on imagined professional settings. Specifically, this part investigates the assumption of a professional role when solving professional role-related dilemmas (i.e., in imagined professional conditions). Part 3 focuses on the coordination of different sub-systems of the self, personal, and professional, and the regulation of tension that the ambivalent condition—PERSON in a ROLE—elicits. Drawing on findings from the underlying longitudinal study, this part introduces three general directions of internalization of a professional role (i.e., self-professionalizing, self-personalizing, and self-maintaining) and dynamics regarding how students handle tension throughout three years of studies in a bachelor's program.

The concluding Part 4 addresses the main principles of the socio-cultural construction of professional identity and introduces some of the general implications of the findings in educational context. Based on the ideas presented in this book, this part introduces the internalization of expectations for the professional role as a non-linear and context-sensitive process that does not have a shortcut. When socializing through the professional role, this ontogenetic trajectory can take various directions that indicate role-centered and person-centered ways of being a professional.

What this book is and is not about

Before moving on, I will briefly address some questions to put the process of becoming a psychologist into a larger context: why take an interest in psychologists, why examine the period of bachelor-level studies, and why focus on professional identity?

Who is a psychologist?

The question "Who is a psychologist?" is highly relevant in this book because the process of becoming a psychologist is inseparable from how the term "psychologist" is understood. To reflect briefly on the issue, I will draw on approaches, possibly the most common ones, that allow a smooth introduction into the specific perspective on becoming a psychologist that is used in this book.

The image of the psychologist that we know today is a quite recent product of cultural dynamics that have led to the emergence of an institutionally established, regulated, and maintained professional role that addresses the specific needs or requests from society. The psychologist's role began to be formalized in the field of psychology in coordination with discoveries and developments in other disciplines like physiology, philosophy, and medicine before the foundation of the experimental discipline in 1879 when the laboratory for experimental psychology was established in Leipzig by Wilhelm Wundt.

From the 19th century onwards, different schools of thought and traditions in psychology have provided knowledge about human nature. Their influences reflect the hybrid nature of contemporary psychology that has emerged over time and that now includes different branches like clinical, cognitive, experimental, educational, and industrial-organizational psychology, to name a few. Obviously, this list is incomplete, and creating such a list is not the purpose of this book. Nevertheless, it implies that the generic label "psychologist" embraces specialists and experts from a wide range of areas in psychology who provide different services and who have somewhat different profiles of professional competencies.

Still, who is a psychologist? Perhaps the most common explanation we can all agree on is that a psychologist is member of a profession that requires specific competencies, professional knowledge, and skills (Dall'Alba & Sandberg, 2006). Based on the sociological approach, professions can be defined as "privileged, autonomous occupational groups; they have gained control of specific, socially relevant sections of work. A profession can define professional education and controls the entry to a market" (Mieg, 2008, p. 42).

When building on the conceptualization of a psychologist using social role theory, one may introduce a psychologist more specifically by drawing on professional role expectations for the functions of a psychologist in a society and on the required preconditions of work in the profession (e.g., professional knowledge and skills). To define the functions, one might turn, for instance, to the American Psychological Association (2021), which says that "Psychologists examine the relationships between brain function and behavior, and the environment and behavior, applying what they learn to illuminate our understanding and improve the world around us." In addition, psychologists "conduct basic and applied research, serve as consultants to communities and organizations, diagnose and treat people, and teach future psychologists and those who will pursue other disciplines" (American Psychological Association, 2021). The Australian Psychological Society (2021) explains further, "Broadly speaking, most psychologists provide assessment and therapy to clients, help facilitate organizational or social change, conduct psychological research, or administer psychological tests to individuals or groups."

As to pre-conditions for psychologists' work, professional competencies and personal traits enable one to define a psychologist. For instance, in the professional standard for psychologist-counselors used in Estonia (Eesti Psühholoogide Liit, 2021) in addition to professional skills and knowledge, professional requirements also include personal characteristics and abilities necessary for working in the occupation. For instance, tolerance, empathy, reliability, and creativity are considered to be characteristics that support the achievement of professional goals.

Thus, a detailed answer to the question "Who is a psychologist?" can be found by familiarizing ourselves with different institutional requirements that, for example, structure the preparation of psychologists for professional activities, such as curricula or formal standards describing professional competencies. Irrespective of the sub-field in which specialization takes place (e.g., clinical psychology, school psychology), criteria have been determined that are used to confirm a person's suitability for a professional role in the field of psychology.

However, academic-institutional definitions co-exist with everyday knowledge about psychologists. There are various understandings of who a psychologist is—everyone knows something about psychologists. For one person, they are shrinks working at mental hospitals, another presumes that they are different from "ordinary" people, and a third finds them interesting, yet dangerous, due to their tendency to observe and diagnose people.

To summarize, answers to the question "Who is a psychologist?" cover a wide range of observations, including common-sense understandings and academic-institutional representations of psychologists, that together set up the societal framework for becoming a psychologist and all that needs to be considered to comprehend the process of becoming a psychologist. All these images of psychologists constitute a heterogeneous environment that students are exposed to and that they may contest or accept, negotiate, and renegotiate.

Why explore prospective psychologists' experiences in a bachelor's program?

Why not? Globalizing, digitalizing, performing tasks faster—our increasingly complex, fragmented, and heterogenous world challenges societies and individuals trying to adjust to new conditions, including those in the professional scope of psychologists. Macro-scale tensions at the societal level, issues in interpersonal relations addressing the mental health in modern societies call for the involvement of experts on human issues. Psychologists are qualified to contribute to the functioning of societies at different levels and provide services that meet their needs. How they prepare for their professional future is a relevant research question.

In general, studies in a university and the internalization of a professional role take place during a period of in-betweenness, a socio-culturally established zone of liminality for psychological transition to a new social (professional) position. Thus, university studies make space for becoming through an institutionally established frame of regulations that challenges individuals in their life worlds.

In the university context, the period of undergraduate (bachelor's) studies is a prelude to professional life, and it is decisive in terms of pursuing a career of any specialization requiring university education, including that of a psychologist. In the beginning of their studies the student's prior knowledge of the field of psychology is limited, and broad and systematic exposure to professional knowledge is about to occur. As found by Cant and Higgs (1999), students' experiences in the formal academic-educational structure lead to changes in their preconception of the profession. What it "really means to be a psychologist" is yet to be discovered. This period embraces the students' exploration of their relationship with the professional role. Some may find that psychology is not what they wanted to study, while others may be surprised by how interesting and complex the field is. Exposure to "academic reality" has various consequences—it can redirect a student's focus to another occupational area or increase their interest in the chosen profession.

Institutions of higher education are formal settings in which, guided by a curriculum, professional socialization is systematically and purposefully carried out to "produce graduates who display mastery of theoretical ideas, competence in applying theory in complex workplace settings, and professional dispositions that foster ethical and reflective professional practices" (Trede, Maclin, & Bridges, 2012, p. 365). Studying in a university is a transformative and non-linear process of "internalization of the specific culture of a professional community" (Shahr, Yazdani, & Afshar, 2019, p. 1). The academic-institutional route provides an institutionally confirmed way to *officially* become a psychologist by showing that the individual has completed the relevant training and has engaged in formal educational activities. Obtaining an academic degree and being awarded a professional qualification typically legitimates one's position as a psychologist in a society. Figuratively speaking, a course of study in psychology at a university is the legitimate "seedbed" of preparation for the professionals on human issues called psychologists.

However, the professional socialization is not exclusively related to the academic-institutional factors. It begins before academic studies in a university—individuals' predispositions take shape first of all in informal settings of communities (Miller, 2013) and continues after studies are over when various conditions continuously shape an individual's competencies and self-perception as a professional. They are formed in professional communities and workplace contexts in which new professionals encounter the realities of their role (Shahr et al., 2019) being also continuously negotiated in informal settings.

To conclude, the educational-academic system has a compelling influence on how an individual becomes a psychologist, however, inputs from different informal and non-academic social contexts become reference frames for the psychologist-to-be during their studies in university.

Why professional identity?

The approach used in this book presents an exploration into the process of becoming a psychologist in terms of the construction of professional identity. Professional identity is undoubtedly a relevant topic to discuss within the context of individuals navigating the uncertainties of their professional future (Watzlawik & Kullasepp, 2016). As a brief introductory, though the constructs of *identity* and the *self* have captured scientific interest for more than a century and have been extensively discussed in scholarly and practical discourses across different disciplines and from different theoretical perspectives, there is still no consensus about the meaning of these concepts (Bruner, 1959; Erikson, 1968; Stryker & Burke, 2000; McAdams, 2011). Further, identity has been defined as people's understanding of what type of people they are, "what it means to be a 'certain kind of person'" (Gee, 2000,

p. 100), and as "the subjective concept of oneself as a person" (Vignoles, Regalia, Manzi, Colledge, & Scabini, 2006, p. 309). Burke (2004) states that "Identities are the sets of meanings people hold for themselves that define 'what it means' to be who they are as persons, as role occupants, and as group members" (p. 5).

As to professional identity, it has been described as people's subjective understanding of themselves as professionals (Beijaard, Meijer, & Verloop, 2004) and as a self-concept based on attitudes, values, and experiences (Van Zandt, 1990; Ibarra, 1999; Slay & Smith, 2010). Haverkamp Robertson, Cairns, and Bedi (2011) define professional identity as "a multifaceted construct involving acquisition of discipline-specific knowledge, skills, and attitudes; internalization of the values and philosophy of the discipline; adoption of the discipline's code of ethics and standards of practice; acceptance of a professional interpersonal style; and having pride in the profession" (p. 257).

Professional identity has an important part to play in university studies and later in working life (Nyström, 2009). Based on the literature, professional identity, as "an important cognitive mechanism that affects workers' attitudes, affect and behavior in work settings and beyond" (Caza & Creary, 2016, p. 4), acquires its significance as a factor related to job satisfaction, motivation level, self-efficacy, occupational commitment (Day, 2002), and career success (Slay & Smith, 2010) and is also linked to how professionals experience events within professional settings, how they make sense of their work environment, and how they evaluate their professional practice, and interpret professional issues (Trede et al., 2012; Leijen, Kullasepp, & Toompalu, 2018).

Given the wide scope of the topics relevant in comprehending the process of becoming a psychologist, it is unavoidable that many themes are underrepresented in this book. It is a complex phenomenon that can be discussed within various contexts and analyzed in terms of different functions. Also, the aim of this book is not to offer a comprehensive list of the features that qualify an individual as a psychologist, to provide a set of the most appropriate elements in the professional identity of a psychologist, or to introduce the personal characteristics most suitable for the role of a psychologist. Numerous existing sets of professional standards contain this knowledge and are introduced elsewhere. Instead, the intent of this book is to examine *how* psychology students construct their professional identity when assuming their new professional role during their studies in a bachelor's program—a period when the students have their first systematic and thorough exposure to the field of psychology through the academic structure of the university.

There is an extensive body of scientific literature on experts and specialists working in the field of psychology, including counseling psychologists, therapists, school psychologists, work psychologists, and clinical psychologists (Bruss & Kopala, 1993; Brott & Myers, 1999; Johnson & Campbell, 2002; Carli, 2007; Montesarchio & Venuleo, 2007; del Rio & Molina, 2007), as well as studies of psychology students in connection with the organization of their studies (Rupert & Kent, 2007; Przyborski, Benetka, & Slunecko, 2007; Castro-Tejerina, 2014) that deal with different aspects of professional socialization. Yet, what characterizes the *process* of entry into professional role, is still to be explored for a more rigorous understanding, and it is in the focus of this book. Identity is continually constructed and altering (Gergen, 2009) that, indeed, has to be investigated through its dynamics and changes.

However, what is also needed here is to comprehend how the complex process of internalizing a professional role involves the coordination of two aspects of the self—I as a professional and I as a person, the intriguing topic that frequently stimulates debates in the international scientific community (Rønnestad & Skovholt, 2003; Leijen & Kullasepp, 2013; Marlowe, Appleton, Chinnery, & Van Stratum, 2015; Leijen et al., 2018). This book aims to explore how these aspects of the self are expressed, evaluated, and negotiated and it contributes to the discussion on the construction of professional identity as a cultural development. With a focus on intrapsychological dynamics, it examines how professional identity emerges through the complex dialogical relations within the self. Based on the example of a specific cohort of students in an Estonian university, the universal mechanism behind the internalization of a professional role is addressed in the chapters.

Summary

In this book, the process of becoming a psychologist is approached in terms of the construction of professional identity—a crucial "tool" that enables individuals to navigate the uncertainty of (professional) life. Despite the existence of an extensive body of research, there is still a need to discuss the *process of emergence* of professional identity (of psychologists or any other profession) and how different aspects of the self are coordinated when internalizing the professional role. Focusing on processes at the intrapsychological level, this book provides insight into this complex process of emergence of a novelty in the self when socializing through the professional role.

Becoming a psychologist through professional socialization has different phases. These include the pre-period before university studies when the trajectory of professional development begins, formal studies of the profession in an educational institution, and the post-period after studies have concluded. This book addresses professional socialization through a bachelor's program, a catalytic period that re-configures students' developmental trajectories.

References

American Psychological Association (2021, September, 4). Science of Psychology. https://www.apa.org/education-career/guide/science

Australian Psychological Society (2021, September 4). What does a psychologist do? https://psychology.org.au/for-the-public/about-psychology/what-does-a-psychologist-do

Beijaard, D., Meijer, C. P., & Verloop, N. (2004). Reconsidering research on teachers' professional identity. *Teaching and Teacher Education, 20*(2), 107–128. 10.1016/j.tate.2003.07.001

Brott, P. E., & Myers, J. E. (1999). Development of a professional school counselor identity: A grounded theory. *Professional School Counseling, 2*(5), 339–348.

Bruner, J. S. (1959). Myth and identity. *Daedalus, 88*(2), 349–358. http://www.jstor.org/stable/20026501

Bruss, K. V., & Kopala, M. (1993). Graduate school training in psychology: Its impact upon the development of professional identity. *Psychotherapy, 30*(4), 685–691. 10.1037/0033-3204.30.4.685

Burke, P. (2004). Identities and social structure: The 2003 Cooley-Mead Award Address. *Social Psychology Quarterly, 67*(1), 5–15.

Cant, R., & Higgs, J. (1999). Professional socialization in educating beginning practitioners. In J. Higgs, & H. Edwards (Eds.), *Challenges for Health Professional Education* (pp. 46–51). Melbourne: Butterworth-Heinemann.

Carli, R. (2007). Psychology training in Italy. *European Journal of School Psychology, 4*(2), 179–209.

Castro-Tejerina, J. (2014). "Psytizens": The co-construction of the professional identity of psychology students in the postmodern world. *Integrative Psychological and Behavioral Science, 48*(4), 393–417. 10.1007/s12124-014-9279-x. PMID: 25155299.

Caza, B. B., & Creary, S. J. (2016). The construction of professional identity. In A. Wilkinson, D. Hislop, & C. Coupland (Eds.), *Perspectives on Contemporary Professional Work: Challenges and Experiences* (pp. 259–285). Cheltenham, UK: Edward Elgar Publishing.

Dall'Alba, G., & Sandberg, J. (2006). Unveiling professional development: A critical review of stage models. *Review of Educational Research, 76*(3), 383–412.

Day, C. (2002). School reform and transitions in teacher professionalism and identity. *International Journal of Educational Research, 37*(8), 677–692. 10.1016/S0883-0355(03)00065-X

Eesti Psühholoogide Liit (2021, September, 4). Kutsestandard. http://www.epl.org.ee/wb/media/files/n6ustaja/Psuehholoognoustaja%20kutse_Kutsestandard.pdf

Erikson, E. H. (1968). *Identity: Youth and Crisis*. New York: WW Norton.

Gee, J. (2000). Identity as an analytic lens for research in education. *Review of Research in Education, 25*, 99–125. 10.2307/1167322

Gergen, K. J. (2009). *Relational Being: Beyond Self and Community*. New York: Oxford University Press

Haverkamp, B. E., Robertson, S. E., Cairns, S. L., & Bedi, R. P. (2011). Professional issues in Canadian counselling psychology: Identity, education, and professional practice. *Canadian Psychology/Psychologie canadienne, 52*(4), 256–264. 10.1037/a0025214

Ibarra, H. (1999). Provisional selves: Experimenting with image and identity in professional adaptation. *Administrative Science Quarterly, 44*(4), 764–791. 10.2307/2667055

Johnson, W. B., & Campbell, C. D. (2002). Character and fitness requirements for professional psychologists: Are there any? *Professional Psychology: Research and Practice*, *33*(1), 46–53. 10.1037/0735-7028.33.1.46

Leijen, Ä., & Kullasepp, K. (2013). All roads lead to Rome: Developmental trajectories of student teachers' professional and personal identity development. *Journal of Constructivist Psychology*, *26*(2), 104−114. 10.1080/10720537.2013.759023.

Leijen, Ä., Kullasepp, K., & Toompalu, A. (2018). Dialogue for bridging student teachers' personal and professional identity. In: *Dialogical Self Theory in Education: A Multicultural Perspective* (pp. 97−110). Springer. 10.1007/978-3-319-62861-5_7.

Marlowe, J. M., Appleton, C., Chinnery, S.-A., & Van Stratum, S. (2015). The integration of personal and professional selves: Developing students' critical awareness in social work practice. *Social Work Education*, *34*(1), 60–73. 10.1080/02615479.2014.949230

McAdams, D. P. (2011). Narrative identity. In S. J. Schwartz, K. Luyckx, & V. L. Vignoles (Eds.), *Handbook of Identity Theory and Research* (pp. 99–115). Springer Science + Business Media. 10.1007/978-1-4419-7988-9_5

Mieg, H. A. (2008) Professionalisation and professional identities of environmental experts: The case of Switzerland. *Environmental Sciences*, *5* (1), 41–51. 10.1080/15693430701859653

Miller, S. E. (2013). Professional socialization: A bridge between the explicit and implicit curricula. *Journal of Social Work Education*, *49*(3), 368–386.

Montesarchio, G, & Venuleo, M.E. (2007). Constructing psychotherapists' social roles. *European Journal of School Psychology*, *4*(2), 403–413.

Nyström, S. (2009). The dynamics of professional identity formation: Graduates' transitions from higher education to working life. *Vocations and Learning*, *2*(1), 1–18. 10.1007/s12186-008-9014-1. ISSN 1874-785X. S2CID 143402240.

Przyborski, A., Benetka,G., & Slunecko, T. (2007). Psychology curriculae and the challenge of Bologna: An answer from a cultural science perspective. *European Journal of School Psychology*, *4*(2), 211–225.

del Rio, M.T., & Molina, M.E. (2007). Psychotherapists at dialogue: Passing thorough microgenetic trajectories. *European Journal of School Psychology*, *4*(2), 377–382.

Rønnestad, M.H., & Skovholt, T. M. (2003). The journey of the counselor and therapist: Research findings and perspectives on professional development. *Journal of Career Development*, *30*(1), 5–44. 10.1023/A:1025173508081

Rupert, P. A., & Kent, J. S. (2007). Gender and work setting differences in career-sustaining behaviors and burnout among professional psychologists. *Professional Psychology: Research and Practice*, *38*(1), 88–96. 10.1037/0735-7028.38.1.88

Shahr, H. S. A., Yazdani, S., & Afshar, L. (2019). Professional socialization: An analytical definition. *Journal of Medical Ethics and History of Medicine*, *12*(17), 1–14. 10.18502/jmehm.v12i17.2016

Slay, H.S., & Smith, A. (2010). Professional identity construction: Using narrative to understand the negotiation of professional and stigmatized cultural identities. *Human Relations*, *64* (1), 85–107.

Stryker, S., & Burke, P. J. (2000). The past, present, and future of an identity theory. *Social Psychology Quarterly*, *63*, 284–297.

Trede, F., Macklin, R., & Bridges, D. (2012). Professional identity development: A review of the higher education literature. *Studies in Higher Education, 37*(3), 365–384.

Van Zandt, C. E. (1990). Professionalism: A matter of personal initiative. *Journal of Counseling and Development, 68*(3), 243–245. 10.1002/j.1556-6676.1990.tb01367.x

Vignoles, R., Manzi, C., & Scabini, (2006). Beyond self-esteem: Influence of multiple motives on identity construction. *Journal of Personality and Social Psychology, 90*(2), 308–333. 10.1037/0022-3514.90.2.308

Watzlawik, M., & Kullasepp, K. (2016). Career as affective Journey: How constant flux challenges the search for career pathways and counseling. *Integrative Psychological and Behavioral Science, 50*, 492–506. 10.1007/s12124-016-9349-3

Chapter 2

Theoretical framework: A socio-cultural approach to professional identity construction

Professional identity through the lens of cultural psychology

This book aims at enriching our understanding of the process of becoming a psychologist by primarily relying on the interdisciplinary field of cultural psychology that is founded on the basic idea that all human cognitive, affective, and behavioral forms of existence are regulated by socially constructed meanings (Valsiner & Rosa, 2007). Cultural psychology is the field that connects culture and psychology, an attempt that can be found in the works of scholars arguing for reciprocal embeddedness of the mind and culture. In this approach, humans are conceived of open systems that emerge through mutually developing interactions with other open systems. The idea of context-bound development is nicely provided by Vygotsky (1978, p. 57) who pointed: "Every function in the child's cultural development appears twice: first, on the social level, and later, on the individual level; first, *between* people (interpsychological), and then *inside* the child (intrapsychological)." However, the position that individuals' development is not "context free" is accepted widely by many other.

Another axiomatic given in cultural psychology is mediation. Specifically, the semiotic perspective in cultural psychology explains the development through the semiotic mediating system—humans constantly use and construct signs and make sense of experiences. By interpreting occurrences in the world they create the reality that frames and channels their experiences (Salvatore, Tonti, & Gennaro, 2016; Salvatore, Valsiner, & Veltri, 2019). Semiotic mediation organizes psychological processes and is an inherent part of psychological functioning (Salvatore, 2012; Valsiner, 2017).

Drawing on these assumptions, professional identity is discussed in this book as a semiotic process of self-regulation that unfolds in dialogical relations with the individual's socio-cultural surroundings. These mutually developing relationships, as introduced above, are established through the construction and use of signs and through meaning-making, which is, as Cabell (2010) writes: "an active and constructive process by which the

DOI: 10.4324/9781315519616-3

person cultivates their self and environment" (p. 26). In that sense, becoming a psychologist is about building semiotic devices that enable the regulation of one's experiences in the world and the establishment of a relationship with the professional role.

Further, in accordance with assertions about humans' affective nature:

> *human psychological life in its sign-mediated forms is affective in its nature.* We make sense of our relations with the world, and of the world itself, through our feelings that are themselves culturally organized through the creation and use of signs. The realm of feelings is central for construction of personal cultures. The mental – reflexive (or "cognitive") – side is an emergent semiotic tool to organize the affective relating with the world.
>
> (Valsiner, 2007, p. 301)

the professional identity is manifested in affective relations with the individual's surroundings. This cultural organization of feelings can be further explained by the cultural material that is available for us in surroundings and that we barrow to make sense of our experiences—to navigate in lives' uncertainties. Specifically, in a socio-cultural conceptualization, professional identity formation is guided by intra-psychological processes and by social representations that, according to the theory of social representations, a research area in cultural psychology, carry knowledge that enables individuals to make sense of themselves, the world, and their relationships with it (Moscovici, 1988; Wagner, et al., 1999). As set forth by Moscovici, social representations create an order that guides individuals and enables them to understand aspects of the world and communication with each other (Duveen, 2008). Also, social representations that operate at the collective level and inform the formation of identity are one of the key factors that guide a student's entry into a professional role. For example, the way a psychologist is represented in a society is involved in the construction of a personal version of it. It is argued, that mind is inherently transactional—thinking is grounded culturally and historically reflecting specific views of subcultures (Salvatore, et al., 2019), thus, allowing to anticipate re-emergence of the circulating knowledge in society in one's personal way to see the world. However, socially suggested meanings (e.g., psychologist is X) can emerge in the intra-personal domain only in the personal version, built in the involvement of generalized meaning fields that will be discussed later in this chapter. Personal realities are *constructed* and carry marks of the personal experiences from various social, cultural, and historical contexts.

How the cultural material becomes integrated into the intra-psychological regulation systems is described below.

To start with, the construction of personal meaning complexes by using cultural materials available in the environment is possible due to our ability to use signs. This complex process of presenting and representing entails intra-psychological constructive processes of internalization/externalization, which mediate the person-environment relationship (Lawrence & Valsiner, 2003), as well as pleromatization and schematization, that lead to the construction of abstracted feelings and schematic signs, respectively (Valsiner, 2017).

Turning socio-cultural meanings into personal meanings: Personal culture in the making

The integration of co-constructed knowledge into one's self-system and the reorganization of the psychological world are further explained using the lamina model of the intra-psychological world (Valsiner, 2001; Lawrence & Valsiner, 2003). This model posits that individuals are "in constant exchange of perceptual and semiotic materials with the environment" (Valsiner, 2001, p. 198). This occurs through two processes of analysis—internalization and externalization—which lead to the formation of unique meaning systems and to changes in the individual's subjective understanding of the objects they encounter (Valsiner & Rosa, 2007).

In line with the laminal model, the process of becoming a psychologist is organized by social messages and their movement from one layer to the next. However, the inflow of socio-cultural input is regulated. Not every social message enters the system of layers, and not every message moves on to the next layer. The model distinguishes between three layers. In Layer I, messages are noticed but not integrated into the intra-psychological system (which is represented by Layer III). If the message is "taken" to Layer II, it becomes transformed—generalized. If a message arrives in Layer III, it takes on an affective dimension and becomes part of the structure of the intra-psychological phenomenon (Valsiner, 2001). Layer III is regarded as the intra-psychological personal sense-making system as well as the location of the "core self" that regulates the inflow of messages and movement of the incoming social messages to different layers (Figure 2.1).

Consider a hypothetical example that illustrates how the personal sense-making system "recognizes the messages that the person is ready to internalize, and ignores or blocks others" (Valsiner, 2001, p. 202). Two people participating in the same discussion on Topic X are told that psychologists help people. One arrives at the generalized (Layer II) conclusion that psychologists are nice people. When this message about psychologists as nice people arrives at Layer III, it will be transformed again. The message takes on an affective quality and is "taken personally." Because this message became personally meaningful, the individual decides to study psychology (perhaps because of a desire to be a nice person or the personal significance of helping others). At the same time, another person who receives the same message that psychologists help people finds it irrelevant and forgets it.

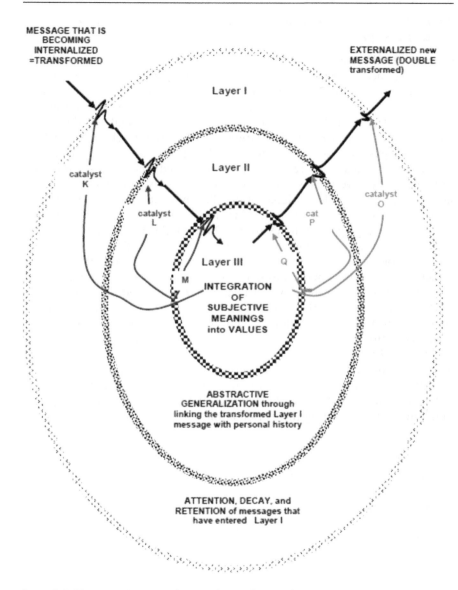

Figure 2.1 The laminal model of internalization/externalization.

Note. From *Culture in Mind and Societies* (p. 346), in J. Valsiner, 2014, Copyright 2007, by Jaan Valsiner. Reprinted with permission.

As suggested by the laminal model, messages that lack certain qualities and are irrelevant from a particular person's perspective are not selected for further analysis and synthesis, and they will be "switched off."

Professional identity as a semiotic process, or "All you need is a sign"

Human affectivity in experiencing the world is organized at different levels of semiotic mediation, ranging from the physiological level to hypergeneralized affective semiotic fields. In the first levels, affective experiences exist in a form of pre-verbal generalization (not encoded in signs). In the higher levels, the affective field is semiotically encoded and articulated through a form of semiosis called schematization. Signs at this level are point-like, schematic signs that depict a simplified world. In contrast, pleromatization is a process of semiosis that results in overgeneralized feelings that cannot be verbalized but nevertheless affect an individual's experiences. Pleromatic signs are the highest-level signs, also called field-like signs, that operate through pleromatic abstracted meaning fields that add an affective dimension to the emerging meaning (Valsiner, 2017; 2021) (Figure 2.2).

Professional identity construction occurs through different forms of semiosis—pleromatization, which provides a generalized concept of what is depicted (e.g., feeling x when thinking about oneself as a psychologist in the future), and schematization, which facilitates a simplified depiction of the world through the use of categories and words (e.g., ideas like "I am not good enough to be a psychologist" and "I am a psychologist"). Both processes feed into each other, as the concept of cultural psychology of semiotic dynamics (CPSD) posits (Valsiner, 2005). In line with the concept of CPSD, the process of becoming a psychologist unfolds through the ongoing construction of dynamic hierarchies of signs that ensure semiotic autoregulation of meaning-making, thus enabling subjective experiences by restricting and simultaneously facilitating their orientation.

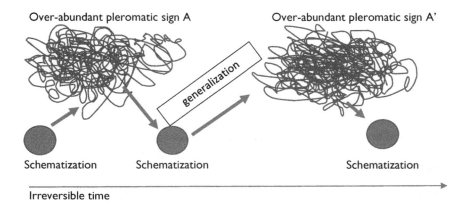

Figure 2.2 Pleromatization and schematization (Modified from Valsiner, 2017, p. 183).

A formal course of study for a profession that cultivates a certain type of psychological functioning to facilitate acting according to the expectations for a professional role should lead to the formation of signs that take control over the process of making sense of experiences. For example, if the role demands X, the person should be capable of being X. Part 3 provides an exhaustive introduction to the semiotic regulation of this intra-psychological ambivalence.

Pleromatic and schematic sides of one identity: "Hidden" richness and simplifications in processes of identity

Consistent with the concept of professional identity as a semiotic process and leaning on the model of hierarchies of signs, two intertwined processes of semiosis—pleromatization and schematization—shape individuals' experiences in assuming the professional role of a psychologist.

In general, professional identity as semiosis is "inaccessible" in all its richness of details, but a simplified version of professional identity is expressed through verbal categories ("I am a psychologist.") Thus, although these two meaning-making processes—simplification of the perceived object and increasing richness of experience—are intertwined and have created mutual feed-forward loops, the "hidden" complexity of experience of I as a psychologist does not appear in full detail in verbally expressed meanings (Figure 2.3).

Based on these starting points, I expand this account of the hierarchy of signs to the concept of identity and suggest that two related but different sides of identity can be distinguished. One is less consciously perceived, if at all, while individuals are aware of the other. In a sense, the pleromatic field-like signs comprise the aspect of identity that is not verbally accessible or encoded in "usual," i.e., point-like signs. This can be regarded as a part of identity that a person is unaware of but passionate about—"I like psychology, but I don't know why" or "They say that I prefer activities that allow me to connect to other people, but I didn't notice that myself." The pleromatic side of identity sets up an inclination to respond in a way that is filled with affective determination but cannot be verbally specified. A verbally expressed identity that claims "I am x" (e.g., a psychologist, policeman, bus driver) is an example of the schematic component of identity. As it is expressed through concrete words, it is an example of a point-like sign. The schematized side of identity attempts to capture the wholeness of subjectivity with the claim "I am a psychologist." Thus, professional identity can appear in unlimited verbal expressions as simplifications of experiences of "I as a person in a professional role" that are not accessible to verbal encoding (e.g., "I feel good when I read psychological texts, but I don't know why.")

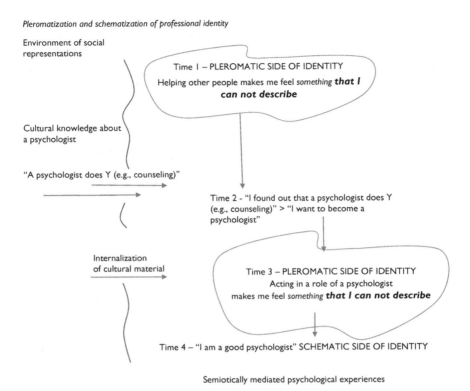

Figure 2.3 Pleromatization and schematization of professional identity.

The construction of professional identity: Regulating the intra-psychological disaccord and accord

Based on the concept of the two different sides—schematic and pleromatic—of identity, the following scenarios can be encountered during studies when assuming the professional role.

In general, professional socialization entails internalization of professional role expectations. Thus, becoming a psychologist (or any other professional) is to negotiate oneself with a professional identity in the context of role expectations. Consider the following institutional expectation of psychologists: Psychologists should be tolerant. In this case, "tolerant," as an orientation of being related to others, refers to a psychological inclination that should be present in semiotically mediated affective relations or one to be cultivated during the training period for the future role. Tolerance (or any other institutionally defined role expectation) is assumed to be displayed or expressed in professional settings.

The following versions of relations between the different sides of identity and the professional role expectations can be found as one enters the professional role:

a   Role expectations (e.g., a psychologist should be tolerant) and the pleromatic side of identity *coincide*.

   a   Schematic side of identity: "I am tolerant (but do not feel like a psychologist)."
   b   Schematic side of identity: "I am tolerant (and feel like a psychologist)."
   c   Schematic side of identity: "I am not tolerant (but it is easy for me to accept others' ideas)
      The scenarios a)a and a)b illustrate that the schematic sides of professional identity are in accord with pleromatic side of identity and the role expectations; however, the schematic side of professional identity sometimes is in opposition with its pleromatic counterpart—i.e., in the versions a)c. In the latter case, persons do not consider themselves as tolerant, although their responses to others and ideas reveal the opposite.

b   Role expectations and the pleromatic side of identity are in *dissonance*; that is, higher abstracted fields of feelings do not generate the orientation that the role prescribes. Again, there are many different combinations regarding the schematization of identity:

   a   Schematic side of identity: "I am not tolerant (but I want to become a psychologist and want to learn how to become more tolerant)."
   b   Schematic side of identity: "I am not tolerant (and don't want to become more tolerant)."
   c   Schematic side of identity: "I am tolerant (and I want to become a psychologist)."
   d   Schematic side of identity: "I am tolerant (and I don't want to become a professional psychologist)."

Various combinations of relations between professional role expectations and the sides of identity set the conditions through which students negotiate their professional identity reveal the complexity behind professional identity construction and entering into the professional role. Reflections like "I think I am tolerant, (although usually I don't like others' ideas)" or, conversely, "I think that I am not tolerant, (although it is easy for me to accept others' ideas)" illustrate a schematization of identity in contrast with the inclination that the higher affective fields tend to generate. These discrepancies can manifest in inner tension and conflicts that one must cope with when assuming the professional role.

However, within the context of the internalization of professional role, the regulation of discrepancy between what IS and what SHOULD BE is central.

Here, an option is to relate becoming a psychologist with the formation of values—considered as higher-order affective phenomena that guide meaning-making (Valsiner, 2007)—that professional socialization entails (Brott & Myers, 1999; Ibarra 1999). From a student's perspective, entering into a professional role requires meeting professional role-related expectations and diminishing the discrepancy, for instance, between institutional expectations and the higher affective fields (or pleromatic side of identity) that regulate meaning-making. In general, different types of discrepancies turn into developmental tasks to address: "I am X, but I should be Y."

The dialogical self

University studies and preparation for a professional future are anticipated to trigger the emergence of new meanings, and manifest in the (professional, role-related) perspective in the self as the outcome of coping with the reality of a new social position as a psychologist-to-be. To comprehend how the professional-role related perspective regulates the dynamics of the construction of professional identity, I apply the Dialogical Self Theory (DST; Hermans, Kempen, & van Loon, 1992; Hermans, 1996; Hermans & Hermans-Konopka, 2010).

In general, DST enables deeper insight into the negotiation of professional identity at the intra-psychological level while it illuminates the expression of different sub-systems in the self when entering into the professional role of a psychologist. It is a useful theoretical tool because it enables a better understanding of how professional identity emerges in the landscape of multiple other identities that bring their own perspectives into meaning-making (e.g., "I as a student," "I as a friend," "I as a colleague," "I as a hard-working person," "I as confident").

Multiplicity within the self

DST is a research field in cultural psychology that introduces the concept of the self in terms of dynamics, multiplicity, and dialogue and depicts the self as extended through the incorporation of others and society (Hermans, Konopka, Oosterwegel, & Zomer, 2017). The concept of the dialogical self is embedded in William James' traditional distinction between I (the self-as knower) and Me (the self as known):

> Whatever I may be thinking of, I am always at the same time more or less aware of myself, of my personal existence. At the same time it is *I* who am aware; so that the total self of me, being as it were duplex, partly known and partly knower, partly object and partly subject, must have two aspects discriminated in it, of which for shortness we may call one the *Me* and the other the *I*.
>
> (James, 2001, p. 43)

By drawing on the metaphor of the polyphonic novel, an idea that starts from Mikhail Bakhtin and from which the idea of the "voice" is borrowed (Hermans, 2001), the dialogical self is conceptualized as a dynamic whole of multiple I-positions that are supplied with voices that make interactions with each other possible.

> we conceptualize the self in terms of dynamic multiplicity of relatively autonomous *I* positions in an imaginal landscape. ... The I has the possibility to move, as in a space, from one position to the other in accordance with changes in situation and time. The *I* fluctuates among different and even opposed positions. The *I* has the capacity to imaginatively endow each position with a voice so that dialogical relations between positions can be established. The voices function like interacting characters in a story.
>
> (Hermans, et al., 1992, p. 28)

In DST (Hermans, 2001), I-positions form from different experiences in a specific historical-social-cultural context. Thus, it is expected that the transition to the position of being a psychology student manifests through the formation of a professional I-position (e.g., I as a psychologist.)

The dialogical self is a position repertoire that consists of external and internal I-positions. External positions, as Hermans (2014) describes, belong to the extended domain of the self and refer to objects in the environment like one's significant other and social groups (e.g., my teacher, my colleague, my grandmother, my supervisor, my fellow student). It is similar to James's theory, which posits that "In its wildest possible sense, however, a man's Me is the sum total of all that he CAN call his, not only his body and his psychic powers, but his clothes and his house, his wife and children, his ancestors and friends, his reputation and works, his lands and horses, and yacht and bank-account" (James, 2001, p. 44). Internal I-positions can be divided into personal positions like I as confident and as social positions (e.g., I as a student, I as a child, I as a colleague); I-positions "receive their relevance from their relation with one or more external positions" (Hermans, 2001, p. 252).

In line with the semiotic-dialogical perspective, I-positions are linked with the construction of meanings (Valsiner, 2002; Mattos & Chaves, 2015). That, in turn, increases possibility for the inner conflicts in the self as new I-positions bring their own view into inner dialogues. Namely, according to Hermans (2001), although I-positions can also exist in agreement and develop harmonious relations with each other, the co-existence of various voices within the self represents potential for conflicts and disagreements between I-positions and may evoke tension in the self. A person can be, for instance, torn between multiple choices—to study psychology or something else, for example. The mother's voice in the self recommends studying information technology, a friend's voice encourages them to go for psychology, the I-position I-as-a-shy-person hesitates, but the I-position I—as-a-helpful-person says that this occupation is a perfect fit.

However, conflicts between different sub-systems of the self (i.e., I-positions) can also feed into the development of the self and have an adaptive function. As Hermans (1996) argues, "Conflict may bring the self into the field of tension, contradiction or disagreement that may have beneficial consequences for its functioning" (p.122). According to DST, the dialogical capacity of the self enables individuals to cope with emerging complexity and a broadening position repertoire that grants an adaptive function to the person. Dialogical relations are considered an innovative activity (Batory, 2010) that supports the construction of professional identity.

In regard to the innovation in the self, Hermans (2013) introduces also the concepts of the third position, the meta-position, and the promoter position, all of which have a role in the innovation and development of the self. The third position can emerge as the result of the reconciliation of two conflicting I-positions by combining them "in the service of its strengthening and further development" (p.15). The meta-position enables distancing from the internal and external positions (e.g., "I as a student," "I as friendly") and reflecting on a situation by simultaneously considering different perspectives—for example, when one critically analyzes an inner conflict. Herman calls this a "helicopter view" (p. 16). Promoter positions are conceptualized as innovators in the self as "they have the potential to synthesize a variety of new and existing positions in the self and organize them at a higher level of integration" (p. 19).

Microgenetic dynamics of ontogenetic trajectories

Several studies on identity development have applied dialogical perspectives when seeking to understand how the personal and professional selves are negotiated in the course of becoming a professional (Alsup, 2006; Akkerman & Meijer, 2011; Ligorio, 2011; Leijen & Kullasepp, 2013; Leijen, Kullasepp, & Ots, 2013). In continuity with this line of studies, I address microgenetic processes in the self by focusing on how different aspects of the self (i.e., I-positions I as a person—a generic term that stands for non-psychologist and refers to all kinds of voices of non-psychologists—and I as a psychologist/professional) are regulated when assuming a professional role.

The migration of individuals to the transitional zone—a university—and to the social position of being psychology students leads to increasing multivocality in the self-system and to manifestation of a generic I-position, I as a psychologist, that represents different perspectives on being a psychologist and expresses the views of a professional group (or modified personal versions that do not coincide with the "original" versions)—the "psychologist's perspective" on objects and events. For example, the

I-position I as a psychologist in the student's multi-vocal self can "demand" that they stay calm in Situation X because, from the point of view of a psychology student, staying calm is what a therapist would do in a therapeutic setting (e.g., "I must stay calm because I am a psychology student and will be a therapist in the future.") However, a psychology student can also create an opposite point of view that holds that a psychologist should express emotions and not suppress them (e.g., "I must express my emotions; otherwise, I cannot work with clients.") As a result, a student may be pulled between different perspectives. This plurality can be translated into ambivalence that, as posited by Abbey and Valsiner (2005), marks the co-presence of differently oriented processes in one whole. Drawing on this idea, assuming a professional role is an inherently ambivalent condition, the typical intra-psychological condition when one is expected to be X when being Y and that is regulated through interactions between I-positions. Thus, the ambivalence known to us from Shakespeare's *Hamlet* may be repeated in the mundane lives of psychology students.

The regulation of different sub-systems of the self: The ontogenetic path under construction

Professional identity construction consists of the regulation of different sub-systems—I as a psychologist and I as a person—within the self. For example, the coexistence of different I-positions is revealed in the following dilemma: Should I behave as a *professional*, or should I respond as a *person* (i.e., a non-professional, non-psychologist)?

Consider the hypothetical example below. The dilemma lies in the question about the proper way to respond in the situation: Should I behave as a person or as a psychologist? "I am not interested in what he is telling me (I-position I as a person), but it seems like he expects that I will listen to him because he knows that I study psychology. Although I really don't want to talk right now about his personal life, I SHOULD do that because in the future I MUST listen my patients (I-position I as a professional [in the future]). Maybe listening to people is a good thing to do. It is important to improve my interaction skills because I am going to work as a clinical psychologist in four or five years (I-position I as a professional). I SHOULD start to learn how to regulate myself (I-position I as a professional). I SHOULD not (I-position I as a professional) show him my REAL feelings (I-position I as a person)."

This example reveals the re-organization of the relationships between I-positions—sequences of temporary dominance of a specific I-position in solution to the dilemma—within the self and how the individual copes with intra-psychological ambivalence by choosing between different perspectives to address an issue that can be handled from a personal or professional position. In general, when assuming this professional role, one must deal with (e.g., reject, adjust, modify, agree with, dominate) the voice of the psychologist among the other voices in the self. Regulation of discrepancy in the intra-psychological domain—I SHOULD feel/be X, but ACTUALLY I feel/am Y—is one of the transitional tasks belonging to the process of entering into the professional role. These conditions in the system potentially entail the emergence of new directions. The example above illustrates the inner dialogue that can lead to the innovation in the self. The meaning of the situation (I don't want listening) changes (listening can be beneficial). It is the new I-position (I as a psychologist), which creates tension and introduces new ways of relating with the surrounding while appearing in the inner dialogue. Part III in this book provides an exhaustive overview of the regulation of intra-psychological tension evoked by internalization of the externally created frame of regulations.

Non-linear transition: I am a psychologist < > I am not a psychologist

From here on, microgenetic processes—the coordination of interactions between different sub-systems of the self—construct the path of ontogeny of the self and play a role in adjusting to the ambivalent condition of being "a person in a professional role" (Kullasepp, 2006; Kullasepp, 2008; Toompalu, Leijen, & Kullasepp, 2017; Leijen et al., 2018).

Consider another hypothetical example. A student reads a self-help book on how to live a happy life. Criticizing the book for applying an overly trivial approach to a highly complex issue makes the student feel like an expert—like a psychologist. The next day, the same student meets a friend who asks for advice. At this moment, the student is aware of just being a student and lacking the required professional competencies to be considered a psychologist. "I am not a psychologist, and maybe that profession is not at all for me," may be the student's conclusion.

Similar cases of fluctuation in opposite understandings—I am X <> I am non-X—shed light on changing relations with the professional role. Any psychological withdrawal from the role (e.g., "I still feel that I am not good enough to consider myself a psychologist, so this is not for me") can potentially feed into further distancing from the field up to the point at which a person decides to exit the field of psychology. That is, once accepted, the self-understanding "I am X" can be switched to its opposite, "I am non-X," and then again to the former. However, it still is being informed by the opposing experience: "I am non-X; I am X."

One's relationship with a professional role is non-linear by nature—the established relations change over time, and the direction of the developmental trajectory changes. As students transition through various dynamic contexts, their professional identity is expressed along a scale of "psychologist-ness" that ranges from "I am a psychologist" to "I am not a psychologist." Between these two poles are an infinite number of different perspectives on the self as a psychologist. At any particular moment, a student can create the self-understanding "I am a very good psychologist because I know how to listen to another person and because last semester all my grades were As" as a function of situational influences, but in time, this can shift to its opposite: "I am not a good psychologist at all, and maybe I should reconsider which profession actually suits me." The fluctuation of the self between different positions—"I am X" and "I am non-X"—regulates the relationship with the professional role. One can experience a strong affective bond with the role (e.g., "Psychology is my calling; I definitely want to become a psychologist") or withdraw from the role by increasing psychological distance from it (e.g., "I no longer feel that psychology is for me.")

Summary

Becoming a psychologist is a process of semiosis; thus, all you need is a sign to become one. It is a movement toward the construction of an intra-psychological semiotic control system that regulates (professional) conduct. In simple terms, to become a psychologist, one must cooperate with institutions that inform one about how to think, feel, and act (e.g., "Psychologists do X; psychologists have y and z characteristics") and create the sign complexes that control one's responses to the world and enable socially suggested ways of being a psychologist (whatever that means).

The formation of professional identity is guided by social representations and by intra-psychological process that analyze socio-cultural input and construct signs. Through the constant construction of temporary hierarchies of signs, social representations, as particular cultural forms (Duveen, 2008), become involved in one's affective relationships with the world.

Studying psychology in a university results in differentiation of the self-structure. The emerging I-position I as a psychologist, along with numerous other I-positions, brings new perspectives on the self. Namely, the dialogical self conceptualizes the self through its connections with society and posits that society forms an inherent part of the self (Hermans, 2001). According to this theory, the self is a decentralized whole consisting of multiple I-positions that develop dialogical relationships with each other. Each I-position has its own perspective on an issue, a story to tell, or an utterance to add to the inner dialogue. In so doing, I-positions bring experiences from different life events and social contexts into the process of constructing a professional identity. The voices of others in the self involve themselves in this process by supporting each other and forming coalitions or by bringing conflicts and disagreements into the self. However, controversies create a fruitful ground for development: "internal conflicts, like any internal tension or contradiction, may be a source of productive self-reflection, self-exploration, and self-dialogue and even lead to creative insights or activities" (Hermans & Hermans-Konopka, 2010 p. 122).

However, at the level of microgenetic processes, internalization of a professional role manifests in the coordination of different sub-systems of the self. These microlevel interactions between the different I-positions form the non-linear trajectory of internalization of a professional role. Becoming always unfolds under ambiguous conditions and without a defined destiny. The source of a developmental direction can be any kind of experience, like a friend's comment or reading a book. Such events can pull a person toward studying psychology or push them away from it. However, the construction of professional identity is a non-linear process that does not have a shortcut. Rather, becoming a psychologist is a longitudinal process of gradual internalization of professional role expectations and linking them with the structure of the self.

References

Abbey, E., & Valsiner, J. (2005). Emergence of meanings through ambivalence [58 paragraphs]. *FQS: Forum Qualitative Sozialforschung* [On-Line Journal], *6*(1), Art. 23. www.qualitative-research-net/fqs-texte/1-05/05-1-23-e.htm

Akkerman, S. F., & Meijer, P. C. (2011). A dialogical approach to conceptualizing teacher identity. *Teachers and Teacher Education*, *27*(2), 308–319.

Alsup, J. (2006). *Teacher Identity Discourses*. Mahwah, NJ: Lawrence Erlbaum Associates.

Batory, A. M. (2010). Diaologicality and the construction of identity. *International Journal for Dialogical Science*, *4*(1), 45–66.

Brott, P. E., & Myers, J. E. (1999). Development of a professional school counselor identity: A grounded theory. *Professional School Counseling*, *2*(5), 339–348.

Cabell, K. R. (2010). Mediators, regulators, and catalyzers: A context inclusive model of trajectory development. Psychology & Society, *3*(1), 26–41.

Duveen, G. (2008). Social actors and social groups: A return to heterogeneity in social psychology. *Journal for the Theory of Social Behaviour*, *38*(4), 369–374. 10.1111/j.1468-5914.2008.00385.x

Hermans, H. J. M. (1996). Voicing the self: From information processing to dialogical interchange. *Psychological Bulletin*, *119*(1), 31–50. 10.1037/0033-2909.119.1.31

Hermans, H. J. M. (2001). The dialogical self: Toward a theory of personal and cultural positioning. *Culture & Psychology*, *7*(3), 243–281.

Hermans, H.J.M. (2013). The dialogical self in education: Introduction. *Journal of Constructivist Psychology*, *26*(2), 81–89. 10.1080/10720537.2013.759018

Hermans, H. J. (2014). Self as a society of I- Positions: A dialogical approach to counseling. *The Journal of Humanistic Counseling*, *53*(2), 134–159.

Hermans, H., & Hermans-Konopka, A. (2010). *Dialogical self theory: Positioning and counter-positioning in a globalizing society*. New York: Cambridge University Press.

Hermans, H. J. M., Kempen, H. J. G., & Van Loon, R. J. P. (1992). The dialogical self: Beyond individualism and rationalism. *American Psychologist*, *47*(1), 23–33. http://dx.doi.org/10.1037/0003-066X.47.1.23

Hermans, H. J. M., Konopka, A., Oosterwegel, A., & Zomer, P. (2017). Fields of tension in a boundary-crossing world: Towards a democratic organization of the self. *Integrative Psychological and Behavioral Science, 51*, 505–535. 10.1007/s12124-016-9370-6

Ibarra, H. (1999). Provisional selves: Experimenting with image and identity in professional adaptation. *Administrative Science Quarterly, 44*(4), 764–791. 10.2307/2667055

James, W. (2001). *Psychology: The Brief Course*. Canada: Toronto/Ontario General publishing company, Ltd.

Kullasepp, K. (2006). Becoming professional: External and intrapsychological level in the service of professional identity construction of psychology students. *European Journal of School Psychology, 4*(2), 337–347.

Kullasepp, K. (2008). *Dialogical Becoming. Professional Identity Construction of Psychology Students*. Tallinna Ülikooli Kirjastus.

Lawrence, J. A., & Valsiner, J. (2003). Making personal sense: An account of basic internalization and externalization processes. *Theory & Psychology, 13*(6), 723–752.

Leijen, Ä., & Kullasepp, K. (2013). All roads lead to Rome: Developmental trajectories of student teachers' professional and personal identity development. *Journal of Constructivist Psychology, 26*(2), 104–114. 10.1080/10720537.2013.759023.

Leijen, Ä, Kullasepp, K, & Ots, A (2013). Õpetaja professionaalse rolli internaliseerimise hindamine õpetajakoolituse esmaõppe üliõpilaste hulgas. *Eesti Haridusteaduste Ajakiri = Estonian Journal of Education*, 1, 72–96. 10.12697/eha.2013.1.05

Leijen, Ä., Kullasepp,K., & Toompalu, A. (2018). Dialogue for bridging student teachers' personal and professional identity. In: F. Meijers & H. Hermans (Eds.), *Dialogical Self Theory in Education: A multicultural perspective* (pp. 97–110). Springer. 10.1007/978-3-319-62861-5_7

Ligorio, M. B. (2011). The dialogical self and educational research: A fruitful relationship. In H. Hermans & T. Gieser (Eds.), *Handbook of the Dialogical Self Theory* (pp. 439–453). Cambridge: Cambridge University Press.

Mattos, E., & Chaves, A. M. (2015). Becoming professionals: Exploring young people's constructions of alternative futures. In. G. Marsico, V. Dazzani, M. Ristum, & A. C. S. Bastos (Eds.), *Educational Contexts and Borders through Cultural Lens* (pp. 131–156). New York: Springer.

Moscovici, S. (1988) Notes towards a description of social representations. *European Journal of Social Psychology, 18*, 211–250.

Salvatore, S. (2012). Social life of the sign: Sense-making in society. In J. Valsiner (Ed.), *Oxford Handbook of Culture and Psychology* (pp. 241–254). New York, US: Oxford University Press, Inc.

Salvatore, S., Tonti, M., & Gennaro, A. (2016). How to model sensemaking. A contribution for the development of a methodological framework for the analysis of meaning. In M. Han, & C. Cunha (Eds.), *The Subjectified and Subjectifying Mind* (pp. 245–268). Charlotte, NC: Information Age Publishing.

Salvatore, S., Valsiner, J., & Veltri, G. A. (2019). The theoretical and methodological framework. Semiotic cultural psychology, symbolic universes and lines of semiotic forces. In: S. Salvatore, V. Fini, T. Mannarini, J. Valsiner, G. Veltri (Eds), *Symbolic Universes in Time of (Post)Crisis. Culture in Policy Making: The Symbolic Universes of Social Action.* (pp. 25–49). Switzerland: Springer, Cham. 10.1007/978-3-030-19497-0_2

Toompalu, A., Leijen, Ä., & Kullasepp, K. (2017). Professional role expectations and related feelings when solving pedagogical dilemmas: A comparison of pre- and in-service teachers. *Teacher Development*, *21*(2), 307–323. 10.1080/13664530.2016.1237985

Valsiner, J. (2001). *Comparative Study of Human Cultural Development*. Madrid: Fundación Infancia y Aprendizaje.

Valsiner, J. (2002). Forms of dialogical relations and semiotic autoregulation within the self. *Theory & Psychology*, *12*(2), 251–265. 10.1177/0959354302012002633

Valsiner, J. (2005). Scaffolding within the structure of dialogical self: Hierarchical dynamics of semiotic mediation. *New Ideas in Psychology*, *23*(3), 197–206.

Valsiner. J. (2007). *Culture in Minds and Societies: Foundation of Cultural Psychology*. New Delhi, India: Sage Publications India Pvt Ltd.

Valsiner, J. (2014). Culture in mind and societies. *Foundations of Cultural Psychology*. New Delhi: Sage Publications.

Valsiner, J. (2017). Semiotic processes: How meanings are made. In M. Raudsepp (Ed.), *Between Self and Societies: Creating Psychology in a New Key*. Tallinn, Estonia: Tallinn University Press.

Valsiner, J. (2021). *General Human Psychology*. Springer International Publishing. 10.1007/978-3-030-75851-6

Valsiner, J., & Rosa, A. (2007). *The Cambridge Handbook of Sociocultural Psychology*. Cambridge: Cambridge University Press. 10.1017/CBO9780511611162

Vygotsky, L. S. (1978). Internalization of higher psychological functions. In M. Cole, V. John-Steiner, S. Scribner, & E. Souberman (Eds.), *Mind in Society: The Development of Higher Psychological Processes*. Harvard University Press.

Wagner, W., Farr, R., Jovchelovitch, S., Lorenzi-Cioldi, F., Marková, I., Duveen, G., & Rose, D. (1999). Theory and method of social representations. *Asian Journal of Social Psychology*, *2*(1), 95–125. 10.1111/1467-839X.00028

Chapter 3

Introduction to the methodology of the study: Grasping the multilinear and unique developmental process over time

The general intent of this book is to discuss *how* psychology students construct their professional identity during their studies in a bachelor's program. More specifically, it investigates how the different I-positions I as a person and I as a professional (psychologist) are coordinated throughout the three years of studies and how the students make sense of their unfolding relationship with the professional role. Thus, through exploring the (micro-) *processes* in the self this book deals with the developmental dynamics of internalization of the professional role.

In this chapter, the philosophical assumptions that have guided the research are put into the perspective and underpinnings methodology is introduced. My decision-making in the research process has been informed by the social constructivist paradigm and by the axiomatic assumptions of cultural psychology.

The central idea of social constructivism holds that knowledge is constructed by making meanings and that construction of knowledge embeds in cultural settings and in social interactions that lead to "generating divergent experiential worlds and stocks of 'knowledge'" (Hammersley, 2013, p. 35). As Creswell (2013) notes: "In social constructivism, individuals seek understanding of the world in which they live and work. They develop subjective meanings of their experiences—meanings directed toward certain objects or things." (p. 24)

Putting the basic philosophical beliefs into the perspective, the psychology students' interpretations of the professional role and their relations with it are unique. Their encounters with environmental properties feed into the emergence of intra-individual and inter-individual differences regarding their understandings, affective responses in relation to professional socialization, generally, their ways they interpret the professional related experiences.

Further, in line with the associated ontological and epistemological beliefs of the interpretive framework, and drawing on the axiomatic understanding about psychological phenomena in cultural psychology, students' experiences are understood as unique. In line with this assumption, this study on the developmental dynamics of the construction of professional identity is located

DOI: 10.4324/9781315519616-4

within the idiographic paradigm (Molenaar, 2004; Molenaar & Valsiner, 2005)—professional identity as a semiotic *process* can exist only in *a unique version* in irreversible time. Thus, instead of looking for "the way" (or "the average way") of becoming a psychologist, in this book, I focus on patterns within each person's experience and highlight unique personal versions of the emergence of professional identity. By mapping out their subjective experiences, we gain an understanding of the dynamics within individuals and a better understanding of the emergence of inter-individual differences in professional identity.

A multiple-case study research strategy

The chosen research strategy for this study is a multiple-case study. As this methodological approach allows in-depth investigation of intricate phenomena to identify unique patterns within the individual and explore underlying principles (Cohen, Manion, & Morrison, 2007), it was adopted in this study to investigate the lived experiences of the students.

Abductive inference: The generalization of knowledge in cultural psychology

To generalize findings from the individual case studies, I draw on the assumption that the universal mechanism that guarantees development "is present in the particulars" (Valsiner 2016, p. 6) and the patterns identified by studying individual cases become the bases for the generalization of knowledge (Valsiner, 2009b).

It has been argued that a different model of general knowledge is required for studying the phenomena of cultural psychology. Salvatore and Valsiner (2010) posit that in addition to inductive and deductive generalization, another option is to follow the logic of abductive inference. According to the logic of this model of the construction of general knowledge, every case of a psychological phenomenon is representative of the group and therefore enables general knowledge (Salvatore & Valsiner, 2010).

Generalization beyond single cases occurs through comparing holistic patterns—trajectories of development—across individual cases (Sato et al., 2007; Valsiner, 2007). Every single case is modeled, and generalization occurs from it. Therefore, the model is validated through the process of construction of knowledge and analysis of the next case—if the new model is consistent with it, it is validated; if it is inconsistent, then it is possible to revise the model. Based on the new knowledge gained, there is also an option to revise the grounding theoretical framework.

Historically Structured Sampling (HSS)

Considering the aim of the study to explore the developmental trajectories of a cohort of psychology students who enrolled in university in the same year,

Historically Structured Sampling (HSS) was applied as the sampling method (Sato et al., 2007). HSS is a methodological tool that attempts to select individual cases on the bases of their trajectories as they unfold through a common temporary state known as the equifinality point (EFP).

HSS is built upon the Trajectory and Equifinality Model (TEM) (Valsiner & Sato, 2006; Sato, et al., 2007; Sato, et al., 2009), a methodology in cultural psychology that is based on the notion of equifinality that implies that sameness is impossible in historical systems; (Valsiner & Sato, 2006; Sato et al. 2007; Sato et al., 2009). Equifinality is the principle that open systems can reach the same state from different initial conditions and through different trajectories (Sato et al., 2007; Sato, 2017). According to HSS, the selection criterion of the participants is that they arrive at the same equifinality point (Sato et al., 2007) established by the researcher and that this study covered the period of undergraduate studies of psychology. The researcher also defines the obligatory passage points (OPP) that are structurally necessary locations in the field, experiences that participants inevitably experience (Valsiner & Sato, 2006; Sato et al., 2007). In this study, the OPPs were enrollment in a university (OPP1) and obtaining a bachelor's degree (OPP2). Between these two points, developmental dynamics were assumed to occur as the participants arrive to the academic environment that guides their professional socialization.

Participants

The sample consisted of a full cohort of psychology students in a bachelor's program from one university in Estonia. The students were admitted in the same academic year (N = 23; 2 male students and 21 female students). Participation in the study was voluntary. Thirteen (N = 13) of the full cohort finished the 48-month-long follow-up. The other ten (N = 10) students who did not complete the study exited for various reasons and at various times. Regardless of whether they had exited the study, the participants were invited to continue their participation at every scheduled time of contact.

To ensure the anonymity of the participants, they are marked with the following fictitious names: Vik, Snap, Uur, Mes, Hei, Ris, Gar, Par, Eri, Ele, Pai, Aet, and Ain. Participants ranged in age from 19 to 20 years at the beginning of the longitudinal study.

The psychology curriculum consisted mostly of courses that provided theoretical knowledge with few practical exercises. A short-term professional internship took place in the last semester of the three-year course of studies. Further specialization in the field (e.g., counseling psychology, school psychology, organizational psychology) was available through graduate studies for a master's degree.

Longitudinal research design

While the aim was to explore the emergence of novelty it was necessary to follow the same cohort over time to detect change over the period of time. For this reason, the longitudinal research design was adopted in this study (Taris, 2000).

Longitudinal research revealed the professional identity construction over a period of 48 months. Figure 3.1 provides the timeline for the longitudinal contact points over the study period and specifies the mixed-method strategies used in data collection. During the period between the two OPPs, the students were contacted three times. The participants were also invited to respond to the follow-up survey 12 months after obtaining a bachelor's degree.

Phase 1 of the study took place nine months after the start of the academic year. At this time, the participants wrote essays, filled out questionnaires, and were interviewed. Phase 2 of the study was carried out in the 19th month, which was also the end of the second academic year. Phase 3 of the study took place in the 33rd month of the students' university studies. Participants were invited to participate 12 months after their studies concluded (Phase 4). All participants held their bachelor's degrees by the final phase of the study.

Methods: Interviews, questionnaires, essays, and theme completion method (DDTC; Double Direction Theme Completion)

In cultural psychology that deals with the psychological dynamics in their complexity (Valsiner, 2009a), qualitative methodology is regarded more fitting (Toomela, 2008; Valsiner, 2017). Considering this, and that

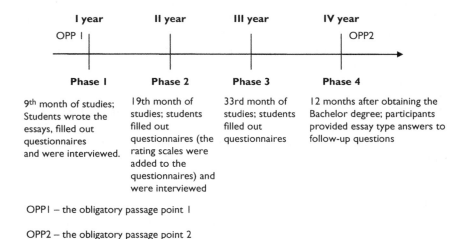

Figure 3.1 The timeline for the longitudinal contact points over the study period.

qualitative research is intended to understand and describe reality through individuals' interpretations (Flick, 2007), to explore the subjective experiences and to gain an in-depth and detailed understanding of participants' meanings of experiences of becoming a psychologist, the qualitative research was adopted.

Exploration of subjective experiences was pursued through semi-structured interviews and questionnaires consisting of open-ended questions. The questionnaires also contained theme-completion tasks (Double Direction Theme Completion; DDTC) (Kullasepp, 2008)—vignettes modeled on a traditional sentence-completion task (Symonds, 1947). In Phase 2 of the study, the rating scales were added to the questionnaires.

The selected excerpts from the interviews, questionnaires, essays, and answers to the follow-up questions presented in this book were translated into English. To confirm the accuracy of the translation, the back-translation method was applied and was carried out by a professional English language expert and by the author of this book.

Interviews and Questionnaires

The semi-structured interviews and questionnaires consisting of open-ended questions were designed to elicit information on the following themes: the students' experiences relating to the professional role, the students' subjective understandings about psychologists (personal representations of psychologists), and experiences linked to different social settings in transitioning to the new social position of being psychology students. The students were also invited to reflect on the changes they had gone through since the beginning of their studies of psychology.

The questionnaires consisted of open-ended questions that allowed participants to describe their experiences in their own words and share meaningful responses to them. The questionnaires provided information about each student's subjective understanding of who psychologists are and how studying psychology affected their lives (e.g., "Has psychological knowledge made your life easier or more complicated? Please explain."), about the perceived differences in the social settings and in the student's interpersonal relationships since beginning studies in psychology (e.g., "Who are these people who make you feel that you have knowledge in psychology. Please explain."), about events or aspects that make studying psychology pleasant or unpleasant (e.g., "What makes studying psychology pleasant or unpleasant for you? Please explain."), and about people's attitudes toward them as psychology students. The questionnaires also contained questions about the perceived influences of studying psychology on the students' lives, and the participants were asked to recall emotional events over the academic year (e.g., "When did you experience the most positive and negative emotions during the previous academic year?") and any doubts they experienced related to their studies (e.g., "Have you experienced doubts about your choice to study psychology?") (Kullasepp, 2006).

Semi-structured interviews enable participants to share detailed insights and personal meanings and are believed to provide a deeper understanding of phenomena (Corbin & Strauss, 2008). The semi-structured interviews for this study were conducted to establish an understanding about the following themes: students' perceptions of the influence of studying psychology on their lives, different events that made studying psychology pleasant or unpleasant for them, and other people's attitudes toward them as psychology students. To captures their images of psychologists, they were invited to reflect on who a psychologist is (e.g., "What did you think before about who a psychologist is, and what do you think now about psychologists?"), on their perceptions of the influence of studying psychology on their self-understanding, and on inter-personal dynamics (e.g., "Have you noticed differences in the ways that you think and behave?").

Essays

The essays were used to investigate how the students construe their pre-studies period. In order to comprehend how the students construed their relationship with the field of psychology before their official studies, they were invited to provide their reflections by writing essays on the aspects of the pre-studies period that, from their point of view, were relevant to their professional choice. Their narratives about their professional journeys toward studying psychology included descriptions of experiences that the students linked to the process of becoming a psychologist.

The essay-type answers to the follow-up questions were used to collect information about whether the students remained in the field after graduating with a bachelor's degree (e.g., studying psychology in a master's program) or distanced themselves from the field of psychology after their studies concluded. The students offered information and opinions about how studying psychology affected their lives after the bachelor's program concluded.

Rating scales

Likert-type rating scales were added to the questionnaires in Phase 2 and Phase 3 of the longitudinal study to gather students' general perceptions of psychologists as different or not different from non-psychologists. The items to be rated were based on data collected in Phase 1 and were developed on the bases of participants' responses to the questions from the interviews and the questionnaires. Participants had to indicate the extent to which they agreed with the statement ("I absolutely agree that, compared to others [non-psychologists], psychologists should …"). The examples of items: [Psychologists should] be more tolerant, be more dedicated to their work, understand better what is needed for well-being, and be better at keeping (personal) relationships. The scale ranged from absolutely disagree to absolutely agree. No statistical analyses were performed with the data.

The utilization of rating-scales in the study was not initially planned, however, it seemed that inviting participants to reflect on the image of a psychologist through the prism of the predefined features of a psychologist could provide some additional information about tendencies in depicting a psychologist. The change in the initial plan was considered to be consistent with the qualitative research methodology. As Creswell (2013, p. 22) writes: "Sometimes the research questions change in the middle of the study to reflect better the types of questions needed to understand the research problem. In response, the data collection strategy, planned before the study, needs to be modified to accompany the new questions."

Double Direction Theme Completion (DDTC) method

The questionnaires contained theme-completion tasks (Double Direction Theme Completion; DDTC) that consisted of vignettes modeled after traditional sentence completion tasks (Symonds, 1947). The DDTC method explicates the microgenesis of ambivalence in person<>role relations. This method, including its coding scheme, was developed to study the psychology students' professional identity formation, and specifically, how different sub-systems in the self (i.e., "I as a person" <> and "I as a professional") are coordinated when solving professional dilemmas (Kullasepp, 2008).

The individual profiles of responses to the Double Direction Theme Completion (DDTC) items provide individual temporal profiles of the coordination of personal orientations and professional role-assuming. Every person is first a person, and only secondly "becomes a psychologist"—that is, incorporates the personally perceived social role expectations set up by the social representation PSYCHOLOGIST. Longitudinal data afford a multi-sided look into the role assumption process, which is expected to be slow (as the socially set course of "studying psychology" extends over N years) and uneven (different aspects of the expected role of the psychologist become linked with features of personal culture at different times, creating different tensions that are either maintained or overcome through semiotic regulators). Thus, the whole process of coordinating the two systems {(I)-ME}-AS-MYSELF and {(I)-ME}-AS-PSYCHOLOGIST is inherently ambivalent but in ways that are always internally inconsistent (Kullasepp, 2008).

The general form of the DDTC items is

> If [SITUATION X happens] then [PERSON-IN-ROLE: psychologist] feels _____ [respondent is directed to construct a direction] because [researcher triggers social suggestion for further direction of the thought process) _____

The technique used in the construction of this method is to insert—based on theoretical considerations of the inevitable centrality of ambivalence in human lives—into the process of constructing answers at the given moment

The DDTC Space. In this study, the DDTC items form a holistic space. That space is organized by the features of the client/patient/person and relationship to him/her (*attractive stranger—familiar person—person linked with familiar person —person in psychological crisis—disliked client— different values—distancing from client*), as well as features of the psychologist's role expectations (*ability/non-ability to help—work hours/non-work hours— confidentiality of client information*). The two domains are structurally linked by one DDTC item ("When a psychologist meets a person in crisis outside working hours, s/he feels ___because__ —the feature of client-in-crisis is set up in link with psychologist-at-work) but not others (Figure 3.2).

The DDTC is integrated here into profiles for each year in the longitudinal study. Based on DDTC, maps of ambivalence profiles were constructed. Maps of profiles of ambivalence (PoA) demonstrate the dynamics of approaching styles over the years. Horizontal lines (see Figure 3.3) refer to tension (or its absence) in responses by the given respondent to the nine DDTC themes (from 1 to 9). Tension—if detected—can be as positive or negative (which may be neutralized or suppressed). The label "prof" refers to professional and "prsn" to personal focus to issue. Missing horizontal lines indicate responses where tensions were not detected. The rule for detection of tension was kept highly conservative—if it is not discernible from the specific DDCT response, it could not be inferred (even if the theme's dilemma suggests it).

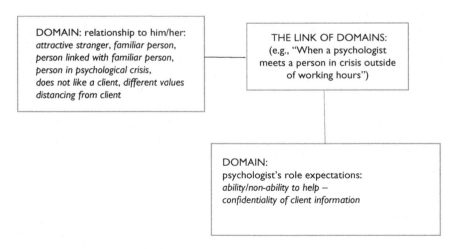

Figure 3.2 The structure of DDTC Space.

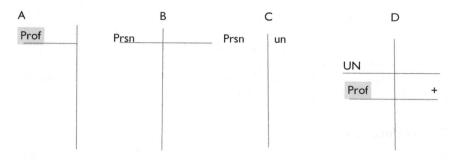

Figure 3.3 A generic example of ambivalence profiles. A—a professional approach, the eliminated tension (e.g., neutral), B—a personal approach, the negative affectivity, C—an unidentified type of tension, a personal approach, D—an unknown approach, the negative tension, and a professional approach, the positive affectivity (marked with +).

The set of DDTC items (see Appendix 1) over the longitudinal study remained the same—like the features of the life of person-as-psychologist depicted in these would remain the same over all work career of any psychologist. What was expected to change was the ways in which the psychology students constructed themselves in relation to the DDTC dilemmas. The respondent is not asked directly ("what would you do if...?") but is viewed as projecting one's own personal-cultural construction of what a psychologist would feel in the given situation into the answer.

Two kinds of data from DDTC.

The DDTC responses are expected to produce (1) interpretations of the suggested situations and (2) ways of suggested solutions to the dilemmas by extending the answers beyond the information given in the item. Thus, any semiotic means (meanings—of various imperatives, or explanations) that are brought into the "because-----" follow-up of the item are the primary data that the DDTC elicits.

DDTC items describe inherently ambivalent conditions. Active denial of such ambivalences, or demonstration that these ambivalences are not there, are also parts of the data. One can consider the method similar to the testing of a null-hypothesis, and relying on evidence that proves that wrong. The data of no ambivalence—under the condition where theoretically ambivalence is expected—requires explanation. This explanation comes by proving that either a previous ambivalence in this case has been overcome, or it has not yet emerged—or that the given item for the given respondent is not relevant.

Furthermore, the data from individual DDTC items reveal respondent-produced semiotic regulators that are brought into the situation for dealing with the ambivalence, and/or explaining how it can be handled. These data give evidence of feed-forward self-regulatory "loops" that are meant to pre-emptively limit (or enhance) a possible event in the future. These feed-forward loops "move through" the personal and professional I-positions, linking them with the realm of actions.

The coding scheme

When coding the responses to the dilemmas from the DDTC, the semiotic regulators were analyzed to identify the perspective to the issue (i.e., professional perspective, personal perspective) and orientation of tension (i.e., negative, positive, and neutral state).

The professional perspective (I-position I as a psychologist)

Perspectives on the issue were coded as professional if the participants' reports included references to moral implications and obligations (e.g., "must," "should be," "forbidden") or to role-related regulations and sets of standards (e.g., ethical codex) and when the need to follow role-related rules was acknowledged in the solutions. (For more examples, see Part 3)

The personal approach (I-position I as a person)

The personal approach to the issue was identified when the meaning of a situation was constructed under the dominant influence of personal concerns and the participant's personal life, such as being influenced by personal relations while in a professional role. If the responses revealed a psychologist's inability to react in accordance with professional role-related regulations (e.g., "a psychologist cannot stay objective"), the response was coded as a personal approach because a non-professional I-position took the lead in generating the affective reaction. Although in the response, regulations and rules were mentioned, the meaning of the situation (e.g., feeling sad because *one doesn't* stay objective) was shaped by a mismatch between a personal quality and a role expectation.

The fluctuation of perspectives

If the solution to the dilemma consisted of both of perspectives—personal and professional—it was coded as the fluctuation of perspectives. In this case, the dominating or leading I-position was not identified.

Directions of developmental trajectories based on the utilization of personal or professional I-position

Based on the identified perspectives in solutions to professional dilemmas each year across the three years, the three directions of developmental trajectories (i.e., self-professionalizing, self-personalizing, self-maintaining cases) were identified.

In order to define the direction of the trajectory of socialization through the professional role, the dynamics of the utilization of leading I-positions (i.e., professional I-position, personal I-position) in solutions to dilemmas were identified. Specifically, the dynamics of the use of both positions was observed in parallel. That enabled to identify, generally, the increasing and decreasing tendencies in the application of I-position, together with their stable distribution in different years. For example, one (1) the occurrence of the professional position in year 1, six occurrences of the same position in year 2, and 9 occurrences in the last year, in parallel with 8 personal positions in year 1, three (3) in second year and zero personal positions in the last year in solutions. This particular illustrative example demonstrates the self-professionalizing case characterized by the increase of professional perspectives in solutions and the decrease of I-position I as a person in responses.

However, different types of patterns of the dynamics of the use of leading positions in solutions may fall into the same general category and are described below:

- the dominance of the professional focus on the issues increased by the 3rd year of studies in parallel with a decrease in the personal perspective (e.g., Uur, Ris, Mes, Vik)
- the use of the professional focus dominated over the personal approach and remained the same in parallel with a decrease in the personal perspective by the 3rd year (e.g., Hei).
- the use of the professional focus increased by the 3rd year, while the use of personal perspective tended to remain the same (e.g., Aet).

The self-professionalizing cases in this study were Vik, Snap, Uur, Mes, Hei, Ris, Aet (7)

Self-personalizing trajectories were identified in cases of the increasing use of personal I-positions by the last year, in parallel with the decreased use of the professional approach in solutions (Gar, Par).

Compared to the other two directions of professionalization, self-maintaining cases (Ain, Eri, Ele, Pai) did not display a clear tendency to incline toward self-professionalization or self-personalization. The common feature of these cases is their tendency to maintain the system (which does not exclude the dynamics). The maintenance of the system appeared in different forms:

- re-establishing or maintaining the state in the use of both types of I-positions over the years (Ain)
- maintaining the frequency of utilization of both types of I-positions in different years that appeared in parallel increase and decrease of the application of professional and personal perspectives, or "synchronized dynamics" (Eri),
- tendency to maintain the frequency of the use of personal and professional perspective by the last year (Ele),
- the ratio of the use of different positions was maintained over the years, meaning the initial ratio was restored (Pai). For example, four (4) occurrences of professional and three (3) occurrences of personal I-positions in the first year and in the last year three (3) and two (2), respectively.

The orientation of tension in solutions across the years

Regarding the orientation of tension in the responses, the following different categories were extracted from the data: positively and negatively oriented affectivity, neutral state, flux (i.e., the fluctuation of handling tension) and unknown. When data on feelings were missing, this category was marked as "unfilled." (e.g., the answer is not provided). Feelings like happy, good, pleased, and proud were coded as positively oriented tension. Feelings like bad, sad, unsure, in tension, angry, inadequate, restricted, stressed, incompetent, and uncomfortable were marked as tension with a negative orientation. The category of neutral was identified when feeling normal, no difference, still the same, or as a bystander were reported. (For more examples, see Part 3).

Description of the profiles of handling tension

The solutions to the dilemmas revealed how the tension in the inherently ambivalent condition, person< >role, was handled between different years, including the prevalence of the specific affective orientation (i.e., negatively oriented affectivity, positively oriented affectivity, or neutral) in solutions between different years.

In general, the participant (Snap) was coded as "positive case" because tendency to incline toward dominance of non-negative affectivity (i.e., positively oriented affectivity, or neutral) in solutions. The participants were labeled as "negative cases" (e.g., Ain, Uur) because showing prevailing negative tension in total. The participants were coded as "balanced cases" due to a more balanced distribution of negative and non-negative affectivity in solutions in total (e.g., Pai, Hei). Some of the participants tended toward the increasingly generating positive affectivity and neutral state (e.g., Mes, Hei) whereat the others toward negative affectivity (e.g., Pai, Eri). One case (Ris) was exceptional, with 13 unknown solutions but with the dominance of negative affectivity in total.

Summary

While focusing on intra-psychological dynamics, this book attempts to establish how professional identity emerges.

In accordance with the axiomatic set of cultural psychology, the current study on ways of internalizing professional identity was rooted in the idiographic paradigm. Various methods of data collection were used in this qualitative research, including questionnaires (which also contained theme-completion tasks), interviews, and essays. The participants were invited to answer follow-up questions after their studies were over. The theme-completion method (DDTC) was developed to investigate how different sub-systems in the self (i.e., I as a person <> and I as a professional) are coordinated when solving professional dilemmas (Kullasepp, 2008).

To explore the individual developmental trajectories of psychology students who belong to the same cohort, non-random, HSS was applied. HSS attempts to select individual cases on the basis of trajectories that unfold through a common temporary state (i.e., an equifinality point). According to HSS, the selection criterion of the participants is arriving at the same equifinality point from their initial points (Sato et al., 2007). The total duration of the longitudinal multiple case study was 48 months. It contained four contact points (i.e., in the 9th, 19th, and 33rd months of studies and in the 48th month after beginning university studies), the first three of which took place during studies in the bachelor's program, while the final contact took place after the studies concluded.

References

Cohen, L., Manion, L., & Morrison, K. (2007). *Research Methods in Education* (6th ed.). Routledge/Taylor & Francis Group.

Corbin, J., & Strauss, A. (2008). *Basics of Qualitative Research: Techniques and Procedures for Developing Grounded Theory* (3rd ed.). Sage Publications, Inc. 10.4135/9781452230153

Creswell, J. W. (2013). *Research Design. Qualitative, Quantitative and Mixed Methods Approaches*. Thousand Oaks, CA: Sage.

Flick, U. (2007). *Designing Qualitative Research*. Sage Publications Ltd. 10.4135/9781849208826

Hammersley, M. (2013). *What Is Qualitative Research?* London and New York: Bloomsbury.

Kullasepp, K. (2006). Becoming professional: External and intrapsychological level in the service of professional identity construction of psychology students. *European Journal of School Psychology, 4*(2), 337–347.

Kullasepp, K. (2008). *Dialogical Becoming. Professional Identity Construction of Psychology Students*. Tallinna Ülikooli Kirjastus.

Molenaar, P. C. M. (2004). A manifesto on psychologyas idiographic science: Bringing the person back into scientific psychology, This time forever. *Measurement, 2*(4), 201–218.

Molenaar, P. C. M., & Valsiner, J. (2005). How generalization works through the single case: A simple idiographic process analysis of an individual psychotherapy case. *International Journal of Idiographic Science, 1,* 1–13.

Salvatore, S., & Valsiner, J. (2010). Between the general and the unique: Overcoming the nomothetic versus idiographic opposition. *Theory & Psychology, 20*(6), 817–833. 10.1177/0959354310381156

Sato, T. (2017). *Collected Papers on Trajectory Equifinality Approach Hardcover.* Chitose Press Inc.

Sato, T., Hidaka, T. & Fukuda, M. (2009). Depicting the dynamics of living the life: The Trajectory Equifinality Model. In J. Valsiner, P. Molenaar, M. Lyra, & N. Chaudhary (Eds.), *Dynamic Process Methodology in the Social and Developmental Sciences* (pp. 217–240). New York: Springer.

Sato, T., Yasuda, Y., Kido, A., Arakawa, A., Mizoguchi, M., & Valsiner, J. (2007). Sampling reconsidered: Idiographic science and the analyses of personal life trajectories. In J. Valsiner & A. Rosa (Eds.), *Cambridge Handbook of Socio-Cultural Psychology* (pp. 82–106). NY: Cambridge University Press.

Symonds, P. M. (1947). The sentence completion task as a projective technique. *Journal of Abnormal and Social Psychology, 42*(3), 320–329.

Taris T. (2000). *Longitudinal Data Analysis.* London, UK: Sage Publications.

Toomela, A. (2008). Vygotskian cultural-historical and sociocultural approaches represent two levels of analysis: Complementarity instead of opposition. *Culture & Psychology, 14*(1), 57–69.

Valsiner. J. (2007). *Culture in Minds and Societies: Foundation of Cultural Psychology.* New Delhi, India: Sage Publications India Pvt Ltd.

Valsiner, J. (2009a). Integrating psychology within the globalizing world. *IPBS: Integrative Psychological & Behavioral Science, 43*(1), 1–16.

Valsiner, J. (2009b). Cultural psychology today: Innovations and oversights. *Culture & Psychology, 15*(1), 5–39. 10.1177/1354067X08101427

Valsiner, J. (2017). Cultural-semiotic self-regulation. In M. Raudsepp (Ed.), *Between Self and Societies: Creating Psychology in a New Key.* Tallinn, Estonia: Tallinn University Press.

Valsiner, J., & Sato, T. (2006). Historically Structured Sampling (HSS): How can psychology's methodology become tuned in to the reality of the historical nature of cultural psychology? In J. Straub, C. Kölbl, D. Weidemann & B. Zielke (Eds.), *Pursuit of Meaning. Advances in Cultural and Cross-cultural Psychology* (pp. 215–251). Bielefeld: Transcript Verlag.

Valsiner, J. (2016). The nomothetic function of the idiographic approach: Looking from inside out. *Journal of Person Oriented Research, 2*(1–2), 5–15. 10.17505/jpor.2016.02

Conclusion to Part I

Part 1 introduced the theoretical framework of this book and its methodology. Chapter 2 brought together the laminal model of internalization and externalization, the concept of hierarchies of signs, and the dialogical self theory to introduce the semiotic-dialogical approach to the construction of professional identity.

In line with the constructivist perspective (Gergen, 1999) identity is not understood as an inborn quality or static entity, but as a process that emerges through various socio-cultural encounters (Hall & du Gay, 2003; Wenger, 1998), in this book, identity is conceptualized—as the semiotic process of affective regulation of one's unique relations with the world that unfolds through the use and construction of signs. These meaning complexes regulate one's relationship with the professional role and enable one to construct self-understanding—"I am a psychologist" or "I am not a psychologist yet."

In terms of cultural psychology, becoming a psychologist is regarded as an intra- and interpersonally unique process (Salvatore & Valsiner, 2010)—there are no identical professional identities of psychologists. Although students from the same cohort encounter the same social academic-educational messages (e.g., attending the same lectures) and are engaged in the same (obligatory or optional) activities (e.g., participating in seminars, conducting research projects), the ways they construe their experience of internalizing the professional role remain different.

In general, entry into the professional role during university studies is guided at the level of social representations and coordinated at the level of intra-psychological processes manifesting in the ongoing transposition of cultural material that shapes psychology students' responses to events and how they build their self-understanding as psychologists. Dialogues between these two organizations—social and psychological—occur through the internalization/externalization of social representations. As the result of constructive interactions with their socio-cultural surroundings, the students build the professional identity that is the

DOI: 10.4324/9781315519616-5

reflection of their migration to the environment of academic-institutional representations and of the transition to the new position in the matrix of social relations.

References

Gergen, K. J. (1999). *An Invitation to Social Construction*. London, United Kingdom: Sage Publication.

Hall, S., & du Gay, P. (2003). *Questions of Cultural identity*. Sage Publications.

Salvatore, S., & Valsiner, J. (2010). Between the general and the unique: Overcoming the nomothetic versus idiographic opposition. *Theory & Psychology*, *20*(6), 817–833. 10.1177/0959354310381156

Wenger, E. (1998). *Communities of Practice: Learning, Meaning, and Identity*. Cambridge University Press. 10.1017/CBO9780511803932

Part II

A psychologist as a sign

Chapter 4

Psychologists emerge everywhere: The academic and non-academic voices in the focus

From the heterogeneity of microsystems to the multiplicity in the self

Becoming a psychologist is not a solo journey in the sense that it embraces mutually developing interactions with the others. It is shaped by both academic and non-academic environments that contribute to the formations of professional identity. A systemic ecological perspective is needed.

One of the organizing theoretical frameworks for comprehending human development within the person's environment is Bronfenbrenner's ecological theory (Bronfenbrenner & Evans, 2000; Bronfenbrenner & Morris, 2006). Based on this model, an environment consists of different layers of systems (i.e., microsystem, macrosystem, mesosystem, exosystem, chronosystem) that interact in complex ways, affect individual's development, and are itself affected by it (Johnson, 2008).

According to the concept of microsystem that is "a pattern of activities, roles, and interpersonal relations experienced by the developing person in a given setting with particular physical and material characteristics" (Bronfenbrenner & Bronfenbrenner, 1981, p. 22), the encounters in the academic and non-academic environment (e.g., interactions with friends, casual acquaintances, therapists, teachers) and experiences in multiple social roles (e.g., a family member, a colleague, a patient) has to be considered of as the contexts where negotiation of professional identity unfolds. Thereat, the bidirectional influences between the microsystems—called a mesosystem (Bronfenbrenner & Bronfenbrenner, 1981), allow to expect that experiences with the non-academic others influence the dynamics in formal educational settings, and vice versa. For example, what students find out about their future professional role (e.g., psychologists are expected to have x or y characteristics that are needed to provide professional services) can influence how they respond in informal relations and in the non-academic settings. Similarly, the stereotypes about psychologists encountered in the non-academic environments may have an effect on students' responses

DOI: 10.4324/9781315519616-7

in the educational practices at the university. The non-academic others' unrealistic expectations about psychologists (e.g., psychologist can read the others' mind, they are particularly interested in observing all the time the others' behavior), can give rise the students' dissatisfaction with academic studies at the university (e.g., I am still unable to read others' mind) or vice versa, the increase of motivation in pursuing academic goals.

Additionally to the microsystems that compose the students' immediate environments, becoming a psychologist is shaped by the system of events that the students themselves cannot influence but that have a direct or indirect impact on their professional socialization. This system is called exosystem, a system in which the students themselves are not active participants (e.g., government's educational policy decisions, major society related factors affecting labor market).

The students' environment includes also a larger system called macrosystem that consists of, for example, overarching values, belief systems, subcultures. An example that could be given is the value attributed in the society to the profession of psychologist, or the stereotypes, which influences the selection by students of the major of psychology.

Lastly, the model highlights chronosystem that refers to time-dimension and concerns changes at all levels of ecological system (Johnson, 2008).

In pages to follow I foremostly address the involvement of the academic and non-academic environments that provide psychologists-to-be the cultural material to construct the professional to comprehend how the personal meanings of the social encounters guide the construction of self-understanding—I as a psychologist—and shape relations with the professional role. Below, first, academic and non-academic settings echoing in the voices of I-positions in the self are explored, followed by the analysis of unique experiences of the three psychology students. Three cases enable us the insight to the re-construction of Self-Other relations when the novel aspect of the self (I as a psychologist) is under construction

Non-academic arenas in becoming a psychologist

The interviews consisted of the questions that invited the participants to reflect on their professional journey and were relevant to their experiences. To the questions concerning when the students experienced that they study psychology, students responded as given below revealing involvement of different voices that can be linked to the microsystems in the non-academic settings (i.e., non-academic voices) in the inner dialogues. Typically, based on the students' retrospective reflections (e.g., Ain, Ris, Eri, Aet), the non-academic others' voices pointed out that the students are (now) the experts on human issues or the helpers who provide support.

Extracts from the interviews

> "When I meet strangers and when they learn what I study, then, it has happened many times that they ask, "What am I thinking right now?" (Ain)
> "I also discuss things with members of my family, and they ask, "and your point of view as a psychologist?" (Pai)
> "Also, my friends and acquaintances come to me more often to talk about their problems and ask for the advice." (Eri)
> "When friends ask questions related to their personal lives, or when I see stressed-out persons, or in my family, when my parents have intensive periods and they need help." (Ain)

The non-academic voices in the self brought to the inner dialogues the perspectives to include into negotiation on the professional identity and to adopt with the expressed (new) social expectations. The non-academic voices became a part of assuming a professional role by recommending the directions of professional development—the friends' and the close ones' voices in the self "told" students to change, to be different (than before). The following extracts exemplify some of the suggestions, illustrating that there is more than one—academic-institutional—frame of reference for negotiating the professional identity. Participant Aet reported: "My parents, for example, when I become nervous, they note all the time that you are becoming a psychologist. They think that a psychologist must be very calm." Another student, Ain, pointed: "I have the feeling that people expect more from me, because I study psychology. They rely on you, and what you say can be taken too seriously, maybe they trust me too much."

The non-academic environment guides the transition to the social position of a psychologist and shapes the psychology students' experiences. A psychologist must be calm, a psychologist's personal life has to be in order, psychologists have to be reliable in personal relations, emerge in students' autodialogues as the frame of (new) regulations extending also to the sphere of personal life. The voices suggest to the psychologists-to-be that the border between personal and professional life has to be re-negotiated. One is expected to function as a psychologist not only in professional settings but also in informal relations.

Drawing on the reports, the students, too, identified themselves as psychologists in the non-academic settings, turning everyday settings into the informal playground where to practice the professional role and shape I-position I as a psychologist. For example, based on the findings, students had started to apply their professional knowledge outside the academic context, in informal settings. In addition, it seems that an emerging psychologist's voice in the self brought about the themes related to the interpersonal interactions (e.g., the precision in expressing oneself, trying to understand the other person, letting the other person speak without interruption) into the inner dialogues and made interpersonal skills topical.

Extracts from the interviews

> "In conflict situations, when I try to solve problems, I use the knowledge I have learned. Then it is necessary to be very careful in exactly what you say." (Ris)
> "But also, with clients at the workplace, I observe them and analyze them. I also believe that my family, friends, and acquaintances evoke that feeling in me [that I study psychology]. I use my knowledge from school when I interact with them." (Ain)
> "With a friend, my parents—I try to understand my mother when I feel that I don't, and then I try to link it to the psychological knowledge I have learned. It is a good feeling; it helps me to understand and bring knowledge into practice." (Gar)
> "I try more and more not to interrupt people when they are talking and to listen to them more carefully. Sometimes I think how a professional psychologist could give advice to his/her friend...I think that I should not proceed on the basis of my own experiences, I try not to act on the basis of my own personal experiences." (Ain)

Academic others in the inner dialogue

Further, while non-academic informal situations provided an arena mostly for positioning oneself as an expert on human issues and being helper or supporter, then academic settings fostered the professional identity formation through the sense of belonging to the group of psychologists, through the feeling of membership. Specifically, the same question: "When do you feel that you are studying psychology or experience the effect of psychology studies?" received responses such as the following: "With the other psychology students, feeling of belonging together. It makes me feel good that I don't have to explain.", "With psychology students—the feeling of belonging together.", "With other psychology students—it is good if you can talk about psychology freely and not be afraid that they will laugh at you and say 'what rubbish you are talking about'." "People who study psychology or have finished it already. They evoke positive emotions, but not because they study psychology, just because they are nice. Also, with people who know well the "inner life" of humans.", "Other psychology students. We have experienced the same things and we understand the same jokes.", "Other psychology students. We share inside jokes and experiences. This makes me feel happy, it kind of allows me to escape from the reality."

Border under negotiation: psychologists <> non-psychologist

In terms of the semiotic perspective, becoming a psychologist is the semiotic process of re-negotiation of the borders. Based on co-genetic logic that "the figure, ground, and separating them boundary are mutually co-definitive" (Valsiner, 2007, p.129), the emergence of psychologist's identity co-occurs with semiotic distinction with non-psychologists (i.e., A co-occurs with non-A).

> A border enables us to define our own identity while distancing ourselves from the others in a correlative way at the same time. A semiotic border triggers a dynamic process in which the counterpart, the alterity, the otherness, the strangeness are involved. It is impossible to define a Me without a non-Me.
> (De Luca Picione & Valsiner, 2017, p. 534)

Accordingly, becoming a psychologist and the emergence of I-position I as a psychologist is the process of re-construction of border—re-negotiation of the "us" and "non-us" (Tajfel & Turner, 2004)—the process of re-considering relations with "non-psychologists" along the dimension of I ("us") "psychologists" <> "non-psychologists" ("non-us") relations. The entry into the professional role is accompanied by identification with the academic others like fellow students with whom the respondents experienced perceived similarities and membership to the group of psychologists. Thereat, the voices linked to the non-academic contexts emphasized students' differences from non-psychologist.

Building on the socio psychological perspective, assuming a professional role entails identification with the specific social group (e.g., the psychologists) and self-categorization that allows expecting novelty in the way persons think about themselves and about the relations with the others. Thus, while social groups "provide their members with an identification of themselves in social terms" (Tajfel & Turner, 2004, p. 283), the psychology studies lead to re-construction of self-understanding in terms of the future professional role—a psychologist.

Unfolding bordering across years

More detailed analysis of the three cases from the underlying study below—participants Snap, Mes, and Uur—exemplifies the essential and typical findings concerning the formation of I-position in academic and non-academic settings across the three years of studies, shedding light on the continuous formation of I-position I as a psychologist in the inner dialogue between multiple external and internal I-positions.

Respondent Snap's transition during studies of psychology

In the first year of bachelor's studies, Snap's reflection reveals an emerging I-position, I as a psychologist where the non-academic and academic settings both have shaped Snap's professional identity. We can notice in Snap's reports that the interactions with friends and colleagues at the workplace (while studying, Snap had a job that was not related to psychology) provided experiences, that outlined in Snap's self, Snap's position I as a psychologist. Other people's voice in Snap's self provided Snap with an opportunity to make sense of the position in social matrix of relations: who am I in this situation, what others think who I am in this situation.

Extracts from the interviews with Snap.

"It seems to me that my old friends' opinion about me has changed—they think that I have become more understanding than I used to be—they have a different attitude toward me. People at my workplace, they like to think that someone [Snap as a psychologist] observes them."

To the question: "Do your colleagues behave differently when they discover that you study psychology?" Snap answered: "Yes, some of them become so open, they ask questions. My friends have said that in the long-term perspective they want me to counsel them, but I think that they are joking. But surely, they expect greater understanding. They say "You are a psychologist. You keep secrets" and I do. Now, yes, when expectations are higher, you want to live up to the expectations. For sure, expectations are higher. I must behave differently."

Snap's becoming a psychologist occurs under the guidance of different microsystems—the friends' and colleagues' voices—external I-positions in Snap's self—expressing expectations (e.g., friends expect that their secrets will be safe with Snap). Snap's use of the semiotic regulator MUST (I must behave differently) refers to the I-position I as a psychologist in informal settings when socializing with friends. To the question: "When do you feel that you have studied psychology?" Snap responded: "I would like to socialize with lecturers of psychology, it gives me a kind of special feeling."

In the second year of studies, we can observe an ongoing formation of Snap's professional identity through encounters in the academic and non-academic contexts. "I have to hear the stories of my friends, I feel that I must listen to them, I know their secrets. I try to take a friend's position—like a friend is listening to a friend, it is good that people trust me." Again, the reports reveal the involvement of I position I as a psychologist, in the coordination of psychological functioning under the ambivalent conditions (i.e., I positions I as a psychologist and I as a non-psychologist (i.e., a friend) are both presented in the self). The semiotic regulator MUST (i.e., I must listen to them) reveals the ongoing internalization/externalization of professional role expectations; the psychologist's voice in the self has brought regulations or norms (i.e., must) into the inner dialogue Snap has to deal with.

Snap's answer to the question: "When do you feel that you study psychology?" was: "With my supervisor. Actually, with people who are not psychologists, because it makes it possible to feel that I am different from them "at that level." Being with other psychology students from our class makes me feel nothing special, we don't talk all the time about psychology."

What is more, Snap's comment: "Actually with people who are not psychologists, because it makes it possible to feel that I am different from them 'at that level'." illustrates how the non-academic environment offers opportunities for the construction of identity of a psychologist. The creation of a border between "us" (i.e., psychologists) and "them" (i.e., non-us or non-psychologists), and the identification with the specific group (i.e., psychologists), refers to an emerging I-position of I as a psychologist in the Snap's self. The non-academic others support Snap experience the feeling of being in transition.

Snap's report in the third year of studies implicitly indicates the tension that the different I positions—I as a PERSON (non-psychologist) and I as a PSYCHOLOGIST—generate and move the inherently ambivalent condition of entry into the professional role into the focus. "I expect my friends to think that I am their friend regardless of my education (and it is so!), they don't, should not, think that as a psychologist I am better than they are, and vice versa."

Eventually, we can also observe how the interactions with the in-group members like other psychologists, psychology students, and the supervisor are involved in becoming a psychologist during the studies at university. Snap reported: "When I participate in experiments or spend time with well-known psychologists. For example, it is a good feeling to meet my supervisor at the university. With other psychology students or at parties with faculty members."

Respondent Hei's transition in the academic and non-academic contexts.

Respondent Hei's reflection across the three years of psychology studies resembles Snap's experiences, in general terms. Although the details of assuming the role of a psychologist remain different, Hei, for instance, feels the influence of psychology studies when interacting with children, emerging as a psychologist through encounters in the academic and non-academic contexts similarly to other students who participated in the study. The friends and family members, fellow students, and clients at work, are all involved in Hei's transition and in negotiation on the professional identity.

As to the extracts from the interviews and questionnaires, in the first year of studies of psychology, Hei responded to the question: "When do you feel that you study psychology?" as follows: "With the other psychology students, we have found a special language. With children—they need people to encourage them. Also, with close friends, I try to understand them and listen to them more than before."

While I am now becoming a psychologist, I try to understand and listen more to my friends (than I used to) illustrates self-regulation when becoming a psychologist. Rethinking one's own behavior in relation to interactions with others from non-academic environment is part of Hei's entry into the professional role—emerging psychologist's voice in the self tells Hei to listen more to friends indicating to transformations in the self-structure and emergence of I-position I as a psychologist.

Therefore, we can also see that for Hei the other psychology students form the "us"—group (i.e., in-group)—they have a special language that marks a border between those who know and share a special language and those with whom the special language is not shared. The fellow students' voices in the self seem to foster the feeling of belongingness to the group of psychologists (or psychology students). The keyword here is "a special language" that explicitly points at identification with psychologists.

To the question: "When do you feel the effect of studying psychology?" Hei responded: "At the workplace, with clients. Life is easier now, it concerns interactions with others, I understand people better. Especially kids. I know a lot important things, how to influence their development, how to behave with them in certain situations."

Psychologist's voice in the self enables a feeling of improvement of the interaction skills (implication: as a psychologist one has knowledge that allows them better understand others).

Meaning complex of a psychologist (e.g., someone who has the knowledge about interactions) regulates Hei's relations with the others (e.g., I understand people better now). Because I am studying psychology and I have special professional knowledge > I have to be doing something better/in a different way (from the non-psychologists), is a semiotically constructed reality for Hei.

The responses in the second year of studies shed light on the continuing emergence of I position, I as a psychologist: "Life is complicated, because you can face prejudice against psychologists in society, that they treat crazy people and people don't understand who a psychologist is, and what psychology is."

The identification with a specific group of psychologists is accompanied by the tension rising when Hei perceives the prejudice against psychologists. According to Hei, it makes life more complicated. Emerged I position, I as a psychologist, in the self that makes Hei vulnerable to others' opinion about psychologists.

In addition to the academic context, the non-academic settings constitute the arena where the new identity is also negotiated for Hei. "Now, when I interact with people, I know how to more effectively listen, observe, analyze them. As to other psychology students—it evokes positive feelings, we have much in common—talking about the same things. Friends and parents—I can give them knowledge, it is a positive feeling. It also makes this knowledge clearer for myself."

In the last year of studies, becoming a psychologist manifests continuously in the construction of self-understanding—due to her studies of psychology, Hei views herself as more competent on human issues. Similarly to the reports from the previous years of studies, interactions with fellow students and informal relations provide the socio-cultural setting that shapes her I-position, I as a psychologist: "I understand the human psyche better, and based on that [knowledge], I am better at evaluating human relations and behavior," and "With psychology students. With them I can share experiences and knowledge. Also, with parents—I can talk about what I know. With friends and acquaintances—they ask for advice and help, I feel good, I see that they value my specialty."

Respondent Uur's becoming a psychologist through various developmental contexts

Uur's responses, similarly to Snap and Hei, illustrate the role of academic and non-academic settings in assuming a professional role. We can observe the non-academic others' voices—external I-positions—in the inner dialogues that tend to lead to a rise in tension within the self. It seems that being positioned by others as a psychologist, or an expert on human issues in the informal relation has an effect on the dynamics within the self. In the first year of studies, Uur responded to the questions: "When do you feel that you study psychology? " and "Has your life become more complicated?" as given below:

> "Sometimes when my friends talk about problems, and then they add— you as a psychologist. They are like a little bit more watchful. But it has happened for a few times that a stranger says 'psychologist' in a teasing way, as if psychologists should know the answers.",
>
> "Mostly people from the university—students and lecturers. Maybe because we talk about psychology.", and "Life is now more complicated, because friends and acquaintances think that I am kind of an expert and they expect me to analyze their behavior when they ask me."

Similarly, Uur's experiences in the second year of studies shape the I-position, I as a psychologist. For instance, during the interview Uur answered: "Another person asked me, what do you think, because they knew that I studied psychology, and then I was not sure that what I said was right, but I tried to look sophisticated, to approach it from a different perspective than they do, and then I felt smart and proud."

External I-positions lead to the attempt to "look sophisticated," which was accompanied by positive feelings. Forming I-position has started the move toward desired self-concept.

The following extracts from the interviews illustrate an inherently ambivalent nature of assuming the professional role. To be more specific, Uur's responses reveal a conflict due to the role-related expectations that are in contradiction with Uur as a PERSON (i.e., non-psychologist)."We were with friends in a cafe and one person with antisocial appearance entered, and again, my friends asked me what would have been the reasons behind that [that this person had become antisocial], and then I said that I am a psychologist from 8am until 5 pm. After that I want to be a normal person who looks at an antisocial person and wants them to go away." and "I don't want to talk about psychology with my friends. I am no longer a psychology student in school; sometimes I feel that I am the target of interest, they all want to know what I think about somebody. Now I want to be a normal person like everyone else."

Alike other participants in this underlying study, the formation of professional role related I-position was supported by identification with the others from the academic settings in the second year of studies, as well as in the last year of studies. The question: "When or with whom do you feel that you study psychology?" received the following answers: "People from the university and psychology students. They are part of my life and I enjoy it. Sometimes, I am proud that I am one of them.", "At the university with other students and lecturers and at the workplace. In school I feel that I have a long way to go, at work I feel competent. It is a good feeling when you know what you are talking about."

And eventually, Uur's reports in the last year of studies reveal a continuous emergence of I-position. Uur reported that: "I think that all my life is tied to psychology, this is inside me and I already consciously use the psychological knowledge I have learned, but also unconsciously." and "First of all, at the workplace when interacting with people, when I evaluate them. The ability to assume something and apply a respective theory makes me feel good and proud of myself It is a good feeling when you can assume something and apply a theory, I feel proud. It is enjoyable and fun to apply knowledge about psychology in everyday life."

Different microsystems that re-appear in students' inner dialogues and in reflections of experiences are high of significance in organizing the process of identity. The voices of friends, colleagues, fellow students, professors guide the construction of self-understanding and differentiation of the self. I-position I as a psychologist receives different feedback that supports its continuous formation. Identity is a process of re-construction of borders that additionally to the forming self-understanding manifests in re-negotiation of Self-Other relations (Kullasepp, 2021; Fontal, Marsico, Ossa, Millan, & Prado, 2021; Español & Cornejo, 2021). As the findings enable to argue, becoming a psychologist re-organizes "us"<>"non-us" relations. Former friends become experts or someone who is different because they are psychologists. Novelty in the interpersonal dynamics, in turn, reflects in the inner dialogues in the self creating new possibilities for the development.

Summary

Becoming a psychologist is a complex and multilayered process unfolding under the influence of various microsystems that function as an immediate playground to practice "being a psychologist" and relate to the professional role. Thereat, the formation of professional identity takes place through the academic-educational practices, in parallel with the input from everyday settings in the non-academic environments; it involves informal and formal relations that the social structure makes available for them. Based on the findings, the non-academic and academic microsystems seem to provide different socialization experiences when assuming professional role. Friends' voices within the self suggest "You are a helper" and recommend to adopt the supporter's perspective in informal relations (e.g., to help others), whereas fellow students' and academic staff's voices suggest "You are one of us." Additionally, the others' voices in the self when recommending certain developmental directions and changes, implicitly refer to the representations and to the knowledge about psychologists circulating in the socio-cultural surrounding. The voices in the self reflect the cultural knowledge about a psychologist that regulates not only the intra-psychological but also inter-personal dynamics—a sign "a psychologist" operates also on the inter-personal dimension (re-)organizing the relations between people.

Although in this chapter the attention was foremostly paid to micro-systems, or more precisely, to I-positions that represent the social others in the self, and to their influence, the organizing influence of macro- and exosystems cannot be underestimated in professional identity construction. The historical, social, and cultural environmental conditions have an impact to interpersonal interactions, activities in academic and non-academic settings.

References

Bronfenbrenner, U., & Bronfenbrenner, U. (1981). The ecology of human development: Experiments by nature and design. Retrieved from http://ebookcentral.proquest.com. Created from tallinn-ebooks on 2019-07-12 01:59:38.
Bronfenbrenner, U., & Evans, G. W. (2000). Developmental science in the 21st century: Emerging questions, theoretical models, research designs and empirical findings. *Social Development*, *9*(1), 115–125. 10.1111/1467-9507.00114

Bronfenbrenner, U., & Morris, P. A. (2006). The bioecological model of human development. In R. M. Lerner & W. Damon (Eds.), *Handbook of child psychology: Theoretical models of human development* (pp. 793–828). John Wiley & Sons Inc.

Español, A., & Cornejo, M. (2021). Border selves: Experiences, positions, and inner-others from the Spanish-Moroccan Border. In K. Kullasepp, & G. Marsico (Eds.), *Identity at the Borders and Between the Borders* (pp. 53–72). Springer International Publishing.

Fontal, A., Marsico, G., Ossa, J. C., Millan, J. D., & Prado, A. (2021). The dynamic functionality of borders: A study from a cultural perspective. In K. Kullasepp, & G. Marsico (Eds.), *Identity at the Borders and Between the Borders* (pp. 37–52). Springer International Publishing.

Johnson, E. S. (2008). Ecological systems and complexity theory: Toward an alternative model of accountability in education. *Complicity: An International Journal of Complexity and Education*, 5 (1), 1–10.

Kullasepp, K. (2021). An intra-psychological perspective on borders: On the example of becoming Estonian. In K. Kullasepp, & G. Marsico (Eds.), *Identity at the Borders and between the Borders* (pp. 89−107). Springer International Publishing.

De Luca Picione, R., & Valsiner, J. (2017). Psychological functions of semiotic borders in sense-making: Liminality of narrative processes. *Europe's Journal of Psychology*, *13*(3), 532–547. 10.5964/ejop.v13i3.1136

Tajfel, H., & Turner, J. C. (2004). The social identity theory of intergroup behavior. In J. T. Jost & J. Sidanius (Eds.), *Key Readings in Social Psychology. Political Psychology: Key Readings* (pp. 276–293). New York, NY, US: Psychology Press.

Valsiner, J. (2007). *Culture in Minds and Societies: Foundation of Cultural Psychology*. New Delhi, India: Sage Publications India Pvt Ltd.

Chapter 5

A sign of a psychologist as an organizer

Consistent with the basic axiom in cultural psychology that a semiotic mediation process cannot be separated from the psychological functioning (Salvatore, 2012), this chapter moves on to explore the involvement of social and personal representations in the construction of professional identity.

Based on the theoretical assumption of cultural psychology, we can observe how psychology students construct and organize their world through the ongoing processes of internalization and externalization that enable the integration of novel cultural material and innovations in the structure of self. It can be assumed then, that the transition to the social position of psychology student reflects in how the students construct their self-understanding, and make sense of their relations with the surrounding, including with the professional role. Metaphorically speaking, becoming a psychologist is expected to appear in looking to the world through the "lenses of a psychologist"—a fuzzy and ambiguous concept. However, this chapter narrows down "a psychologists' way of thinking" to how the students construed their relation with the professional role and worldview.

"I am different now"

To investigate emerging I-position I as a psychologist, the psychology students were instructed to reflect on the changes in themselves since the beginning of studies of psychology. The questions like: "What do you think, has something changed in you since the psychology studies began?," "What do you think, have studies of psychology changed you somehow?" and "Have you tried to change something in you because you become a psychologist?" provide an insight into the tendencies in construction of professional identity. To guide the participants reflect more broadly on their experiences as a psychology student, the questionnaire incorporated the question: "Have the studies of psychology made your life easier or more complicated?"

First, the findings, introduced in detail elsewhere (Kullasepp, 2008a, 2008b, 2011a), revealed some main tendencies in the students' descriptions

DOI: 10.4324/9781315519616-8

of the changes they had undergone since their enrollment in the university. Mostly, these reported changes were related with the personality features (typically, the students found that they became more confident, calmer, and tolerant), interaction, and self-regulation skills.

For example, one student (Par) reported: "The studies have not changed my life too much, but I feel that I have changed. I am now calmer, smarter. I am not so nervous anymore, I am more self-confident. I stay calm now, I don't scream anymore that 'this or that is right'. I am convinced now that I am not right every time." Another student (Uur) reflected: "The studies have changed me a lot. I am very self-confident now. Maybe I also try to be more tolerant and understanding. I try more to monitor myself, I also monitor other people, this has changed during the last year."

What concerned perceived improvement of interpersonal competencies then students reported that they understand now other people better. One participant (Gar) found that: "When I interact with people, I analyze their behavior more and I understand them better than before." The student, called Eri, pointed: "What is different comparing me and others due to my psychology studies is that thanks to psychology I can see behind others' behavior." The participant also found that their worldview had become broader: "My studies have taught me to see life more broadly." and "Everything is not black and white anymore." Similarly, the student (Uur) found that: "Before everything was so black and white. Now is everything much more complex." and "I feel that my worldview is broader and I see the reasons behind events, or at least I know how to find them and analyze possible alternatives. Maybe even the way I think has changed."

Studies of psychology were also linked by the participants with improved skills of self-analysis. Ain, one of the participants, reported that: "Now is easier for me to understand myself. I am better at self-analyzing." In line with Ain's impression of changes, the student Uur said: "I think that I now understand better who I am and why I do what I do."

Additionally, the prospective psychologists reported that the studies have changed their views on life. There were the students who outlined the positive effect of studies on their lives, however, for others internalization of social role of psychologist was associated with life that has become more complicated.

Among the reasons of easier life changes like improvement of social competencies (i.e., specific skills and knowledge) were mentioned. The participant Pai said that life is a bit easier, not as complicated: "Life tends to be easier than more complicated—I am better at listening to people, I try to understand people and their problems to analyze them."

Behind the complicated life was, as the students reported, the understanding of the complexity of reality (life is not anymore black or white) and that was linked, for instance, with to diversity of perspectives to the situations. For instance, the student Mes, reported: "I would say that on the contrary—everything is actually more complex, I have developed a lot. In some sense life is complicated—I understand that behind something can be so many different reasons and situations—opinions are very often relative."

Comparing how the psychology students described themselves with how they represented the psychologists many similarities were detected in the descriptions. As for the findings, following main categories were used to depict a psychologist over the three years of studies: personality qualities (e.g., psychologist is empathetic, tolerant), the interpersonal competencies (e.g., good listening and self-expression skills), the cognitive attributes and specific thinking style (e.g., tendency to analyze, broad view of life) (Kullasepp, 2011a, 2011b).

In regard to the findings collected when the ratings scales were applied that enabled to investigate how the respondents depicted a psychologist in comparison to non-psychologist, some of the features observed like tolerance, trustability, dedication to work, together with being better at keeping their personal relationships, to name a few, scored maximum by at least one of the participants.

Putting the findings into the developmental perspective allows assuming involvement of personal representation of psychologist in formations of professional I-position—the image of psychologist tended to be constructed around the similar features than the descriptions of undergone modifications since the beginning of studies of psychology.

Re-negotiation borders between what IS and what SHOULD be

On the example of case Gar below we can observe further how the transition to the social position of psychologist across years unfolds in the involvement of a psychologist and regulates meaning-making of the experiences. Gar was one of the participants who set up the developmental directions drawing on the personal representation of the psychologist. Gar's attempts to become a psychologist—to change—through regulating the emotional-psychological and social functioning illustrates how socio-culturally pre-ordered way of "being a psychologist" appears in the intra-psychological level in self-regulation. Based on Gar's case, a sign of psychologist, when emerging in the meaning-making process, organizes the experiences, blocking some potential developmental directions and suggesting others (Kullasepp, 2006, 2008b, 2014).

As a first-year student, Gar explained: "A psychologist must put a soul into the work. I do study psychology passionately. I also want to improve my verbal expression skills." Then, a year later she reported having problems with delivering a presentation in front of the audience that she had overcome due to the dedication to the future professional role: "Many students are afraid to perform, but they shouldn't. I also had that problem before. When we have the classes, for example, and some of us have to report in front of the class, then they all push me to do that. OK, I can do it, for myself [while] a psychologist must have performing skills."

Being engaged in the improvement of interaction skills is one of Gar's transfer strategies to overcome the boundary that hinders considering herself as a psychologist. We can also observe an image of a psychologist in action that determines the directions of the trajectory of development. In response to the question: "What is needed for psychological work?" Gar explained: "I know how to listen to people. I feel so much empathy inside me. I don't only hear people, but I follow their thought. I hope that once I graduate, I'm better at expressing myself. Now I'm not good enough at expressing my thoughts. Empathy is probably the most important feature [when doing psychological work]. My stress resistance is low, I have to work on it. Actually, I'm afraid that I'm too empathetic. Psychologists must love their work, they must give themselves fully to their work because others' well-being depends on them. Psychologists must be more interested in the patient than in themselves."

The tension between what is (empathetic) and what should be (less empathetic) is a developmental task to solve—the student has to construct the self-understanding of being less empathetic (than before) to consider herself "more psychologist." Likewise, the student finds that it is important to work on stress resistance.

In the final year of her studies, Gar was continuously looking for opportunities to improve her interaction skills: "When I work as an educator, I can improve my performance skills and skills of verbal self-expression."

The student was available for an interview a year after receiving the bachelor's degree, this time as a student in the master's program specializing in clinical psychology. The report casts light on the professional I-position that is "in action" when Gar positions in informal settings. Gar reported: "A counselor should be tolerant, and not imposing his/her personal views on others. Like yesterday, I had a visitor, a friend of my friend who claimed that smoking cannabis, as he actually does, is harmless. I said that there is no reason why we should argue, we just have different opinions. Later on, I wanted to comment on his views, but I didn't. I thought that maybe in the future I have patients like he is. I cannot impose my views upon people. I also hold myself back, when people talk, and try not to interrupt them."

To sum, what can be observed over the years is an ongoing self-regulation. The repeating "request" regarding improvement of the interaction skills and modification of the personality features creates semiotic borders separating the PRESENT self from its FUTURE version (e.g., as a psychologist I should have x quality, but I am lacking that quality) leading to the creation and application of the personal transfer strategies in order to overcome the self-created boundaries—"I tell myself what needs to be changed in me as a psychologist."

Summary

The formation of professional identity unfolds through the use of cultural material to re-organize the self. The social-institutional representations available in the surrounding are one of the sources on the bases of which professional I-positions are created. They enable specific perspectives and points of view in the inner dialogues in the self. The case of Gar brings fore that the personal meanings attributed to the activities matter while enabling to re-negotiate the border between the PRESENT and FUTURE version of the self. These activities become the transfer strategies. The main criterion for the strategy is its relevance in supporting "moving towards" the future self—to transfer from state A (i.e., non-psychologist) to B (i.e., psychologist). For example, attributing a certain meaning to listening another person more carefully feeds into the changes in self-understanding—"If I am listening more carefully another person, I am more like a psychologist." In other terms, engaging in activity X may lay foundation to the emerging identity allowing psychological transition and entering into a new reality. If I do X then I am (more like) a psychologist.

References

Kullasepp, K. (2006). Becoming professional: External and intrapsychological level in the service of professional identity constrction of psychology students. *European Journal of School Psychology, 4*(3), 337–347.

Kullasepp, K. (2008a). Are you like this…or just behave this way? *The International Journal for Dialogical Science, 19*(3), 69–92.

Kullasepp, K. (2008b). *Dialogical Becoming. Professional Identity Construction of Psychology Students*. Tallinn: Tallinna Ülikooli Kirjastus.

Kullasepp, K. (2011a). Creating my own way of being a psychologist. *The Japanese Journal of Personality, 19*(3), 217–232.

Kullasepp, K. (2011b). Why become a "Shrink"?. The psychology studies as an extention of self. In: S. Salvatore, J. Valsiner, J. T. Simon, & A. Gennaro (Eds.). *YIS: Yearbook of Idiographic Science* (pp. 95–114). Rome: Firera Publishing Group.

Kullasepp, K. (2014). Through the professional role to the world of new meanings. In: S. Salvatore, A. Gennaro, J. Valsiner (Eds.). *Multicentric Identities in a Globalizing World YIS: Yearbook of Idiographic Science* (pp. 111–132). US: Information Age Publishing Inc.

Salvatore, S. (2012). Social life of the sign: Sensemaking in society. In J. Valsiner (Ed.), *The Oxford Handbook of Culture and Psychology* (pp. 241–254). Oxford: Oxford Press.

Conclusion to Part II

The main theme discussed in this part was the differentiation of the structure of self by using the cultural tools, with the focus on connections between the social and personal representations (e.g., psychologist) and formation of the I-position (e.g., I as a psychologist).

Becoming is the process of construction and re-construction of the personal meaning complexes that affect relations with the professional role and with the world. In that sense the central developmental task related to the internalization of the future professional role is to demolish and re-construct the hierarchies of signs. The sign of a psychologist, thereat, can be considered inherently involved in this ongoing semiotic construction of the self, a part of the process of becoming a psychologist.

The chapters in Part 2 examined the microlevel (i.e., intra-psychological level) dynamics of assuming a professional role. Chapter 4 brought together the concept of ecological model (Bronfenbrenner & Bronfenbrenner, 1981) and the dialogical self. The emphasis in this chapter was on the extended self that incorporates the voices related to experiences in the various sociocultural environments. In the dialogical self these different environments (e.g., micro-, mesosystems) become interrelated with each other as the relevant I-positions have a voice to bring their own views into the dialogue. Interpersonal interactions with family members in past, encounters with the academic others, stereotypes and attitudes against the psychologist in a society, belief systems reflecting in the discourses circulating in a society, emerge in a form of the I-positions affecting negotiation over professional identity.

As the findings suggest, the presumption that the professional identity construction unfolds mostly under the control of academic settings overlooks the complexity of relations between the self and the larger socio-cultural surrounding. The non-academic contexts are as crucial as the non-academic ones. They became the "everyday arenas" where the students internalized/externalized professional identity and they did it in various of ways.

DOI: 10.4324/9781315519616-9

In general, the identity formation in the non-academic settings provided the feeling of being different from the others, differently from the academic environment that seemed to evoke feeling of belonging to the professional group of psychologists through the assumed similarities among the members of professional community. To conclude, the general tendency in becoming a psychologist was the use of the semiotic tools to create the structure of oppositions—"us" and "non-us" (i.e., psychologists and non-psychologists). An input was received from both of the environments (i.e., academic and non-academic).

Chapter 5 dealt also with how the students constructed their I-position I as a psychologist. Exploration of personal representations of psychologists and how the students described themselves revealed some overlapping, indicating that a sign of a psychologist became to organize their meaning making. In general, the construction of prosocial orientation and focus on the interpersonal competencies were present in the students' subjective reflections on their changes since their enrollment in the university.

To sum, becoming a psychologist is a semiotic process the directions of which are affected by the socio-cultural surroundings as they enable cultural (semiotic) tools for re-organizing psychological functioning and to construct the psychological organization.

Reference

Bronfenbrenner, U., & Bronfenbrenner, U. (1981). The ecology of human development: Experiments by nature and design. Retrieved from http://ebookcentral.proquest.com Created from tallinn-ebooks on 2019-07-12 01:59:38.

Part III

Becoming a psychologist: The multiple life trajectories

Chapter 6

Thirteen pathways to entering the professional role

Introduction

Part II gave a glimpse into how students make sense of the dynamics in non-professional settings and how they connect these experiences with the forming I-position I as a psychologist. The focus in Part III is on *imagined* professional settings. Specifically, this part investigates the assumption of the professional role when solving professional-role related dilemmas—that is, *imagined* professional conditions. These two types of conditions—the coordination of I-positions in non-professional and imagined professional settings—are distinct in terms of the expectations set by the social representation of the role. Unlike the dynamics of non-professional settings, the client/patient dynamics in professional settings are framed by professional practice guidelines. The following pages introduce the assumption of the professional role in *imagined* professional settings in terms of coordination of different I-positions and ways of handling tension. Based on these microprocesses, the trajectories of directions of entry into the professional role are created.

According to the semiotic-dialogical approach to internalizing a professional role, becoming a psychologist is a semiotic process that unfolds in the intra-psychological dialogues between the I-positions. The developmental trajectory of becoming a psychologist is formed from microgenetic processes that coordinate sub-systems in the self. These coordination processes enable depict distinct profiles of role-assuming and describe the dynamics of relations between the I-positions I as a person and I as a professional when they move along a professional path. As every person is first a person and only secondly "becomes a psychologist" by incorporating the personally perceived social role expectations set by the social representation PSYCHOLOGIST, then the assumption of the role is an ambivalent condition. Thus, the whole process of coordinating the two systems {(I)-ME}-AS-MYSELF and {(I)-ME}-AS-PSYCHOLOGIST is inherently ambivalent and is regulated using semiotic devices that may lead to the generation of different types of tensions (Kullasepp, 2008).

Additionally, this chapter presents the students' reflections on their experiences in the pre-period before and the post-period after their studies in the bachelor's program to provide a richer view of their unfolding professional trajectories. Becoming a psychologist in the academic-educational structure of a university is just one episode along the professional path. However, given that the pre-studies phase is inseparable from the period of official studies, addressing the initial conditions of professional socialization enables a deeper understanding of the dynamics of the professional trajectory's emergence, in line with Huynh and Rhodes (2011) who have underlined importance of exploring the personal motives of psychology students to pursue the field of psychology.

However, after the equifinality period, which includes the whole period of studies in a university, developmental trajectories are expected to diverge. Thereafter, every student continues on a unique professional pathway. To explore how the participants construed the impact of the studies of psychology to their lives, the students' reflections were collected after they had obtained their bachelor's degree (48 months after the beginning of studies).

Thirteen unique trajectories of becoming a psychologist

To investigate the coordination of the different sub-systems in the self when solving professional tasks, the theme completion method (DDTC; Double Direction Theme Completion) was implemented. The students' reflections on the pre- and post-period of undergraduate studies of psychology were collected via essays and via responses to the follow-up questions.

The students (Vik, Snap, Uur, Mes, Hei, Ris, Gar, Par, Eri, Ele, Pai, Aet, Ain- numbered a–m) were presented with the nine dilemmas (9) from the DDTC three times since the beginning of their studies of psychology (for more information see Chapter 3). Each dilemma described a situation that could occur in professional practice as a psychologist. Participants were instructed to respond to the dilemmas with answers—report the feeling that the specific dilemma would generate in psychologist if it were the real life situation and provide also the reason behind the reported feeling (e.g., When a psychologist is in X situation then they feel Y, because Z).

The trajectories of coordinating different sub-systems in the self and regulation of tension

In general, by applying the DDTC method, it was possible to identify the temporary dominance of the I-positions "I as a person" and "I as a psychologist" (i.e., professional). Three developmental directions (i.e., self-professionalizing, self-personalizing, and self-maintaining) were found across the 13 case studies, and here the cases are grouped according to these directions. Vik, Snap, Uur, Hei, Mes, Aet, and Ris (N = 7) form the group of self-professionalizing cases. Gar and Par (N = 2) belong to the group of self-personalizing cases, and the self-maintaining cases are Ain, Pai, Eri, and Ele (N = 4). (More about the description of the three identified directions of developmental trajectories are in Chapter 3).

Additionally, the solutions to the dilemmas revealed how the tension in the inherently ambivalent condition, person< >role, was handled between the different years, including the prevalence of the specific affective orientation (i.e., negatively oriented affectivity, positively oriented affectivity, or neutral) in solutions and the dynamics of handling tension (i.e., increasing or decreasing negatively oriented or non-negatively positively oriented affectivity) between the different years.

In general, one participant (Snap) tended to incline toward dominance of non-negative affectivity. Par, Eri, Aet, Ain, Ele, Gar, Ris, and Uur were labeled as "negative cases" showing prevailing negative tension in total. Pai, Hei, and Mes were the cases with a more balanced distribution of negative and non-negative affectivity in solutions. Some of the participants tended toward increasingly generating positive affectivity and neutral state (e.g., Mes, Hei) whereas others toward negative affectivity (e.g., Pai, Eri). One case (Ris) was exceptional, with 13 unknown solutions but with dominance of negative affectivity in total.

The participants' responses to 9 dilemmas from DDTC across the years and a detailed analysis are presented below along with the essays in the beginning of the description of each case and responses to the follow-up questions. The first are the responses of students who formed the group of self-professionalizing cases (7) presented below, followed by the group self-personalizing (2) and self-maintaining (4) cases.

Self-professionalizing cases

Respondent 6a—Vik

Vik mentions having a long-term interest in psychology. In Year 1, Vik's reflection on her reasons for studying psychology revealed her interest in the field years before enrollment in a university. However, despite reporting a long-lasting interest in psychology, Vik did not continue studies in a master's program. Instead, her undergraduate studies of psychology culminated with her withdrawal from the field. As she reported, she never wished to work as a psychologist.

> *I decided to study psychology because of a sincere interest. The first time I noticed that interest was when I was an 8th-grade student. We had psychology classes in school. I like to talk to people, listen to them, understand how they think about life. Psychology was fascinating because when you study psychology, you can realize why people behave how they do, how criminals think, why they do harm, and what influences human behavior. Psychology seemed so mysterious to me and also so necessary because you can apply it in every situation. Psychology makes it easier to understand your own behavior and easier to analyze yourself, and you can also help other people as well. All my friends supported my decision to go to study psychology. Studies of psychology have not changed my life directly, but they have opened my eyes and made me think more and consider others. I am sure that I would make the same choice again. I continuously want to study psychology.*

Although she continued to be interested in psychology four years after beginning her studies and after obtaining a bachelor's degree, Vik reported:

> *I changed my field .... In the workplace, I use different strategies to reach goals more effectively and faster. Now I am better at realizing what people want to see and hear. The main thing I got from my psychology studies is perhaps that I am now more tolerant and my interaction skills have improved .... Psychology has influenced my personal life; the way I see life and relations is 'broader,' not so black and white anymore. But I think that this is also caused by age; I am more mature now...I have been thinking that maybe it is a smart step to go to study something that would later become the profession I work in. I didn't study psychology because I wanted to work in this field but because I had an interest in it .... I have noticed that people have a kind of attitude when they become aware of my education. They tend to think that I am a person who observes and analyzes them.*

The outcome of studying psychology from Vik's point of view is that it changed her interaction skills and personal characteristics, making her more tolerant. However, although she does not work as a professional psychologist, in everyday life, Vik experiences being treated as if she is a psychologist. External I-positions (the voices of people around her) tell her that "You are a psychologist."

In very general terms, Vik represents the case: "I am interested in the subject of psychology but not in being a psychologist as my profession."

Solutions to the items from DDTC

Theme 1   Providing confidential information to third parties

"When a psychologist has a dilemma whether to give out information on his/her patient, then s/he feels ____ because ____."

Year 1 ... insecure, because the rules of ethics do not allow to give out information without the patient's consent.

Year 2 ... dispirited, because s/he cannot break confidentiality.

Year 3 ... confused, because it is an important aspect (confidentiality, the contract) in the psychologists' code of ethics

---

When solving this dilemma, the respondent seems to seek guidance from the professional perspective, since the solutions Vik offered under the study period of three years kept referring to ethics and/or a set of rules that pertain to the profession. It is also apparent that semiotic regulators like "forbidden" and "is not allowed" tended to bring about negative tension for Vik.

Theme 2   Disliked client

"When a psychologist does not like his/her client (s)he feels ____ because ____."

Year 1 ... the same, because s/he has to put aside his/her own opinion about the patient, the patient must be treated objectively.

Year 2 ... still the same, because the psychologist does not select a client on the basis of their external picture [i.e., the physical appearance].

Year 3 ... like usually, because the psychologist does not have to like the client's physical appearance (n)or their nature. The client should be viewed objectively.

What we see here is that Vik manages to eliminate tension in responses by taking a professional approach which remains the same over the years. The only thing changing is the semiotic regulators that are indicated in the solutions. For instance, when in the first year, the use of moral imperative "must" can be observed accompanying a reference to the professional demand of objectivity, in the second year, the semiotic regulator is changed to "does not," which entails an implicit indication to the bases of professional conduct. Lastly, in the third year, Vik's response once again points to objectivity as a demand of the role. Hence, Vik's solutions for this dilemma is remained dominated by the utilization of the "I as a professional" perspective.

Theme 3   An attractive patient

"When an attractive person (of the opposite sex) comes in for a session, then psychologist feels ____ because ____."

Year 1 ... like with any other patient, because the psychologist should not prefer anybody.

Year 2 ... like s/he did before meeting the patient, because the psychologist doesn't let him-/herself be affect by physical appearance.

Year 3 ... good, because it is pleasant to meet a beautiful person.

In year 1, Vik approaches this dilemma from a professional perspective where the utilization of moral imperative "should not" seems to eliminate the tension. In the second year, however, the external control (i.e., the role-related rules) is no longer so explicit—instead, Vik indicates that "a psychologist *does not* let her-/himself be affected"—but the perspective still remains professional. Hence, it appears that over time the external control tends to be replaced by an internal one and professional conduct will thereafter be guided by the set of internalized rules one has about their professional role.

By the third year of study, Vik's perspective on this dilemma becomes personal. The attraction toward a patient is no longer perceived as something that needs to be regulated in professional conduct and the feelings reported when solving this dilemma are positive (good).

All in all, the following sequences of assuming professional role could be identified from Vik's answers: from the external "a psychologist should not" to the internal "a psychologist does not" (implying that professional conduct is in accord with the regulations), and eventually to a shift in the construction of meanings that promote the domination of the perspective "I as a person."

> **Theme 4   Unable to help**
>
> "When a psychologist understands that s/he is unable to help his/her client, s/he feels ____ because ____."
>
> Year 1 ... limited, because helping this person remains beyond his competence.
>
> Year 2 ... incompetent, because s/he is not able to solve the client's problem, but must refer the patient further (to another professional).
>
> Year 3 ... incompetent, because his/her skills and competencies are insufficient for solving patient's problem.

Regarding the realization of being unable to help the patient, Vik conveys negative tensions in the years 2 and 3 (unknown for year 1), and her focus remains role-centered throughout the study period. In the third year, the lack of professional competencies is creating negative tension.

> **Theme 5   Close relations**
>
> "When a psychologist is to consult a person s/he has a close connection with, s/he feels ____ because ____."
>
> Year 1 ... inadequate, because his/her advice could most likely be influenced by their previous experiences and conversations.
>
> Year 2 ... unprofessional, because the advice s/he will be giving is probably subjective rather than objective.
>
> Year 3 ... driven to the corner, because the psychologist should not counsel a close person as his/her previous experiences affect the counselling process.

Here we can see a movement from the personal perspective to professional role enactment by the third year, when the utilization of imperative "a psychologist should not" indicates the implementation of professional role regulations.

> **Theme 6 Common acquaintances**
>
> "When a person whose problems involve people close to the psychologist comes in for an appointment, the psychologist feels ____ because ____."
>
> > Year 1 ... inadequate, because people who are close to her/him can indirectly influence the course of counselling and then it is not objective anymore.
> >
> > Year 2 ... incompetent, because he/she should not disclose information about the other people, she may use the information unsuspectedly.
> >
> > Year 3 ... incompetent, because the psychologist must refer the patient to another professional as s/he is not allowed to see to this patient on the professional level.

Regardless of the perspective Vik has taken on this issue, negative tension has remained present in all of the student's responses over the years. In the first year, the possibility of close relations violating the objectivity of a psychologist was acknowledged; however, compared to the solutions provided in the second and third years, the semiotic regulators that generate negative tension tend to be related to Vik's personal rather than professional experiences. Although it has "a voice" in the dialogue, Vik's "I as a professional" seems to be suppressed, giving more ground to "I as a person." (Year 1). The second- and third-year answers reflect Vik's adjustment into the professional role through the utilization of role-related moral imperatives, like a psychologist "should not" (Year 2), "must" and "is not allowed" (Year 3).

> **Theme 7 Inability to keep the distance**
>
> "When the psychologist feels that s/he cannot distance him-/herself from the patient's problems, s/he feels ____ because ____."
>
> > Year 1 ... exhausted, because s/he gets too involved with this problem and it will also begin to affect his/her personal life.
> >
> > Year 2 ... inept, distressed, because the patient's problems follow the psychologist into his/her personal life.
> >
> > Year 3 ... too involved, because the psychologist must be able to keep the distance from the patient. Otherwise s/he will burn out.

During the first two years, the semiotic regulators reveal a personal centeredness that does not seem to eliminate negatively oriented tension in responses. Both of the provided solutions showed the dominance of "I as a person" perspective, which in turn appeared to generate tension within professional settings due to the influence professional relations are perceived to have on the private sphere of life.

In the third year, the focus is changed and an emergence of a professional approach can be noted. Again, the semiotic self-regulator "must" refers to the professional role, however, the character of tension remains unclear.

Theme 8   Different values

"When a person whose values differ greatly from those of the psychologist comes in for an appointment, the psychologist feels ____ because ____."

Year 1 ... the same, because that person's opinions and values may be different.

Year 2 ... good, because people have different value systems.

Year 3 ... obligated to be neutral, because s/he should not to press his/her own values onto the patient.

The first two perspectives Vik describes indicate the utilization of a so-called third position that (in line with dialogical self theory (DST)) represents a compromise between the personal and professional positions of the self and thereby has an ability to generate neutral state and positive affectivity. In year 3, Vik's response includes a moral imperative "should not" as well as references to the obligation to stay neutral—a demand pertained to the professional role of a psychologist.

The semiotic regulators Vik uses appear to generate positive (good) tension and neutral state (still the same).

Theme 9   Encountering a person in crisis after working hours

"When a psychologist meets a person in crisis outside of working hours, s/he feels ____ because ____."

80 Becoming a psychologist

> Year 1 ... calm, because his/her workday is over and after the workday is over s/he doesn't have to think about work.
>
> Year 2 ... staunched, because there is time for work, and during one's leisure time work is out of the picture. One person cannot help everyone.
>
> Year 3 ... as a bystander who is not related to that situation, because after the workday is over, the psychologist doesn't have to deal with work issues.

Over the years, we can observe the role-related semiotic regulators that liberate Vik from negative tension regarding the decision of providing service after working hours. Compared to the cases in the present study, Vik's approach to this particular dilemma is somewhat extreme, with the professional role being depicted as something that can easily be "left aside," "stepped out of," or "turned off and on." It is like a mask that can be removed after the carnival ends. Thus, Vik indicates that being a psychologist stops under certain conditions that are defined and framed by the official regulations controlling formal relations (Figures 6.1 and 6.2).

Summary of case Vik

Throughout the years, Vik's solutions to the dilemmas are characterized by the domination of the professional I-position. In total, 19 professional positions, six (6) personal positions, and two (2) uses of third positions were identified in Vik's responses. Moreover, the findings reveal a tendency toward decrease of the utilization of personal perspective—when in Year 1 five (5) professional positions and three (3) personal I-positions were applied, then in Year 3 the number of personal positions had decreased to one (1) while the application of professional I-positions increased to 8.

Furthermore, across the years Vik's application of I-positions maintains a role-focus when it regards certain themes—i.e., providing information to third parties, disliked patient, unable to help, working with a client one doesn't like, being unable to help a client, and encountering a person in crisis after working hours were the themes that Vik solved by applying only the professional approach.

Like the other cases in this study, the themes regarding close relations and inability to keep the distance were solved mostly from the personal perspective. In the last year of this study, all of the above mentioned dilemmas as well as the theme of different values, were solved from a professional I-

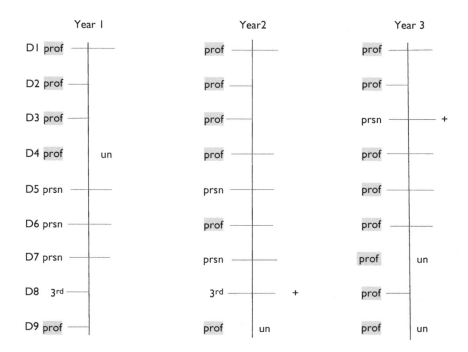

Figure 6.1 Temporary profiles of coordination of perspectives (i.e., professional, personal, 3rd position) and handling tension (i.e., positive and negative affectivity, neutral) in solutions to nine (9) dilemmas.

Note: Prof—the professional approach; Prsn—the personal approach; 3rd—the third I-position; Flux—the fluctuation of perspectives; UN—unknown; X—no answer provided.

position and, characteristic to Vik, by using moral imperatives like *should not, is not allowed, must*.

Regarding the reported feelings, negatively and non-negatively oriented affectivity (i.e., neutral and positive) tended to be unbalanced across years (i.e., 13 and 10, respectively). Concerning the respondents' profile of affectivity regulation, Vik belonged to the group that did not manage to eliminate negative affectivity across years. Nevertheless, the themes that did appear to evoke negatively oriented tensions in Vik included sharing confidential information to third parties, having close relations and (a) common acquaintance(s) with the client.

In Vik's responses to the dilemmas, affective relating with another person (e.g., in cases of working with a client one dislikes, and counselling a client

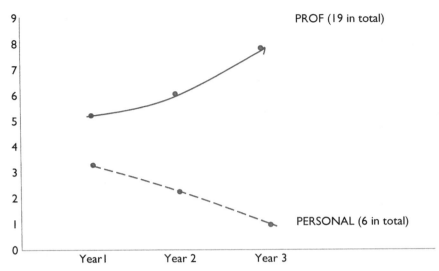

Figure 6.2 Trajectories of coordination of different sub-systems (i.e., professional, personal) in the self across the years.

Note: Occurrences of domination of professional and personal I-positions in the solutions to the dilemmas.

one finds attractive) was acknowledged as a risk, whereas the use of semiotic regulators like *must stay objective, should be looked objectively, should not prefer anybody*, and *doesn't let affect anybody* appeared to generate a neutral state or positively oriented tension.

Unlike the more typical approach used among the students from this cohort, Vik applied semiotic regulators that, instead of generating negative affectivity, revealed the acceptance of inter-individual differences as a natural part of heterogeneous world. Coordinating the dynamics of a sub-system within the self enabled Vik to avoid the emergence of negative affectivity.

Furthermore, in non-professional settings (e.g., in the dilemma of a person in crisis), applying semiotic regulators like "working hours are over" appear to enable the construction of two different and clearly separated worlds—i.e., the "personal" and the "professional." Yet, that so-called separation disappears when the person in the psychologist's role has to consult a person he or she knows personally (e.g., in the case of close relations). The same happens in case of common acquaintances.

In general, the role-related moral imperatives like *must*, *should* or *should not* seem to evoke both positive and negative tensions, depending on the specific dilemma. For instance, the obligation to be neutral (e.g., *should not* press onto patient his or her own values) generates a neutral response, but when the psychologist *should not* counsel a close person, he or she feels "driven to the corner."

Moreover, when dilemmas like working with a client one either dislikes or finds attractive, having different value systems and encountering a person in crisis brought about negatively oriented tensions in many other respondents' reports (see below), then Vik's interpretation of conditions revealed the psychologist's ability to coordinate the dialogue between their different I-positions in a way that in most of cases resulted in the generation of positive affectivity or neutral state. Several other students from the same cohort saw these dilemmas more challenging regarding the elimination of negative tension.

Finally, by the last year of study, Vik's focus shifted from self-centeredness to role-centrality regarding solutions to dilemmas like having close relations with the client as well as being unable to keep the distance from the client's problems. However, in the case of working with a client one finds attractive, the shift of focus was opposite.

Respondent 6b—Snap

Snap represents the example of an abrupt shift in one's professional trajectory—Snap never planned to study psychology, yet it happened. In the first year of studies, Snap was convinced that the choice was right. Four years later, we can find Snap working in the field, although the respondent was not sure about making the same decision again in the future. Again, we can see that relatives, family members, and friends are involved in an individual's inner dialogues when they are negotiating their professional future.

In Year 1:

> *I had never planned to study psychology. But finally, I decided for the humanities because I understood that, actually, I am a people person. All my relatives were sure that I was not going to be a psychologist, and so I surprised them. They were very scared. I found that I don't have to explain anything to them, at least as long as my family and friends understand me. When I made the decision, I felt firm. Especially after being accepted to the university. I have always thought that life goes on a predestined course. I do not create a catastrophe out of all the setbacks in life. I am sure that my studies have changed my life. I have discovered very interesting books and people. I am not 100 percent sure that I would make the same choice because I see new specialties that are needed every day.*

In Year 4:

> *When I do psychological work, I need to have psychological knowledge ... It is important that you have specific terminology, knowledge about ethics, probably have developed the ability to be empathetic. Studies helped me to establish a network of professional connections. My work requires the ability to analyze. I don't know if studies help in my personal life or not. It's weird to apply it in personal life. That you know how is true, but ... I probably analyze people more; I no longer have "rose-colored glasses.*

Solutions to the items from DDTC

Theme 1   Providing confidential information to third parties

"When a psychologist has a dilemma whether to give out information on his/her patient, then he feels _____ because _____.")

> Year 1 ... obligated to do it, because there are certain situations when it will be done and when it is necessary
>
> Year 2 ... obligated to calculate in sober ways, because s/he is obligated by law and the danger of losing good relationships with the patient. If it is needed then it is needed—otherwise there can be a mess
>
> Year 3 ... understands that s/he needs supervision and better code of ethics, because the psychologist is a professional and is not needlessly talking about her/his patient with others. When it comes to providing information, then of course s/he needs a reason for that—for instance if the patient is a danger to others or to him- or herself. It could be useful to alter the name of the

As we can see, tension is eliminated (neutral) over the years (in the last year feeling remains unclear) through the utilization of semiotic regulations that emphasize restrictions related to the professional practice, i.e., obligations, law, code of ethics. Snap's response in the third year also includes suggestions about proper professional behavior (i.e., altering the patient's name before giving out any information). The tension is handled through the use of professional perspective in solving this dilemma.

Theme 2   Disliked client

"When a psychologist does not like his/her client s/he feels ____ because ____."

> Year 1 ... bad, because maybe s/he has something personal against that patient. If their physical appearance is not to one's liking, then one is not fit to be a psychologist
>
> Year 2 ... a bit bad, because it should not affect him or her
>
> Year 3 ... not professional, because any kind of feelings that s/he has for patient must be suppressed

Regarding this dilemma, negatively oriented tension is present in Snap's responses every year. Nevertheless, a change can be seen among the semiotic regulators that in year 2 and 3 ("should not" and "must," respectively) begin to bring in more of the profession-centered perspective. Both aforementioned regulators referred to the role expectations set for a psychologist.

In fact, Snap's response in the first year could be interpreted as a fluctuation of perspectives with a direction from personal toward a professional viewpoint.

Theme 3 Attractive patient

"When an attractive person of the opposite sex comes to a session at a psychologist's, then s/he feels ____ because ____."

Year 1 ... as a special one, because the psychologist gives her/him help

Year 2 ... excited, because he/she works with a beautiful person, but a psychologist doesn't allow to show it

Year 3 ... pleased, because the client chose her/him. But maybe she/he won't be exited sexually, if we were to talk about what is actually allowed

When in the first year, the respondent interpreted agency in reverse, by reporting the feelings of the client instead of the psychologist; year 2 brought about a change—with the character of tension being positive (feeling exited) and the perspective professional (i.e., referring to the regulations related to professional activity). By adding a comment "the psychologist does not show it," Snap indicates the knowledge of expectations set for his/her professional role. By the third year, Snap's approach takes a professional perspective, explicitly referring to the rules and restrictions of his/her work role ("what the psychologist actually can/is allowed to do"). The possibility of getting sexually excited seems to be overruled by professional role expectations. However, both approaches are coded as the fluctuation of perspectives as the personal "voice" is also present and is "silenced" by the use of professional regulations.

Theme 4 Unable to help

"When a psychologist understands that s/he is unable to help his client, s/he feels ____ because ____."

Year 1 ... happy, because s/he knows that somebody else is certainly smarter than s/he is, somebody to whom s/he can send the client or with whom one could consult oneself

Year 2 ... incompetent, because s/he didn't find the solution to the problem

Year 3 ... like a professional, because s/he was able to send the patient to another professional who fits better to that client, who is more knowledgeable of the subject matter

Here we can clearly observe the dynamics of tension direction and retention of the role-centered approach on the issue over the years. For instance, the positive orientation of tension (happy) reported in the first year, is replaced by a negative one (incompetent) in the second year due to the realization of having failed in the professional role. In the third year, Snap conveys feeling "professional" (coded as unknown) as (s)he sees the solution in an opportunity that is available to psychologists in their professional role, i.e., referring the patient to another, more competent colleague.

Theme 5   Close relations

"When a psychologist is to consult a person s/he has a close connection with, s/he feels ____ because ____."

Year 1 ... as a normal person, because people who are close to him/her are special and they are similar to him or her

Year 2 ... in a forced situation, because all people close to him/her know what is his/her profession and wait from him/her a lot

Year 3 ... like a professional, because he/she explained to a person who is close to him/her that it is not allowed and sent him/her to another professional

---

The personal perspective that was echoed in responses during the first two years, changes in the third year to a professional viewpoint where a set of role-specific rules are applied to the regulation informal relations ("not allowed"). Negative tension appears only in the response given in the second year. Tension in the last year remains unclear.

Theme 6   Common acquaintance

"When a person whose problems involve people close to the psychologist comes in for an appointment, the psychologist feels ____ because ____."

Year 1 ... in a good position, because s/he probably knows people who are close to her/him and can probably talk about them, something that could be helpful

Year 2 ... in a special position, because s/he knows these people and knows who they actually are

Year 3 ... obligated to refer the person to others, because s/he is not able to do work professionally due to so close a relationship.

> Of course, she can also feel little bit bad, when too many patients who have come to him are referred further

During the first two years, the informal relations were considered to benefit the professional one through the information that they can provide for the counselling process. The semiotic regulators accompanying the solutions during the first two years of this study created a positive tension (good; Year 1) and made the psychologist feel as a special one (Year 2). In the third year, close relations are admitted to affect the professional conduct of psychologist who is obligated, according to the professional regulations, refer the person further (i.e., the fluctuation of perspectives that is accompanied by the flux of handling tension).

Theme 7 Inability to keep distance

"When a psychologist feels that s/he cannot distance oneself from the patient's problems, s/he feels ____ because ____."

Year 1 … like a patient, because patients' problems remind him/her of his/her own problems that s/he has not been able (probably) to solve

Year 2 … in the same way, because s/he cannot keep a distance and relate to the patient with official coldness

Year 3 … sorry for the client, because the client has to be most probably referred further if they cannot solve that problem explicitly in their interaction.

Similarly to the dilemma of common acquaintances, an emergence of self-professionalization can be observed in Snap's responses to this situation over the years. When in the first two years, Snap approaches the dilemma from a personal perspective, negative tensions arise through the affect that patient's problems are perceived to have on the psychologist. In the third year, however, the respondent finds support from the moral imperative pertained to the professional role—"a psychologist has to." Nevertheless, negatively oriented tension remains.

Theme 8 Different values

"When a person whose values differ greatly from that of the psychologist's comes to a session, then s/he feels ____ because ____."

> Year 1 ... that everything is fine, because s/he must not allow his- or herself to be disturbed by that
>
> Year 2 ... obligated to understand him/her, because this is her/his work
>
> Year 3 ... good, because s/he sees that the other person also respects his/her own personal world view and it may even be that the client's worldview is better than his/her own

Regarding this case, positively oriented tension or neutral state was generated over the years. During the first two years, Snap's strategy for solving this situation involves the application of moral imperative "a psychologist must not" and a reference to the obligations that pertain to the professional role. In last year, however, negative tension is eliminated by the utilization of a third position.

Theme 9   Encountering person-in-crisis when workday is over

"When a psychologist meets a person in crisis outside working hours, s/he feels ____ because ____."

> Year 1 ... as usual, because s/he probably saw such cases throughout the day
>
> Year 2 ... badly, because s/he doesn't have to help him/her, if s/he doesn't want that, but maybe s/he understands how the other person feels at the moment
>
> Year 3 ... as a "mean dwarf," because s/he has something else to do after the workday. But if that stranger is going to do harm to her/himself then s/he could intervene

When solving this dilemma in the first year, Snap managed to generate neutral state by focusing on the routine of psychologist's daily work, hence, by applying the professional perspective. The second year brings a change in the focus as well as the character of feelings reported—Snap turns to personal perspective and admits feeling "badly." It is no longer a professional role that generates negative tension, but Snap's personal ability for empathy.

In the last year, the character of tension ("feeling like a mean dwarf") and I position Snap reported remain unidentified (Figures 6.3 and 6.4).

90 Becoming a psychologist

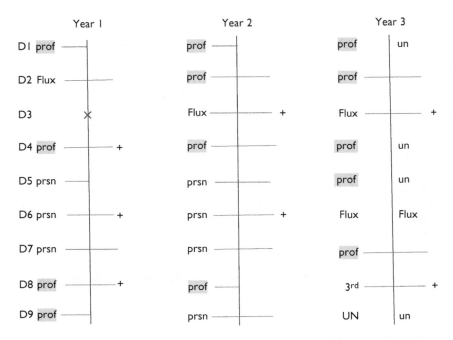

Figure 6.3 Temporary profiles of coordination of perspectives (i.e., professional, personal, 3rd position) and handling tension (i.e., positive and negative affectivity, neutral) in solutions to nine (9) dilemmas.

Note: Prof—the professional approach; Prsn—the personal approach; 3rd—the third I-position; Flux—the fluctuation of perspectives; UN—unknown; X—no answer provided.

Summary of case Snap

With the dominance of professional role-orientation in solutions to the dilemmas (i.e., 13 occurrences of dominating professional I-positions compared to 7 dilemmas that were regulated under the guidance of personal I-position), Snap falls into the category of self-professionalizing cases. The domination of professional perspective in Snap's answers can be observed throughout the years. When in Year 2, Snap's solutions to the dilemmas included the domination of personal perspective in four (4) cases out of 9, then by Year 3 it had dropped down to zero (0) case out of 9.

More specifically, the profile of I-positions in Year 3 consisted of five (5) dominating professional positions, none of leading personal I-positions, two (2) fluctuations of perspectives (the presence of both of perspectives in a solution to the dilemma without the clear dominating I-position), and one (1) third position (more about the 3rd position in Chapter 2).

Thirteen pathways 91

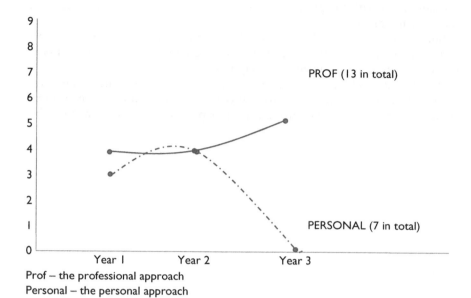

Figure 6.4 Trajectories of coordination of different sub-systems (i.e., professional, personal) in the self across the years.

Note: Occurrences of domination of professional and personal I-positions in the solutions to the dilemmas.

Regarding the regulation of tensions rising in the inherently ambivalent conditions, Snap exhibited the domination of non-negative affectivity (i.e., positively oriented tension and neutral state) over the negative tension (i.e., 12 and 9 times, respectively). However, one fluctuation of handling tension was also identified when Snap solved the dilemma of a common acquaintance.

When analyzing the tensions reported according to the dilemmas, it appeared that there were certain situations where the semiotic regulators Snap chose to apply would not help eliminate the negatively oriented tension (e.g., when working with a client one dislikes and when being unable to keep the distance from the client's problems). However, there were also situations that tended to evoked mostly non-negative affectivity (i.e., neutral and positive) in Snap throughout the years—for instance, providing confidential information to third parties, working with a client one finds attractive, and different value systems from the client.

Moreover, regarding the dynamics of perspective throughout the years of study, Snap's approaches to ambivalent situations changed in six (6) cases out of nine (9), and three (3) of these changes had a direction toward the externalization of professional I-position. These three dilemmas included working with a patient one dislikes, having close relations and common acquaintances with the patient, and being unable to keep the distance from the patient's problems.

Similar to Vik, but unlike many other respondents in this study, Snap's responses do not explicitly indicate that a psychologist will provide support to the person in crisis outside working hours.

In conclusion, characteristic to Snap's general profile was the domination of non-negative affectivity. Snap's responses were dominated by professional perspective, giving ground to self-professionalizing tendency by Year 3.

Respondent 6c—Uur

Uur, like Snap, did not have a long-term interest in the field of psychology, and their choice of studies was accompanied by doubts.

The internalization of the professional role and formation of the I-position "I as a psychologist" culminated in Uur's case in the "inner demand" to listen to other people when they want to talk, which is an example of institutionally guided cultural development. An external demand appears in psychological functioning to regulate one's relations with one's surroundings. Uur has turned from an "ordinary" person into someone who MUST listen to others.

In Year 1:

> *Actually, I did not know for a long time what to study. The only thing I knew was that it must be related to people. I was also interested in the topic of how advertising influences people. I found psychology after discussions with my school counselor. The other choice was social work. My family was surprised. They thought that I would go to study economics. Friends were very positive. I also doubted whether psychology is what I want to do.*

Uur's response in Year 4:

> *I am sure that interaction and counselling skills help me here a lot. I think that the fact that I am a psychologist makes it easier for other people to interact with me .... In my personal life, I don't think so much about my education .... To compare who I was before my studies of psychology to who I am now—now I am more tolerant and have a wider view of the world. One more thing—it is so hard for me to say NO when someone wants to talk. I feel that I must listen to them.*

Solutions to items from DDTC

Theme 1 Providing confidential information to third parties

"When a psychologist has a dilemma whether to give out information on his/her patient, then he feels ____ because ____."

> Year 1 ... tempted, because it is actually forbidden to do so
>
> Year 2 ... unconfident, because mostly it is not ethical
>
> Year 3 ... worried, because none of the solutions are very good

Regarding the choice of perspective, a change appears from the external control of temptation (a psychologist must not; year 1) to the recognition of professional ethics (year 2) indicating progress in the internalization of professional role.

Nevertheless, by the third year, Uur's focus on ethics has moved toward the pragmatism of psychologist's professional conduct, which still includes an negatively oriented tension.

In terms of I-positions utilized when solving this dilemma, all Uur's responses represented the professional perspective (i.e., references to the external rules and regulations controlling professional demeanour). In regard handling tension, in the second and third professional approach was accompanied by negative affectivity. However, in the first year the orientation of tension remained unknown.

Theme 2   Disliked client

"When a psychologist does not like his/her client s/he feels ____ because ____."

> Year 1 ... bad, because a prejudice has already emerged and it can begin to disturb her/him
>
> Year 2 ... uncomfortable, because it could begin to affect his/her opinion about the patient
>
> Year 3 ... uncomfortable, because it should not become visible to the patient and work should proceed as well as usual

Similarly to the previous dilemma, the case of not liking one's patient also brought about negative tension for Uur in all the three years of study.

Still, by the third year, a movement can be seen in the choice of perspective from personal to professional through the change of semiotic regulator (CAN→ COULD→ SHOULD NOT).

Theme 3 Attractive patient

"When an attractive person of the opposite sex comes to a session with the psychologist, then s/he feels ____ because ____."

Year 1 ... watchful, physical appearance can start to affect their opinions about the patient's characteristics

Year 2 ... uncomfortable, because it could affect her/his opinion about the patient

Year 3 ... careful, because it is forbidden to let oneself be disturbed by that

The ambivalence regarding the effect attraction could have on psychologist's work is acknowledged by Uur throughout the three years, however, it becomes explicitly connected with the professional role and its regulations (e.g., "a psychologist cannot let him-/herself be disturbed by it") only by the third year.

Theme 4 Unable to help

"When a psychologist understands that s/he is unable to help his client, s/he feels ____ because ____."

Year 1 ... as though s/he is breaking the patient's trust, because s/he must direct the patient to some other psychologist

Year 2 ... unhappy, because it is his/her calling to help people

Year 3 ... careful, because s/he must find a person who is competent enough to help that human being

In the case of recognizing one's inability to help the patient, a movement from professional to personal perspective and back again can be noticed during the course of three years. When in the first year, Uur's response indicates a role-based focus ("a psychologist must"), the second year brings to light an internalized general self-organizer ("calling") which, by the third year, returns to the perspective of professional role enactment ("a psychologist must find").

> **Theme 5 Close relations**
>
> "When a psychologist is to consult a person he has a close connection with, s/he feels ____ because ____."
>
> Year 1 ... uncomfortable, because it is difficult to stay objective
>
> Year 2 ... in tension, because it is difficult to remain a bystander or to stay neutral, as the problems can be too close to home.
>
> Year 3 ... uncomfortable, because s/he must not let it happen that earlier information and previously created opinions about the patient interfere

The need for differentiation between professional and personal relations is reported each year, however, only by the third year does the personal perspective in Uur's responses (not staying objective, difficult to remain a bystander) transform into a professional role-regulating imperative (psychologist must not).

> **Theme 6 Common acquaintance**
>
> "When a person whose problems involve people close to the psychologist comes in for an appointment, the psychologist feels ____ because ____."
>
> Year 1 ... bad, because s/he cannot stay absolutely objective
>
> Year 2 ... in tension, because it is difficult to stay as a bystander or neutral
>
> Year 3 ... uncomfortable, because s/he must distance herself/himself for that time period from her/his own person and from their own well-being

Similarly to the previous dilemma, the need for differentiation between personal and professional relations is also acknowledged here throughout the years. The personal perspective prevalent during the first two years (i.e., cannot stay objective, difficult to stay as bystander or neutral") is replaced by a professional one by the third year (i.e., must distance).

> **Theme 7 Inability to keep distance**
>
> "When a psychologist feels that s/he cannot distance herself/himself from the patient's problems, s/he feels ____ because ____."
>
> Year 1 ... bad, because s/he then takes them home and then the family will also suffer because of that
>
> Year 2 ... tempted, because on the one hand s/he wants to help, but on other hand s/he can hurt herself/himself
>
> Year 3 ... bad, because in some sense s/he failed and now must ask colleagues to help her/him

Once again, a similar pattern can be seen in Uur's responses that regards handling tensions by a gradual move from the personal focus on the issue (i.e., the impact on myself and my family) to a professional role-based mapping of an action plan (i.e., must ask).

> **Theme 8 Different values**
>
> "When a person whose values differ greatly from that of the psychologist's comes to a session, then s/he feels ____ because ____."
>
> Year 1 ... [no answer provided by the participant], it is difficult to see things from his/her perspective
>
> Year 2 ... challenged, because it is difficult to understand her/him
>
> Year 3 ... bad, because it is right to send the patient to somebody else

While recognizing the discrepancy of perspectives at first, by the year 3, the person becomes secondary to the profession.

The imperative aspect in handling cases that do not correspond to the value set of the psychologist, is referring the patient to a more suitable colleague.

Taking on the psychologist's role allows for new ways of social distancing (by referrals) in addition to the need for psychological space in immediate relations with the patient.

> **Theme 9   Encountering person in crisis after working hours**
>
> "When a psychologist meets a person in crisis outside working hours, s/he feels ____ because ____."
>
> Year 1 … ready to help, because s/he probably wants to help him/her
>
> Year 2 … as though s/he is facing a dilemma, s/he wants to help, could help, knows how to help, but sometimes one must have a rest too and one cannot help the whole world
>
> Year 3 …, that s/he has the power to help (if it were so), but this does not belong to her/his duties

Regarding offering assistance after working hours, the focus once again moves from person-centered to role-centered over the course of three years ("does not belong to her/his *duties*" in year 3) (Figures 6.5 and 6.6).

Summary of case Uur

Uur is different from all other respondents in this study in the assuming of the professional role. By the last year of study, an abrupt change had occurred in Uur's choice of perspective. Namely, unlike the previous years that were dominated by the application of personal perspective, in Year 3, all dilemmas were solved from a professional I-position. To illustrate this shift—when in Year 1, professional perspective was applied in two (2) cases out of nine (9), and a year later in only one (1) case out of nine (9), then by Year 3, professional perspective covered all nine cases.

Moreover, the decline in Uur's tendency to apply personal perspective also altered the trajectory of her entry into the role—by the last year of the study, Uur became self-professionalizing, exhibiting a movement toward increasing the internalization and externalization of professional role. Like in most cases, when the professional perspective to an issue is taken, the use of moral imperatives (e.g., *should, is forbidden, must, should not*) can be observed. Regardless of the shift in perspective, the semiotic regulators Uur utilized tended to continuously generate only negatively oriented tensions. In fact, throughout the three years of study, not a single positive or neutral feeling was identified in Uur's responses. However, there were nine (9) responses where the character of feelings reported remained unknown.

Additionally, an interesting tendency appeared in solving the dilemma of helping a person in crisis outside working hours—namely, a gradual

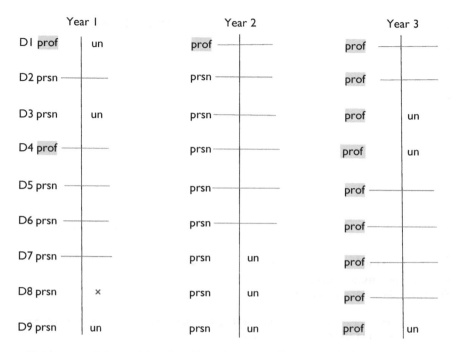

Figure 6.5 Temporary profiles of coordination of perspectives (i.e., professional, personal, 3rd position) and handling tension (i.e., positive and negative affectivity, neutral) in solutions to nine (9) dilemmas.

Note: Prof—the professional approach; Prsn—the personal approach; 3rd—the third I-position; Flux—the fluctuation of perspectives; UN —unknown; X—no answer provided.

emergence of professional perspective. It seems that the utilization of professional I-position allows the psychologist to distance oneself from the situation. "I as a professional" appears to somehow validate one's decision not to get involved.,

So far, three self-professionalizing cases that represent a similar trajectory in assuming the professional role have been described. However, they all remain different in terms of how they utilize I-positions as well as regulate affectivity across the years. For example, Snap stands out with the domination of positive affectivity, whereas Uur represents the opposite case with the prevalence of negatively oriented tensions.

100 Becoming a psychologist

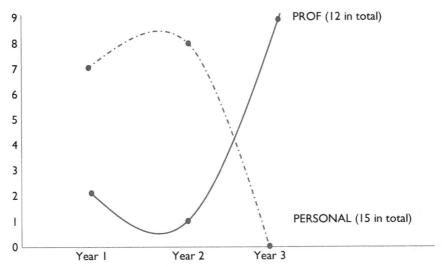

Prof – the professional approach
Personal – the personal approach

Figure 6.6 Trajectories of coordination of different sub-systems (i.e., professional, personal) in the self across the years.

Note: Occurrences of domination of professional and personal I-positions in the solutions to the dilemmas.

Respondent 6d—Mes

According to Mes's report, her journey in psychology was triggered by various factors, among them a psychology course in school and her wish to understand the problems of young people. Like other participants, she was curious about the bases of others' behavior and wished to understand herself better. Her motivation to study psychology was also triggered by noticing people who had problems. Her reflection shows that other people supported her professional decision. Mes's growing interest in the field of psychology also appeared in the research she conducted in high school. After obtaining her bachelor's degree, she continued to be interested in the field.

In Year 1:

> *I became interested in psychology quite early; it tended to be an interest in understanding myself better, and I was also interested in filling out popular science tests. I became curious—who are the people who invent tests like these? They were so senseless. Later, in high school, we had classes on psychology. And now I became interested; I even conducted brief research. Additionally, my interest increased because I saw that so many young people have serious problems. I asked questions like 'Why it is so?' So finally, I was here to start with studies of psychology. I had supporters, like family members, relatives, and friends. I had made it clear to them before why I wanted to study psychology. Of course, they also offered alternatives and warned me that I would have to learn how to distance myself from others' problems. How have the studies changed my life? Actually, I don't know, I think not too much. In some sense, I have started to see people differently; for sure, I have more knowledge now. But at the moment, I feel that it is like a big mixed cocktail, that I don't know how to use this knowledge. Still, I think that if I should decide one more time, I would make the same choice.*

In Year 4, Mes reported:

> *When I do psychological work, I need to have professional knowledge. It is important that you can use specific terminology, that you have knowledge about ethics; [studies of psychology] probably developed my ability to be empathetic. My studies helped me to establish a network of professional connections ... I don't know if the studies of psychology help in personal life or not ... It's weird to apply it in personal life*

Solutions to the items from DDTC

> **Theme 1 Providing confidential information to third parties**
>
> "When a psychologist has a dilemma whether to give out information on his/her patient, then he feels ____ because ____."
>
> Year 1 ... hesitation, because s/he doesn't know exactly what s/he should do
>
> Year 2 ... confident, because s/he can ask advice from a supervisor or look for that through APA regulations
>
> Year 3 ... confident, because s/he knows that there are rules about when it is allowed to give information

In the first year, Mes' choice of perspective when deciding on providing confidential information to third parties remains unclear. In the second and third year, however, professional role based focus appears to dominate Mes' responses to this situation, allowing the respondent to eliminate negatively oriented tension within the self system. It seems that the possibility to lean on well-defined professional conditions, i.e., rules and regulations, evokes the feeling of confidence in Mes.

> **Theme 2 Disliked client**
>
> "When a psychologist does not like his/her client s/he feels ____ because ____."
>
> Year 1 ... bad, because s/he must ignore this unpleasant feeling and continue to interact with the client
>
> Year 2 ... bad, because s/he should help the person, and at the same time, not all people need to be liked and if your cooperation doesn't fit, then you can refuse to work with the client
>
> Year 3 ... self-confident, because not all clients need to be liked by the psychologist

When under certain conditions, role-related rules can be perceived as useful tools for regulating an ambivalent situation (e.g., in the previous case of providing information to third parties), there are also circumstances where defined regulations can become a source of negative tension. For instance, in the first year of study, when coping with the situation of disliking one's patient, Mes reported to feel bad due to the role-prescribed demand ("a psychologist must") that one has to ignore their own unpleasant feelings and continue to work with the patient.

Similarly to the first year, Mes also reports negatively oriented tension in the second year, however, this time the choice of professional perspective also includes an acknowledgment of psychologist's right to give up the patient if the collaboration is considered inefficient.

Thus, Mes' recognition of professional role related rules and regulations appears to expand during the studies as he/she discovers how a psychologist can benefit from them: e.g., in the first year, the possibility to refer a patient to another colleague is not acknowledged, instead a psychologist is viewed to have an obligation to ignore his/her own negative feelings and proceed with work.

Theme 3   Attractive patient

"When an attractive person of the opposite sex comes to a session at a psychologist's, then s/he feels ____ because ____"

   Year 1 ... calm, because the patient remains a patient

   Year 2 ... like a psychologist, because the patient is a patient regardless of his/her sex

   Year 3 ... as usual, because the patient is a patient

When having to work with a patient that the psychologist considers attractive, Mes finds support from the utilization of professional perspective throughout the three years of study. Over the three years Mes reported neutral state (i.e., feeling calm, like a psychologist, usual), indicating that professional role provides Mes with a kind of filter or a lens which allows him/her to maintain neutrality in a work situation.

Theme 4   "Unable to help" ("When a psychologist understands that s/he is unable to help his client, s/he feels ____ because ____"

   Year 1 ... unhappy, because s/he is not able to help the patient and must refer the patient further

> Year 2 ... disturbed, because on the one hand s/he wants to help the patient, but knows that it is not in his/her power to help everyone
>
> Year 3 ... self-confident, because s/he knows that it is impossible to help everyone

When it regards being unable to help a patient, Mes reports negatively oriented tensions in the first two years and a positive feeling (self-confident) in the last year of study. The choice of perspective for solving this situation is professional in the first year, recognizing the psychologist's option to refer the patient to another colleague, but remains unclear in the next two years. Nevertheless, feeling self-confident in the third year appears to stem from Mes' acknowledgment of the fact that one cannot help everyone.

Theme 5   Close relations

"When a psychologist is to consult a person he has a close connection with, s/he feels ____ because ____"

> Year 1 ... bound, because s/he has often had contact with that person
>
> Year 2 ... more bound, because s/he has often had contact with the person who is close to him/her and s/he knows a lot about him/her
>
> Year 3 ... more concerned and bound, because a psychologist should not counsel people who are close to her/him, it is more difficult to distance oneself from a person's problems when that person is close to them

Regarding solving this situation, Mes' responses reveal the impact a personal history of close relations can have on one's feelings about and performance in a professional role.

By the third year, Mes' focus on the issue becomes professional as moral implication pertained to the professional role are applied ("a psychologist should not counsel people close to him/her").

When in the first two years the character of tensions reported remains unclear, in the third year, it is negatively oriented.

> **Theme 6 Common acquaintance**
>
> "When a person whose problems involve people close to the psychologist comes in for an appointment, the psychologist feels ____ because ____."
>
> Year 1 ... more competent, because s/he knows different aspects of that problem
>
> Year 2 ... confused, because a psychologist can have a more different picture about the people who are close to here/him
>
> Year 3 ... more bound with the case, because s/he knows more about what concerns that problem. Trust and ethics should be held to a high degree.

When in the first year, Mes takes a personal perspective to this issue, perceiving his/her personal history of relations to be useful in the professional settings, in the second year, this same personal history becomes a source of confusion. It is now acknowledged that the patient and the psychologist may have different understandings about their common acquaintances.

When in the first year, Mes reported feeling a positively oriented tension (i.e., more competent) and in the second year, a negatively oriented tension (i.e., confused), by the third year the orientation of tension reported remains unclear.

However, the approach for solving this issue in the last year includes a flux of personal and professional perspectives, acknowledging that one's connection to the case is stronger due to the personal relations and at the same time recognizing the importance of holding trust and ethics to a higher degree when dealing with this situation.

> **Theme 7 Inability to keep distance**
>
> "When a psychologist feels that s/he cannot distance herself or himself from the patient's problems, s/he feels ____ because ____."
>
> Year 1 ... bad, because the patient's problems torture him/her. S/he needs supervision
>
> Year 2 ... disturbed, because the patient's problems are continuously with him/her
>
> Year 3 ... disturbed, because s/he realizes that the patient's problems disturb her/his own life

106 Becoming a psychologist

When it regards being unable to keep the distance from patient's problems, Mes' choice of perspective remains personal throughout the three years, acknowledging the influence this situation has on his/her life after working hours. Correspondingly, the reported tensions also remain negative during the entire study time.

Theme 8   Different values

"When a person whose values differ greatly from that of the psychologist's comes to a session, then s/he feels ____ because ____"

Year 1 ... that it is harder to solve the patient's problems, because approaching the patient is now more difficult

Year 2 ... confident, because s/he can give up the client

Year 3 ... [answer not provided], because it is very difficult to council person with very different values system

---

Concerning working with a patient whose values differ greatly from those of the psychologist, the dynamics of handling tensions and choosing a leading perspective can be observed in Mes' responses.

To begin with, the utilization of personal perspective and recognizing the difficulty of approaching a patient with a different value system appear to create negatively oriented tension for Mes in the first and last year of study.

In the second year, however, Mes manages to eliminate this negative tension by applying professional perspective, acknowledging the psychologist's right to give up the patient (i.e., refer him/her to another specialist). The final year brings the personal perspective back in focus, referring to the difficulties of counselling a patient with a different value system.

Theme 9   Encountering person-in-crisis when workday is over

"When a psychologist meets a person in crisis outside working hours, s/he feels ____because ____"

Year 1 ... concerned, because the problems related to that person come to mind

Year 2 ... as a supporter, because s/he has a wish to help that person

Year 3 ...obligated to help, because even if the workday is over s/he should help him/her

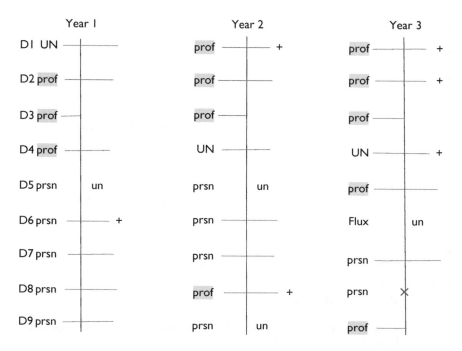

Figure 6.7 Temporary profiles of coordination of perspectives (i.e., professional, personal, 3rd position) and handling tension (i.e., positive and negative affectivity, neutral) in solutions to nine (9) dilemmas.

Note: Prof—the professional approach; Prsn—the personal approach; 3rd—the third I-position; Flux—the fluctuation of perspectives; UN—unknown; X—no answer provided.

When coping with encountering a person in crisis after working hours, Mes' responses shift from personal to professional over the course of study. For instance, when in the first year, Mes expresses feeling concerned about the problems related to this person intruding the psychologist's personal space, then by the third year Mes only focuses on the role prescriptions, stating that a psychologist should provide assistance even after working hours (Figures 6.7 and 6.8).

Summary of case Mes

The direction of Mes' trajectory when entering the professional role can be considered as self-professionalizing. For instance, by the last year of study, the number of leading professional I-positions applied when solving the dilemmas had reached to five (5) out of nine (9), while a domination of personal perspective was in only two (2) cases out of nine. In comparison, in

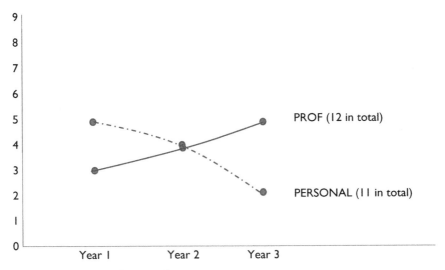

Prof – the professional approach
Personal – the personal approach

Figure 6.8 Trajectories of coordination of different sub-systems (i.e., professional, personal) in the self across the years.

Note: Occurrences of domination of professional and personal I-positions in the solutions to the dilemmas.

the beginning of this study (i.e., in Year 1), the abovementioned measures were three (3) and five (5), respectively. Nevertheless, the general profile of the distribution of dominating personal and professional perspectives in solutions appeared to be fairly balanced (i.e., 12 professional, 11 personal, one (1) flux and three (3) unknown perspectives).

Moreover, Mes was one of the students who's entry into the professional role over the years is characterized by declining generation of negative affectivity. When in Year 1, Mes reported the presence of negative tensions in six (6) cases out of nine (9), then by Year 3, it had dropped down to two (2) cases. Nonetheless, when looking at the distribution of negatively and non-negatively (i.e., positive and/or neutral state) oriented tensions throughout the three years of study, it appears to be relatively balanced, with a total of 12 negative and 10 non-negative responses.

Furthermore, across the years, there were two (2) dilemmas that Mes solved only from a professional perspective—i.e., working with a patient one finds attractive and counselling a client one dislikes. Although, these two situations were similar regarding the presence of an affective component when relating with a client/patient (be it negative or positive), only the case of disliked person was considered disturbing in professional settings. In fact, attraction appeared to be easier to ignore or regulate semiotically than disliking the client. Still, a gradual internalization of role expectations can be noticed over the years in Mes' solutions to the dilemma of disliked client. By the last year, an acceptance of negative feelings was achieved by recognizing that *"not all clients need to be liked by the psychologist."* However, when it regards working with a patient one finds attractive, Mes stated already in Year 1 that *"patient is patient."* Thus, it can be speculated that the person-professional ambivalence was more difficult to regulate in the occurrence of negatively oriented tensions than in the case of attraction. Nevertheless, several students in this study still considered attraction as a source of risk in professional context.

Unlike respondents that interpreted close relations between a patient and a professional as beneficial for professional practice, Mes referred to the problematic side of this type of interaction. Regarding the dilemma of common acquaintances, the emergence of professional role expectations can be observed in Mes' responses as the years pass: for example, in the Year 1, ethics and trust were not highlighted, then in Year 3, the importance of these regulations was explicitly outlined.

What is more, throughout the years, there was one dilemma that Mes solved only from a personal perspective, and that was always accompanied by the reporting of negatively oriented tension—it was the situation that regarded the psychologist's inability to keep the distance from the patient's problems; an ability of high importance for successfully carrying out the professional role of a psychologist. Mes' reflection on that issue revealed difficulties in separating personal and professional aspects of identity within the self. Like several other students in this study, Mes was also unable to find semiotic regulators that would have eliminated negative affectivity.

However, somewhat interesting dynamics were observed regarding the internalization of professional role in Mes' solutions to the dilemma of being unable to help a client. Namely, Year 3 brings out a shift in feelings reported when solving this situation—it went from feeling unhappy (Year 1) and disturbed (Year 2) to self-confident (Year 3); the latter being the result of recognizing the limitations of one's professional role, i.e., that it is impossible to help everyone.

Respondent 6e—Hei

Hei's professional path began "unexpectedly"—she was not sure what her professional future would be. She had alternative options to studying psychology. Hei was not sure about the exact initial conditions that triggered her professional choice. However, we can see that personal contact with a psychologist in her past might have been affected her interest in the field. However, despite the "unexpected" beginning of her studies, she reported that she would make the same decision again. After obtaining a bachelor's degree, Hei has continued in the field. Like other participants, her professional role is reflected in the dynamics of informal relations shaping her professional identity.

Year 1:

> The idea to study psychology came unexpectedly. I attended other entrance exams in other subjects. But all these fields seemed to be so far away from me. One moment, I just realized that this is what I want to study. One of my best friends is a psychologist who is always there for me if I want to talk. Maybe that has influenced my decision to study psychology, too. I also remember that one of my teachers said something like psychology fits me well. Father is probably the only one who still is not on my side. He wanted me to study something else, and [he said] that I am too good to study psychology. It is so interesting to study psychology; it has given me a lot of very useful knowledge. It can only be rewarding in the future. For sure, I would make the same decision again. I can deal with something that is interesting.

Hei in Year 4:

> I do psychological work. Psychology studies gave me a lot, and I use this knowledge. I also became more interested in the field of psychology. Clinical psychology is very interesting. In my personal life, my friends tell me that I read them as if they are open books, but I don't want to believe what they say. Many of them said that it is good to talk to me, always. That they can count on me and that they trust me. One of my closest friends says that I am such a smart mouth and don't stop before I am sure that I other is convinced that I was right. Sometimes I feel that I use the 'psychologist talk' and draw others' attention with that. I am fond of who I am now, and I know that if I continue in this way, I will have a future. I think that if I continue working in the professional field, my professional skills and knowledge will improve and develop. In my personal life, I have noticed that when I say that I am a psychologist, people start to ask questions. I have not experienced negative reactions.

Solutions to the items from DDTC

Theme 1 Providing confidential information to third parties

"When a psychologist has a dilemma whether to give out information on his/her patient, then s/he feels ____ because ____"

Year 1 ... confident, because s/he knows that his/her ethical demands do not allow him/her to do it

Year 2 ... confused, because s/he doesn't know how s/he should behave so that all parts could be satisfied and so that the right decision can be made

Year 3 ... confident, because s/he is familiar with the code of ethics

---

When it concerns providing confidential information to third parties, Hei tends to utilize professional perspective throughout the three years, referring to ethics and to making a "right" decision. In terms of tension, the semiotic regulators applied by Hei managed to evoke both positive and negative feelings.

Theme 2 Disliked client

"When a psychologist does not like his/her client s/he feels ____ because ____"

Year 1 ... patient, because as a psychologist you don't have the choice to select clients whom you like

Year 2 ... disturbed, because that person is not pleasant to her/him

Year 3 ... little bit bad, because the client's behavior has been disagreeable

---

In the first year of solving this situation, Hei's choice of perspective is professional as references are made to role-related prescriptions (i.e., not having a choice to select clients).

The orientation of tension expressed, however, remains unknown.

112 Becoming a psychologist

In the second year, the leading position becomes personal, evoking a negative feeling in Hei.

Lastly, in the third year, the respondent's choice of perspective is unknown, but the orientation of tension reported is negative.

Theme 3   Attractive patient

"When an attractive person (of the opposite sex) comes to a session at a psychologist, then s/he feels ____ because ____."

Year 1 ... curious, because the psychologist is also a human being

Year 2 ... as usual, because an externally attractive patient should not disturb her/his work

Year 3 ... confident, because it should not change anything in his/her work

---

When having to work with an attractive patient, a shift can be observed in Hei's responses from personal toward a professional perspective. For instance, in the first year, attraction is not acknowledged as a distraction in professional relations, instead the emphasis is put on the psychologist as human being.

However, in the second and third year, the utilization of moral imperative "should not" refers to the recognition of role-related rules and restrictions.

Regardless of the choice of perspective, Hei manages to generate neutral state and positive affectivity in the responses throughout the three years of study.

Theme 4   Unable to help

"When a psychologist understands that s/he is unable to help his client, s/he feels ____ because ____."

Year 1 ... indignation, because s/he would surely wants to do more to help

Year 2 ... helpless, because s/he realizes that s/he must turn to other specialists, because s/he realizes that s/he cannot help in everything

Year 3 ... good, s/he always has the choice to direct the patient further

Hei's solutions to being unable to help a patient are conveyed mostly from the professional perspective, except for the first year, when the choice of perspective remains unknown. In the second and third year, Hei finds support from an option available to psychologists, i.e., the possibility to refer the patient to another specialist—hence, applying a professional approach.

Nevertheless, when in the second year, Hei reports feeling helpless because of having to refer the patient to another specialist as a result of failing to provide the assistance needed, then in the third year, this same option is viewed as a resource and thus greeted with a positive feeling (good).

Theme 5   Close relations

"When a psychologist is to consult a person s/he has a close connection with, s/he feels ____ because ____."

Year 1 ... weird, because s/he knows all personal facts about that person

Year 2 ... good, because with friends and acquaintances it is easier to talk, also it is easier to convince them

Year 3 ... good, because s/he can help a person close to her/him, but s/he must also remember about ethics and refer him/her further if possible

---

In solving this case, Hei's choice of perspective shows a gradual emergence of professional position in responses. In the first two years, the responses convey personal relations' involvement in professional practice, indicating its strengthening influence on professional functioning (i.e., easier to do one's job because of knowing the patient's history).

In the third year, however, the utilization of professional position is accompanied by an additional reference to professional ethics, denoting the emergence of professional "voice" in Hei's inner dialogue. However, the response also consists of the personal "voice" (i.e., the fluctuation of perspectives).

Theme 6   Common acquaintance

"When a person whose problems involve people close to the psychologist comes in for an appointment, the psychologist feels ____ because ____."

> Year 1 ... confused, because s/he can face a dilemma—to reveal that s/he knows the "source of the problem" or not
>
> Year 2 ... little bit useless, because the work ethic does not allow one to speak about facts that are related to a person who is close to her/him
>
> Year 3 ... incompetent, because it can happen that s/he is not able to set aside his/her own point of view

When working with a patient whose problems are related to people close to the psychologist, Hei's choice of perspective that is professional in the first two years of study, turns personal by the third year. However, regardless of the leading I-position, the reporting of negatively oriented tensions prevails in Hei's solutions to this situation throughout the study.

Theme 7 "Inability to keep distance" ("When a psychologist feels that s/he cannot distance oneself from the patient's problems, s/he feels ____ because ____"

> Year 1 ... stressed, because being at home s/he is also thinking about the patient and does not dedicate himself/herself completely to her/his family
>
> Year 2 ... harassed, because s/he is thinking intensely about something else
>
> Year 3 ... that s/he must give up that patient, because it will influence the patient-psychologist relation

Similarly to the fifth dilemma, solving this case, also reveals a gradual emergence of professional position in Hei's responses over the years. The personal perspective that takes prevalence during the first two years becomes secondary to the professional "voice" by the third year when the obligation and need to follow role-related rules are acknowledged.

The orientation of tensions expressed stays negative in the first two years and unidentified in the third year of study.

Theme 8   Different values

"When a person whose values differ greatly from those of the psychologist comes to a session, then s/he feels ____ because ____"

> Year 1 ... interest and understanding, because every single psychologist knows that people and their values differ, and this is something that one must understand
>
> Year 2 ... understanding, because all people cannot have the same values
>
> Year 3 ... good, because people and their values *are* different, and this is more interesting than disturbing

Unlike the other dilemmas, this case generated positively oriented feelings for Hei in the year 1 and year 3 as he/she viewed the difference of values as a given and even a positive thing; however, the orientation of affectivity in the second year remains unidentified.

Moreover, Hei's choice of perspective is professional in the first year, when references are made to professional knowledge and to regulations (must). In the second and third year, Hei applies a third position (more about in Chapter 2).

> **Theme 9 "Encountering a person in crisis after working hours" ("When a psychologist meets a person in crisis outside working hours, s/he feels ____because ____"**
>
> Year 1 ... obligated and conscientious, because s/he helps anyway, this is not the kind of job that depends on worktime
>
> Year 2 ... involved in the situation, because a psychologist does not work only from 9 AM to 5 PM, if it is in his/her power to help, then s/he will do it
>
> Year 3 ... obligated to help the person, because the person in crisis is in a very difficult state and can be a danger to her/himself

When encountering a person in crisis after working hours, Hei maintains a professional perspective throughout the three years, emphasizing the role-related obligations that call for a psychologist's intervention (Figures 6.9 and 6.10).

Summary of case Hei

In this study, Hei represents a case of self-professionalization trajectory. Hence, throughout the years and across the dilemmas, characteristic to Hei's entry into the professional role is the domination of "I as a professional"—in total, the

116 Becoming a psychologist

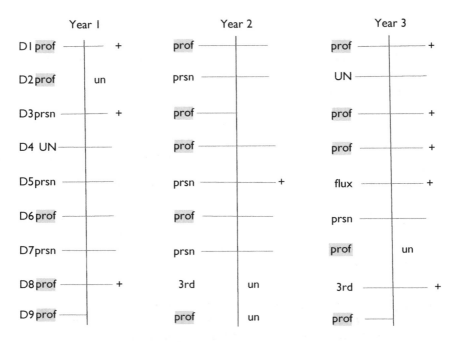

Figure 6.9 Temporary profiles of coordination of perspectives (i.e., professional, personal, 3rd position) and handling tension (i.e., positive and negative affectivity, neutral) in solutions to nine (9) dilemmas.

Note: Prof—the professional approach; Prsn—the personal approach; 3rd—the third I-position; Flux—the fluctuation of perspectives; UN —unknown; X—no answer provided.

latter was identified in 15 cases compared to 7 personal, two (2) third positions (in terms of Hubert Hermans), one (1) fluctuation of perspectives, and two (2) unknown perspectives.

Regarding the regulation of tensions, Hei belonged to the group of students that, as the years passed, exhibited an increase in reporting nonnegative affectivity in their solutions.

Moreover, across the years, there were two dilemmas that Hei solved exclusively from a professional perspective: i.e., (1) encountering person in crisis after working hours, and (2) providing confidential information to third parties. In the latter case, Hei interpreted professional regulations as a source of confidence (in Year 1 and Year 3) that in turn led to positive affectivity. Hence, the regulations appeared to bridge the ambiguity of conditions (i.e., being a person in a social role) and thereby provide a feeling of confidence.

However, the case of encountering a person in crisis after working hours revealed Hei's emerging professional identity as well as the vague borders

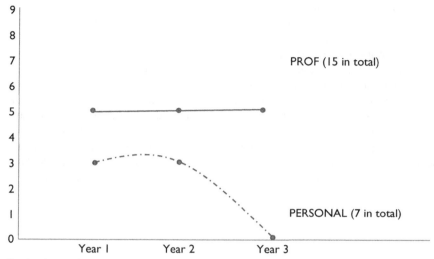

Figure 6.10 Trajectories of coordination of different sub-systems (i.e., professional, personal) in the self across the years.

Note: Occurrences of domination of professional and personal I-positions in the solutions to the dilemmas.

between professional and non-professional settings. The semiotic regulators that Hei applied here (e.g., *the job does not depend on worktime*, and *the psychologist does not work only from 9 AM to 5 PM*) tended to generate a feeling of obligation and "push the psychologist into action." Thus, unlike Vik that finds the psychologist to be a bystander who should not have to think about work after working hours, Hei demonstrates an opposite meaning to this situation. Interestingly, although both respondents display the same trajectory of entry into the profession—i.e., the self-professionalization—their use of professional perspective is affected by a unique, and clearly different personal culture.

Furthermore, when having different value systems with a client associated with negative affectivity for several participants, then Hei applied semiotic tools that enabled a more positively oriented perspective to this issue. Hei's position regarding this dilemma was that the psychologist must acknowledge that everyone is different.

What concerns the tension that having personal relations with the client can potentially bring into professional settings, Hei did not regard this as a threat. Unlike in the case of having common acquaintances, personal relations with a client were interpreted as helpful when doing professional work (e.g., making it *easier to talk* to the client). Nonetheless, in Year 1, the psychologist was reported to feel weird in this situation. By the last year of study, Hei acknowledges the importance of being aware of ethics and regulations when working as a psychologist.

Lastly, regarding the dynamics of the application of I-positions and the emergence of self-professionalizing trajectory by the last year of study, attention should also be given to the dilemmas where the solution strategies changed in time, since these mark the gradual internalization of professional role expectations. For Hei, these dilemmas included (1) an attractive patient and (2) inability to keep distance. For example, when working with an attractive patient Hei's approach shifts from personal (i.e., feeling *curious*, because *the psychologist is also a human being*) to professional (i.e., *feeling confident, because it should not change anything in psychologist's work*).

Respondent 6f—Ris

Ris represents cases with developmental trajectories that have been shaped by role models. However, Ris also seems to be a case of growing interest in the field—she reports that she is more satisfied with her studies than she expected. Also, like many other psychology students, Ris mentions that studying psychology provided practical knowledge to apply in life.

> *Psychology seemed important in life, even if I won't work as a psychologist in the future. Another reason why I decided to study psychology is that one close person to me also used to study psychology, and that person has been a role model for me. All the people close to me supported me, except one friend who was not directly against it but also wasn't for it. I was anxious at the beginning. I wanted to know if it [studying psychology)].was the right decision. Now I am very satisfied that I study psychology, even more than I expected.*

Year 4:

> *Psychology helps me to see things through other people's eyes, or at least I am aware of differences in the way we see situations. Thanks to my studies, I am more self-confident in coping with conflict situations. At my workplace, I am working as an educator.*

Solutions to the items from DDTC

Theme 1   Providing confidential information to third parties

"When a psychologist has a dilemma whether to give out information on his/her patient, then he feels ____ because ____"

Year 1 ... confident, because confidentiality is strictly regulated

Year 2 ... between two sides, because s/he should follow rule of confidentiality

Year 3 ... like a donkey between two piles of hay, because situations like this should be rare. Hopefully the psychologist has more ability to decide than that does a poor starving and dying animal

---

Ris' approach to the situation of providing confidential information to third parties maintains a professional focus over the three years. However, some dynamics can still be observed in how the respondent perceived the ambivalent condition over the years.

For instance, when in the first year, the psychologist is reported to feel confident when leaning on the rules and regulations of the profession, the following two years bring about a change in the respondent's understanding of those same regulations.

Namely, Ris' responses given in the second and third year indicate that she begins to consider the regulations as relative instead of rigid guidelines, hence suggesting that assuming the professional role gives one ground to base the application of profession-related rules according to the necessity of the particular situation.

Theme 2   Disliked client

"When a psychologist does not like his/her client s/he feels ____ because ____"

> Year 1 ... insecure, because s/he has doubts about her/himself—whether or not s/he can give the best of herself/himself during the session
>
> Year 2 ... bad, because s/he is not able to be stay impartial
>
> Year 2 ... uncomfortable, because s/he has difficulties being empathetic

---

When it regards working with a patient that the psychologist does not like, Ris expresses negatively oriented tensions throughout the three years of study while a choice of perspective remains personal.

Theme 3   Attractive patient

"When an attractive person (of the opposite sex) comes to a session at a psychologist's, then s/he feels ____ because ____"

> Year 1 ... confused, because his/her impartiality may be questionable
>
> Year 2 ... bad, because attraction should not disturb their psychologist-patient (client) relations
>
> Year 3 ... uncomfortable, because the counselor/client relationship is ruined

Unlike Mes, when having to work with a patient whom the psychologist considers attractive, Ris conveys negatively oriented tensions throughout the three years of study (feeling confused, bad, and uncomfortable) and it appears to stem from a realization of the effect one's personal attraction could have on one's professional functioning. For instance, in the first and last year, the negative tensions Ris reported seem to result from an understanding that his/her professional conduct (more specifically, his/her ability to remain impartial as well as the effectiveness of the patient-psychologist relationship) is jeopardized due to his/her personal feelings. Meanwhile, in the second year Ris acknowledged that the patient-psychologist relationship *should not* be disturbed by this attraction, thus conveying a professional role related demand.

Theme 4   Unable to help

"When a psychologist understands that he is unable to help his client, s/he feels ____ because ____"

Year 1 ... obligated to direct the patient further to somebody else, because that "someone else' may be able to help the patient more

Year 2 ... sad, because regardless of having given the best of her/himself, patient's problem is deeper than s/he had guessed

Year 3 ... calm, because s/he knows that s/he must direct the patient elsewhere

---

When coping with the situation of being unable to help a patient, Ris' choice of perspective over the years shifts from professional to personal to professional again.

In the first year Ris focuses on his/her professional obligation to refer the patient to another specialist if needed, in the third year, this same obligation, once being acknowledged as an option provided by the profession, eliminates negative tension within Ris' self system and as a result Ris conveys feeling calm.

In the second year, however, the feeling of sadness is reported by Ris as he/she interprets his/her inability to provide help as a personal failure (i.e., regardless of giving his/her best, the problem persists).

> **Theme 5 "Close relations" ("When a psychologist is to consult a person he has a close connection with, s/he feels ____ because ____"**
>
> Year 1 ... more involved, because problems of a person to whom s/he is close affect him/her more
>
> Year 2 ... bad, because close relations hinder the counseling relationship
>
> Year 3 ... bounded, because the relation here is more close than a counselor-client relation

When consulting a person that the psychologist has a close relationship with, Ris maintains a personal focus throughout the three years of study. Moreover, every solution the respondent gives, regardless of the year, highlights the influence personal history is perceived to have on one's functioning in the professional role.

When in the second year, the negatively oriented tension can be identified (feeling bad) in Ris' response, it remains unclear in her first and third year responses.

> **Theme 6 Common acquaintance**
>
> "When a person whose problems involve people close to the psychologist comes in for an appointment, the psychologist feels ____ because ____."
>
> Year 1 ... little bit more motivated, because for her/him it is important that the problems will be solved
>
> Year 2 ... bad, because close relations hinder counseling
>
> Year 3 ... uncomfortable, because s/he finds herself/himself in the crossfire

When having to consult a patient whose problems involve people close to the psychologist, Ris' choice of perspective as well as the character of tension reported remain unclear in the first year of study.

In the second year, however, the tension conveyed is negatively oriented (feeling bad) and appears to stem from the utilization of personal perspective when solving this issue as Ris recognizes that one's personal relations can hinder the work process.

Personal I-position along with the expression of negatively oriented tension also dominates Ris' response in the third year.

Theme 7   Inability to keep distance

"When a psychologist feels that s/he cannot distance herself/himself from the patient's problems, s/he feels ____ because ____"

> Year 1 ... a worsening of his or her mood, because s/he is not able to give the best that he or she can, and what is more, solving the problem can also lead to a lowering of his or her mood
>
> Year 2 ... sucked in, because a close relation can hinder their professional relationship
>
> Year 3 ... the need to direct the patient further to somebody else, because s/he is too personally concerned with the problems

---

Here, we can observe tensions being handled through a gradual move from a personal focus on the issue toward a professional perspective, more specifically, toward the recognition of role-related demand to refer the patient to another specialist when one becomes overly tied to the patient's problem.

Theme 8   Different values

"When a person whose values differ greatly from that of the psychologist's comes to a session, then s/he feels ____ because ____"

> Year 1 ... challenged, because counseling such a person takes more effort
>
> Year 2 ... challenged, because it could be that counseling such person can be more complicated
>
> Year 3 ... challenged, because s/he must be empathetic and professional

---

When having to work with a patient whose values differ greatly from those of the psychologist, Ris approaches the issue through a personal perspective during the first two years of study, referring to the difficulties that may emerge in one's professional conduct because of the perceived mismatch between one's own and the patient's values.

In the third year, however, Ris' choice of perspective becomes professional when the moral imperative "a psychologist must" is applied in the response.

The direction of tension over the years remains unknown as Ris conveys feeling "challenged" when solving this dilemma throughout the study period.

Theme 9   Encountering person-in-crisis when workday is over

"When a psychologist meets a person in crisis outside working hours, s/he feels ____ because ____."

> Year 1 ... connected to that person, because in principle the psychologist could provide emergency help
>
> Year 2 ... connected to the person, because s/he knows that s/he could improve his/her state
>
> Year 3 ... connected to the person, because s/he must decide to help or not

---

Ris' approach to encountering a person in crisis after working hours remains professional throughout the three years of study as (s)he sees his/her professional role and competencies to bound him/her to help the person in need of assistance.

When in the first two years, Ris refers to the psychologist's ability to provide assistance ("a psychologist could provide first aid" and "a psychologist knows that (s)he could improve that person's state," respectively), in the third year, the focus is shifted toward making the decision whether to help or not, accompanied by the utilization of moral imperative "a psychologist must."

The direction of tension remains unknown throughout the three years (Figures 6.11 and 6.12).

Summary of case Ris

Ris belongs to the group of self-professionalizing cases. In total, 15 personal and 11 professional approaches were identified in Ris' responses throughout the years. Nevertheless, in Year 3, the use of personal perspective in Ris' responses decreased, leading to the domination of professional I-position and thereby shifting the direction of Ris' trajectory of entry into the profession.

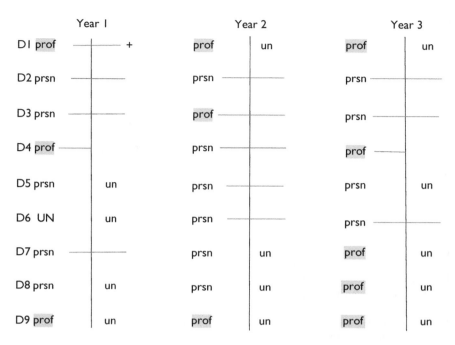

Figure 6.11 Temporary profiles of coordination of perspectives (i.e., professional, personal, 3rd position) and handling tension (i.e., positive and negative affectivity, neutral) in solutions to nine (9) dilemmas.

Note: Prof—the professional approach; Prsn—the personal approach; 3rd—the third I-position; Flux—the fluctuation of perspectives; UN —unknown; X—no answer provided.

Regarding Ris' regulation of affectivity when solving dilemmas, an inclination toward generation of negatively oriented tensions can be observed. In addition to 13 reported tensions of unknown character, negatively oriented tension dominated over non-negative feelings (i.e., positive or neutral state) across the years. Like several other participants, Ris also associated having to work with a patient one dislikes with negative feelings (e.g., insecure, bad, uncomfortable). The approach taken to solve this dilemma remained personal throughout the years of study. However, unlike many other respondents, Ris maintained the abovementioned approach even when encountering an attractive person in professional settings. In fact, no difference was observed in the type of feelings the client evoked in the psychologist as both situations were conceived of as a potential risk to professional relations.

Moreover, similar to other students in this cohort, Ris' tactic when solving the dilemma of sharing confidential information remains professional

126 Becoming a psychologist

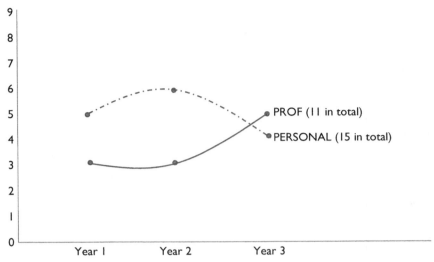

Prof – the professional approach
Personal - the personal approach

Figure 6.12 Trajectories of coordination of different sub-systems (i.e., professional, personal) in the self across the years.

Note: Occurrences of domination of professional and personal I-positions in the solutions to the dilemmas.

throughout the years of study. Nevertheless, it seems that in the beginning of studies this issue is considered as less ambiguous whereas it later becomes a more complex situation without clearly defined principles. For instance, the semiotic regulator of *"confidentiality is strictly regulated"* (Year 1) turns into a metaphor of feeling *"like a donkey between two piles of hay"* (Year 2 and 3), revealing the perceived dependence on the context where the rules are applied. As all other participants, Ris also utilized moral implications like *must* and *should* when taking the professional perspective.

Furthermore, drawing on Ris' profile of responses, assuming the professional role of psychologist can be considered as a demanding task of coordinating two sub-systems of the self—i.e., "I as a person" and "I as a professional"—that leads to the emergence of negatively oriented tensions even if role-related expectations and regulations are acknowledged. For example, affective relating to a client (e.g., in the cases of working with a person one dislikes or finds attractive) as well as having personal relations with a patient (i.e., dilemmas 5 and 6) are perceived to pose a potential threat to one's professional conduct. Meanwhile, encountering interpersonal differences—e.g., having different value systems with a client—are interpreted as something challenging that takes extra effort from the person in the professional role.

Lastly, Ris' solutions to the dilemma of encountering a person in crisis after working hours reveal that the person is expected to operate from a professional perspective even in informal settings, since if the psychologist *could* help, s/he *must* decide whether to do it or not. A gradual emergence of a "stronger" professional identity can also be observed in Ris' responses to this situation, as by Year 3, the moral imperative *must* appears in the solution. When in previous years, there was no obligation to get involved, then in the last year, the psychologist *must* respond. This was also a dilemma that was solved solely from a professional perspective throughout the years.

Respondent 6g—Aet

Her wish to understand herself and others led her to study psychology (implication: psychology enables people to help others and understand others and oneself). Like many other participants, she experienced contradictions in social relations based on her professional decision—Aet's parents did not support her choice. In Year 1, after she had already begun studying psychology, Aet had some doubts regarding her suitability for the role of a psychologist because she found that she was too pessimistic (implication: psychologists are not pessimistic). Moreover, her hesitations seemed to be fueled by the personal domain of life, and she mentioned that "because many people do not believe others' words. True, many believe and trust." In this particular context, not believing what others say indicates an issue in everyday life rather than academic settings and interactions (although it is not totally excluded that the student may not believe what the professors say and may not trust them). It also seems that the ambivalence of being a person in a professional role (i.e., person <> psychologist) leads to inner tension that is expressed in the declaration: "My name is not 'psychologist." Aet in Year 1:

> *I think I changed at the age of fifteen or sixteen. I became serious and started to analyze and observe myself and other people. Since 9th grade, I started to borrow books from a library ... then I was sure that I would come to study psychology. I think that the reasons I chose psychology are my previous experiences (how in childhood, I caused somebody's behavior), for instance. I also had a wish to understand people with similar problems like I had and support them. I also had a wish to get to know more about myself. My parents didn't understand my choice—why do I want to work in a field where I earn nothing? I had to support myself. The time when I took exams to enroll in a university was very anxious. My parents exerted pressure; they wanted me to get in.*

> *I think that it is not possible to hold onto life so tightly. If something will slide from the hand, then it does. Actually, I do not know what I would do if I hadn't enrolled in a university. I was happy when I was admitted to the university, of course.*

> *But it was not good that I had to pay for the studies. The studies themselves have not changed my life. I have been thinking that maybe I wouldn't choose psychology the next time for two reasons: I forced myself too much then, and I would choose something else, not psychology. And a second reason—I must pay for studies.*

> *I am not sure that I am the right person to become a psychologist because I tend to be pessimistic, and these doubts arise day by day because many people do not believe others' words. True, many believe and trust. And maybe there is no need for classification—psychologist, not a psychologist, I can be there for other people as an ordinary human being, for people when they need me. My name is not 'psychologist.'*

In Year 4, Aet commented:

At the moment, I don't have a job. But I used to work a few months ago. It was not psychological work, but I had to interact with colleagues. I am not convinced that the acquired knowledge and skills supported me then [when interacting with colleagues]. Maybe it was my "inner feeling" that helped. Or maybe both. For example, if you have to ask for help, you should know when the right moment is and how to turn to another person. My psychology studies revealed that everyone has feelings, and we should accept it. In my personal life, I have used psychological knowledge—I applied one model recently, and it worked. I felt good—I knew something. I applied it, and it worked. I am not "scanning" people. I don't think that psychological knowledge is the only valid knowledge and that it should guide me in my life. What is disturbing in personal life is that, for most people, a psychologist is like a God or a kind of super person who knows everything and always behaves in the right fashion. Sometimes, I intentionally tell people that I studied something else.

Aet, like some other participants (e.g., Par), reveals that the social expectations for her as a psychologist elicit tension—she feels that she is being "pushed" into the position of a psychologist in informal settings. What is more, we can also notice that "being a psychologist" in informal settings is not an exception but the reality for many participants. Aet's story confirms that, in many cases, persons with a degree in psychology may experience high expectations in everyday life because they "are psychologists." "My name is not a psychologist."

Solutions to the items from DDTC

> **Theme 1   Providing confidential information to third parties**
>
> "When a psychologist has a dilemma whether to give out information on his/her patient, then he feels ____ because ____."
>
> > Year 1 ... like a donkey between two piles of hay, because s/he doesn't know which behavior is correct at the moment
> >
> > Year 2 ... helpless, because it can ruin a psychologists' reputation. Also, because the patient-psychologist relation is based on trust
> >
> > Year 3 ... like a donkey between two piles of hay, because s/he is not sure which of these options is best

When it regards providing confidential information to third parties, Aet does not manage to eliminate negatively oriented tension in his/her responses during the entire study period. Aet's choice of perspective when approaching this issue stays professional over the three years, reflecting over the "right/correct" way to behave as well as the possible consequences to one's behavior (e.g., damaging one's reputation as a professional and jeopardising the patient-psychologist relationship).

Theme 2   Disliked client

"When a psychologist does not like his/her client s/he feels ____ because ____."

   Year 1 ... uncomfortable, because s/he is not able to face unpleasant situations and look past them

   Year 2 ... uncomfortable, because s/he must suppress in herself/himself that unpleasant feeling toward the client. They must ignore, or otherwise not look at that feeling. Stereotypes are deep inside human beings.

   Year 3 ... bad, because s/he simply cannot/is not able to overcome their own prejudices, her/his own feelings

---

Dealing with the situation of having to work with a patient whom the psychologist does not like appears to evoke negatively oriented tension (feeling uncomfortable and bad) in Aet throughout the three years of study. However, Aet's choice of perspective for coping with this situation is changing from personal in the first to professional in the second and back to personal in the third year.

Theme 3   Attractive patient

"When an attractive person of the opposite sex comes to a session at a psychologist's, then s/he feels ____ because ____."

   Year 1 ... excited, because human physiology is that way

   Year 2 ... [answer not provided]

   Year 3 ... normal, because the patient's gender is not important. It is important why s/he came

Thirteen pathways 131

Regarding working with a patient whom the psychologist considers attractive, personal focus prevails in Aet's response in the first year, whereas it becomes secondary by the third year when professional perspective takes over. Aet has managed to generate positive affectivity and neutral state in solutions.

Theme 4 Unable to help

"When a psychologist understands that he is unable to help his client, s/he feels ____ because ____."

Year 1 ... incompetent, because s/he thinks that even though s/he has been trained, it is not enough

Year 2 ... incompetent, because even with all of his/her psychological knowledge s/he is not able to help in the given situation

Year 3 ... bad, because he or she may not have the necessary knowledge or skills to help the patient

---

When realizing one's inability to help a patient, Aet's choice of perspective remains professional and continues to generate negatively oriented tension in the respondent.

More specifically, Aet emphasizes professional training and knowledge as the factors determining one's success within the professional sphere.

Theme 5 Close relations

"When a psychologist is to consult a person he has a close connection with, s/he feels ____ because ____."

Year 1 ... bad, ... [answer not provided] ...

Year 2 ... normal, because you are listening to a person who is close to you whose thoughts and actions are familiar to you

Year 3 ... unpleasant, because a close person is something different than a stranger, you cannot see the larger-scale picture

---

Here, personal perspective dominates Aet's responses in the second and third years, however, a shift can be observed to take place regarding the direction of tension (negative, neutral, negative) reported as well as the choice of semiotic regulators that bring about these tensions.

For instance, when in the second year, close relations are viewed as something that supports the psychologist in his/her professional conduct, then in the third year it is considered as an obstacle, hindering one from seeing the "larger-scale picture."

Theme 6   Common acquaintance

"When a person whose problems involve people close to the psychologist comes in for an appointment, the psychologist feels ____ because ____."

Year 1 ... unpleasant, because discussions and negotiations can hurt himself/herself too, and can influence their attitude toward her/his close relations (by protecting them)

Year 2 ... uncomfortable, because it is difficult to take the stranger's side over that of people who are close to the psychologist. But at the same time it depends on the situation and the relationship (close people to psychologist)

Year 3 ... unpleasant, because the process involves people who are close to the psychologist and to some third person

---

When having to consult a patient whose problems involve people close to the psychologist, Aet's choice of perspective remains personal and the orientation of tensions reported negative throughout the three years of study.

Theme 7   Inability to keep distance

"When a psychologist feels that s/he cannot distance oneself from the patient's problems, s/he feels ____ because ____."

Year 1 ... depressed, because they take it to heart and the psychologist too will worry (too empathetic)

Year 2 ... dispirited, because all that s/he has experienced will come to mind. Disturbed, when problems are similar. Helpful, when the psychologist has overcome similar problems

Year 3 ... tired, because s/he is not able to carry all problems

Similarly to the previous dilemma, solving this situation also yields in the communication of negatively oriented tension and the utilization of personal perspective throughout the entire study period.

More specifically, through the application of semiotic regulators, Aet conveys the influence that psychological work can have on the psychologist's emotional functioning (i.e., feeling tired, depressed, dispirited, disturbed) due to one's personal qualities (e.g., too empathetic) and past experiences. However, applying a personal perspective can lead to generation of different feelings—in the second year, semiotic regulators elicit also positively oriented affectivity (i.e., helpful).

Theme 8 Different values

"When a person whose values differ greatly from those of the psychologist comes to a session, s/he feels ____ because ____."

Year 1 ... guilty, because it is not easy to make something clear to a person who differs from one's own views

Year 2 ... normal, because s/he is able to accept the value system of others

Year 3 ... normal, because s/he knows how to regulate herself/himself to the 'right wavelength'

When working with a patient whose values differ greatly from those of the psychologist, a certain dynamics can be observed in Aet's responses over the years regarding the expression of tension as well as the choice of perspective.

To begin with, in the first year, negatively oriented tension (feeling guilty) is reported due to the perceived difficulty that having different values poses on one's ability to efficiently perform in the professional role (in this case, being responsible for educating the patient).

In the second year, Aet's choice of perspective remains unclear, however, Aet generates this time neutral state.

Lastly, in the third year, Aet manages to maintain neutral state through the application of professional perspective, stating that (s)he "knows how to regulate her-/himself to the 'right wavelength'."

> **Theme 9 Encountering person-in-crisis after working hours**
>
> "When a psychologist meets a person in crisis outside working hours, s/he feels ____ because ____."
>
> > Year 1 ... sorrow, because s/he knows what worries other person has
> >
> > Year 2 ... sad, because they automatically experience empathy
> >
> > Year 3 ... somehow obligated, because s/he wants/may want to help

When solving this situation, the orientation of tension Aet expresses over the years turns from a negative to a neutral state (somehow obligated).

In the second year of study, the perceived "automatic" empathy refers to the domination of personal approach. However, in the first and the third year, Aet's approach remains unknown (Figures 6.13 and 6.14).

Summary of case Aet

Aet appears to be rather the self-professionalizing case: when in the first year, five (5) dilemmas out of 9 were solved from the personal and two (2) dilemmas from the professional perspective, then during the next years, the dominating personal I-positions in solutions decreased to 4, while the dominating professional I-position increased to 4.

Like for many other participants in this study, the semiotic regulators applied across the years generated mostly negatively oriented tensions in Aet. More specifically, Aet's solutions to dilemmas revealed a presence of negative affectivity in 19 occurrences, while five (5) responses indicated a neutral state, and only one (1) positively oriented tension was identified in Aet's answers throughout the years, including one fluctuation of handling tension when Aet referred to positive and negative feelings in solution to the dilemma of inability to keep distance. (Together with the fluctuation in handling tension in the last year of studies, 20 occurrences of negatively oriented affectivity and 7 references to non-negative affectivity were identified.) The positive feeling appeared in the first year of study when solving the situation of working with a patient one finds attractive (i.e., feeling *excited*), however, by Year 3, it was replaced by a professional approach and a neutral state (i.e., feeling *normal*). When in the beginning of studies, Aet's use of personal perspective evokes a reaction to attractive stimulus (i.e., "*because human psychology is that way*"), then by the last year, the

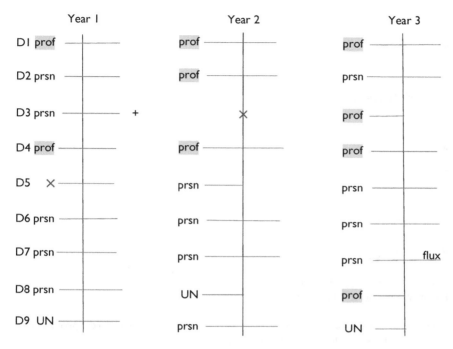

Figure 6.13 Temporary profiles of coordination of perspectives (i.e., professional, personal, 3rd position) and handling tension (i.e., positive and negative affectivity, neutral) in solutions to nine (9) dilemmas.

Note: Prof—the professional approach; Prsn—the personal approach; 3rd—the third I-position; Flux—the fluctuation of perspectives; UN—unknown; X—no answer provided.

internalization of professional role expectations enables Aet to focus on the problem itself, sexual attraction is no longer relevant (i.e., "because *the patient's gender is not important anymore*").

Regarding the dynamics of utilizing I-positions across dilemmas, a change in choice of perspective occurred when solving dilemmas like working with a patient one dislikes, counseling a patient one finds attractive, and different values.

Similarly to other participants across the years of this study, Aet solved the dilemma of providing confidential information to third parties from a professional perspective, whereas the situations involving personal relations (i.e., close relations, common acquaintance) and inability to keep distance were approached from the perspective of "I as a person." Aet's responses reveal a prevailing understanding that relations of the aforementioned character can become an obstacle in professional settings and that inability to keep distance affects a psychologist emotionally.

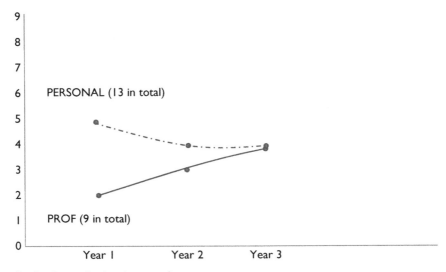

Prof – the professional approach
Personal – the personal approach

Figure 6.14 Trajectories of coordination of different sub-systems (i.e., professional, personal) in the self across the years.

Note: Occurrences of domination of professional and personal I-positions in the solutions to the dilemmas.

All in all, like other students' interpretations, Aet's answers also referred to the difficulties of functioning one experiences while being a person in a social role— drawing the line between personal and professional life is not an easy task for a psychologist.

Self-personalizing cases

Respondent 6h—Gar

Like other participants (e.g., Vik), Gar mentioned having a long-term interest in psychology. Unlike some other respondents (e.g., Par), Gar received support from people close to her for her choice of profession.

Gar, Year 1:

> "I don't remember why I wanted to study psychology, exactly, but I felt that this is something for me. I knew a long time before this summer [of enrollment in a university] that I want to study psychology; I knew in the 9th grade that psychology is my calling. All my close people have supported me; they think that psychology fits me and that in the future it is beneficial."

Gar in Year 4:

> I accepted a job offer because I knew that I could improve the skills that are needed in psychological work ... First, I had the feeling that what I learned at the university does not help. Actually, I think that studies have shaped my worldview. ... In my personal life, the studies have helped me. It is a good feeling to say that I have studied psychology. For most people, it is an interesting subject. I became more tolerant; I can see things from different angles and through others' eyes. People also listen more to the opinion of psychologists.

While Par experiences tension when her education in psychology is mentioned in informal social settings, Gar, conversely, has positive feelings when referring to her professional choice. Gar's lasting interest in the field of psychology also appears in her professional choices—she has accepted work that she feels is helpful in terms of improving the skills needed for work as a psychologist.

Solutions to the items from DDTC

Theme 1 Providing confidential information to third parties

"When a psychologist has a dilemma whether to give out information on his/her patient, then s/he feels ____ because ____."

> Year 1 ... confident, because there are a clear rules, about when it is allowed to give out information, in other cases it is not allowed, it doesn't matter what the explanation is
>
> Year 2 ... confident, because there are rules about when one is allowed to give out information, otherwise the information is confidential
>
> Year 3 ... confident, because there are laws about when you can give out information, and when you cannot do so.

Over the years, Gar manages to generate positively oriented tension in responses to this dilemma through the domination of the professional "voice" over the personal in the dialogue within the self.

All of Gar's solutions refer to the formal (external) regulations, rules (e.g., ethics)—observance of which leads to the emergence of positive affectivity.

Theme 2 Disliked client

"When a psychologist does not like his/her client s/he feels ____ because ____"

> Year 1 ... bad, because s/he is a psychologist and it should not influence his/her work, but a psychologist is also a human being
>
> Year 2 ... incompetent, because s/he must be objective when s/he is working with a patient. Yet, it is so "human" and if it starts to interfere with the work then one should send the client to somebody else because of the well-being of the client
>
> Year 3 ... bad, because s/he must keep her/himself back, must not show it and let it influence the process

Regarding the dilemma of not liking the patient, it is difficult to identify the dominating perspective in the response in year 1 since both positions (i.e., personal and professional) are represented. Hence, the response is identified as a fluctuation, where the first part refers explicitly to professional role regulations and moral implications (i.e., "should not influence"), whereas the second part includes a notion of psychologist "as a human being," bringing forward the personal perspective.

Fluctuation is also present in Gar's response in the second year, however, this time the professional "voice" seems to be dominating. Gar begins by stating that "a psychologist must be objective," but is then recognizing the humane difficulty of remaining objective in a situation where one dislikes the other person. Nevertheless, Gar's response returns to the set of role-specific rules ("a psychologist should refer the patient to another professional").

In the third year, professional perspective prevails in Gar's response through the application of role-related moral imperative ("a psychologist must").

> **Theme 3 Attractive patient**
>
> "When an attractive person of the opposite sex comes to a session at a psychologist's, then s/he feels ____ because ____"
>
> >Year 1 ... good, because people who look good makes one's mood good
>
> Year 2 ... good, it is nice to look at attractive people, so long as it doesn't disturb the work, is everything OK
>
> Year 3 ... good, because s/he has a problem and s/he hopes to find a solution

Encountering an attractive patient is experienced as a positive event for Gar. Interestingly, the positive feelings reported here are not perceived as clouding the psychologist's objectivity, as it was indicated for the negative tension in the case of working with a disliked patient.

Regarding the approach Gar took for solving this dilemma, prominence was first given to the personal perspective. For instance, in the first year, Gar didn't consider attraction as something that could influence the work of a psychologist. Nevertheless, in the second year Gar reconsidered and acknowledged the potential affect from the position of "I as a professional."

In year 3, however, Gar's response concentrated on the patient instead of the psychologist and was therefore coded as unknown.

> **Theme 4 Unable to help**
>
> "When a psychologist understands that he is unable to help his client, s/he feels ____ because ____"
>
> Year 1 ... helpless, because s/he wishes to help everyone who comes to her/him. Yet, s/he has a chance to direct the patient further to someone who is smarter and more competent

> Year 2 ... helpful, because s/he can direct the patient further to more competent people
>
> Year 3 ... guilty (but s/he should not feel this way), because s/he wishes that s/he could help the patient. Although it is impossible to rescue everyone. This is a fact. But you also cannot do anything when you feel it.

Here, we can observe the dynamics of position choice as well as the elimination of negative tension. In fact, the fluctuation of perspectives present in the first year is replaced by a professional focus in the second and a personal one in the third year of studies.

More specifically, the flux reported in the first year embraced personal orientation indicating wish to help everyone, which was followed by a professional focus highlighting an alternative available to the psychologists—i.e., the opportunity to refer difficult cases to more experienced colleagues.

The second year brings about a change in Gar's response, where the negative tension appears to be eliminated through the application of a semiotic regulator (i.e., the option to refer the patient to another colleague), which seems to promote the generation of feeling helpful. As the alternative of referring the patient to another specialist characterizes a professional setting, rather than an informal one, the dominating perspective in Gar's second year response was coded as professional.

The third year, however, brings back the negative tension and the problem-solving focus turns personal. The reported feeling of guilt seems to stem from an internalized semiotic regulator pertained to the person rather than the reflection of professional role expectations.

Theme 5   Close relations

"When a psychologist is to consult a person he has a close connection with, s/he feels ____ because ____"

> Year 1 ... bad, because according to the rules s/he shouldn't officially counsel the person even if s/he wants to help
>
> Year 2 ... bad, because as a professional s/he should not do it
>
> Year 3 ... sad, because s/he knows that close person can expect too much from her/him because s/he knows s/he is a psychologist. Yet, professional counseling is not allowed.

Regarding the dilemma of having close relations with a patient, Gar's answering pattern varies from professional to professional to flux over the course of three years. In the first year, Gar finds support from acknowledging the profession-related rules and uses respective semiotic regulators ("a psychologist should not") to solve the situation.

By the third year, however, a combination of professional and personal perspectives is present in Gar's response, where "I as a person" appears to bring about negative tension (feeling sad) because of having to recognize the expectations of the other person in and outside counselling sessions. Within the same response, Gar also refers to professional role related external regulations through the utilization of semiotic self-regulating devices "it is not allowed" indicating that the role internalization process in the meaning system is active. The perceived discrepancies between the personal and professional perspectives seem to enhance the reporting of negative tension.

Theme 6   Common acquaintance

"When a person whose problems involve people close to the psychologist comes in for an appointment, the psychologist feels ____ because ____."

> Year 1 (the space was left blank), because if need be, s/he can direct the person further to another psychologist so that solving the problem would be objective
>
> Year 2 ... bad, because it is wrong to mix work and one's personal life
>
> Year 3 ... restricted, because it is difficult to be objective

---

During the first two years, Gar's responses to this dilemma are dominated by professional perspective that manifests itself in referring a patient to another specialist in order to avoid the violation of objectivity in professional relations as well as reflecting on the rules defining what is wrong and right in professional conduct. Here, mixing work and personal life is considered a violation of professional role related rules.

By the third year, however, the focus shifts from professional to personal, allowing the perspective of "I as a person" to have a louder "voice" in the dialogue between different sub-systems of the self.

> **Theme 7 Inability to keep distance**
>
> "When a psychologist feels that s/he cannot distance oneself from the patient's problems, s/he feels ____ because ____."
>
> Year 1 ... that s/he must take a break, because otherwise the patient would not get the professional help that s/he was seeking
>
> Year 2 ... stressed, because it disrupts everyday life. It is in the patient's interest that s/he be directed further to somebody else
>
> Year 3 ... incompetent, because s/he must separate his/her life from that of the patient

Over the years, Gar's response pattern regarding managing the inability to keep a distance from a patient tends to refer to professional role related rules through the application of the semiotic regulator "must." The only exception was year 2, when Gar conveyed a personal approach, revealing the difficulties that arise within the psychologist's personal sphere of life due to one's involvement in this profession. However, a professional approach is also present in the response when Gar refers to the patient's interest and that the patient has to be directed further (i.e., the fluctuation of perspectives).

The application of rules and regulations, however, does not seem to eliminate the negative tension.

> **Theme 8 Different values**
>
> "When a person whose values differ greatly from those of the psychologist comes to a session, then s/he feels ____ because ____."
>
> Year 1 ... uncomfortable, because it should not disrupt his/her professional work, but as a person s/he may have difficulties understanding that person
>
> Year 2 ... in conflict, because s/he must stay objective, but the psychologist is also a human being
>
> Year 3 ... [respondent did not understand the question]

Although Gar's solutions regarding coping with different value sets within a professional setting explicitly refer to the application of role-related rules and restrictions, the negative tension in responses appears to result from the presence of personal and professional "voices" in the self.

Being a person in a professional role and trying to understand the viewpoint of another person with a different set of values, can become overwhelming. Especially due to the role-prescribed obligation to overcome the difference for the sake of successful treatment. Here, the application of semiotic devices "should not" and "must" provides support, indicating the internalization of the professional role. Yet, these devices fail to eliminate negative tension.

All in all, the recurrent reference "psychologist is a person" and the use of semiotic devices "should not" and "must" in Gar's responses over the years suggest professional and personal perspectives in the inner dialogue of the self (i.e., the fluctuation of perspectives).

Theme 9   Encountering a person in crisis after working hours

"When a psychologist meets a person in crisis outside working hours, s/he feels ____ because ____."

Year 1 ... touched, because one part of him/her says that s/he should help that person (and s/he should help!)

Year 2 ... competent, because s/he can help that person, and find the place where one gets help

Year 3 ... obligated, because it should never happen that a person in trouble remains without help. This is love for others.

When solving this dilemma, the domination of professional focus in the first two years is replaced by a personal one by year 3.

During the first two years, Gar found support from the application of semiotic regulator "a psychologist should help" and "a psychologist can help" which, combined with having the knowledge about the specific places that can provide help, seemed to generate and promote the feeling of competence (year 2)—thus, giving the professional "voice" prevalence over the personal one within the inner dialogue.

The shift of perspective takes place in the last year of studies when universal ethics are applied to solve the situation. A psychologist no longer intervenes because of the professional role, but because of being human. "One is obliged," as was reported., "because of being a human being."

All in all, the sequence of "should help," and "can help," reveals the dynamics of the professional role internalization process. In a situation

144 Becoming a psychologist

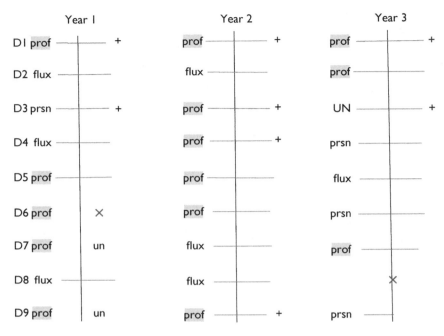

Figure 6.15 Temporary profiles of coordination of perspectives (i.e., professional, personal, 3rd position) and handling tension (i.e., positive and negative affectivity, neutral) in solutions to nine (9) dilemmas.

Note: Prof—the professional approach; Prsn—the personal approach; 3rd—the third I-position; Flux—the fluctuation of perspectives; UN —unknown; X—no answer provided.

where one is not in a formal, externally regulated relationship with another person, Gar focuses on internalizing the professional role, however, the last year of studies brings about a shift in thinking and Gar leaves the professional approach, displaying instead the strong impact of personal I-position when solving this dilemma (Figures 6.15 and 6.16).

Summary of case Gar

With a decline in the utilization of dominating professional perspective and an increase in the use of leading personal I-positions, Gar seems to represent the group of self-personalizing cases, however, by Year 3 the direction of Gar's trajectory of entry into the role shifts and becomes self-personalizing. Compared to other participants, Gar's use of fluctuations of perspectives in the solutions was one of the highest (i.e., 7 solutions thorough the years), together with Pai and Ain.

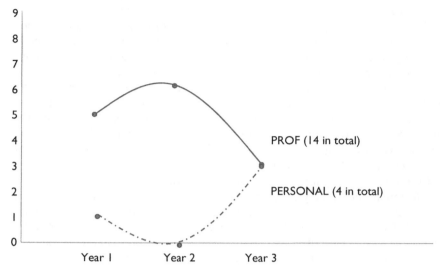

Figure 6.16 Trajectories of coordination of different sub-systems (i.e., professional, personal) in the self across the years.

Note: Occurrences of domination of professional and personal I-positions in the solutions to the dilemmas.

Moreover, as is the case for several other students from this cohort (e.g., Ris and Uur), the regulation of tension that Gar manages using semiotic tools, tended to incline predominantly toward negatively oriented feelings. In fact, there were only two themes—i.e., (1) providing confidential information to third parties and (2) working with an attractive patient—that Gar solved by using semiotic regulators that generated solely positively oriented affectivity. Hence, it can be supposed that leaning on professional role related rules allows Gar experience non-negative feelings. Nevertheless, this strategy does not appear to function for all dilemmas. For example, working with a patient one dislikes, and dilemma of close relations, seem to be somewhat more challenging in terms of generation of non-negative affectivity.

Additionally, the application of moral imperatives like *should not* (Year 1) and *must* (Year 2 and 3) lead to the emergence of personal "voice" which in turn refers to the conflict between different perspectives within the self, e.g., " …. but the psychologist is also a human being" (Year 1), "Yet, it is so 'human,' … ." (Year 2).

What is more, the case of the attractive patient also illustrates Gar's gradual internalization of professional role expectations and the emergence of regulations in their psychological functioning: for example, " ... *because people who look good make your mood good*" in Year 1 becomes "*it is nice to look at attractive people, so long as it does not disturb the work, is everything OK*" in Year 2. In fact, Gar's solution to this dilemma in Year 2 refers explicitly to an understanding of right and wrong in the professional context. Meanwhile, an opposite development can be observed in Gar's responses to the dilemma of encountering a person in crisis after working hours. If in Year 1, the psychologist *should* help, and in Year 2, the psychologist *can* help (which in turn induces feeling competent), then by the third year of study Gar's professional approach is replaced by a personal perspective, where one's "love for others" becomes the guiding meaning of the situation, leading to providing help.

Furthermore, compared to other students in this cohort, Gar's solutions to the dilemmas across the years stand out with a higher utilization of the flux of I-positions (i.e., 7 cases in total), meaning that both I-positions are clearly represented in Gar's inner dialogue, leading to the fluctuation instead of domination of one perspective. As Gar represents the group of self-personalizing trajectory when assuming a professional role, it would be interesting to observe the dilemmas where Gar's approach shifted from professional to personal. These dilemmas were (1) having common acquaintance(s) with the patient, (2) being unable to help the client, and (3) encountering person in crisis after working hours.

In conclusion, Gar's profile of responses indicates that assuming the role of psychologist is tension filled due to the existence of two conflicting perspectives within the self. Regardless of the awareness of rules and regulations that appeared to lead to the reporting of positively oriented feelings, negative affectivity is still experienced on the path of becoming a professional.

Respondent 6i—Par

Like some other students (e.g., Vik), Par mentioned in her Year 1 essay that she had been interested in psychology for a long time; however, unlike Vik, her long-lasting interest was accompanied by hesitations over the choice of becoming a professional psychologist. A wish to improve her knowledge about the principles of human behavior and to understand herself better were mentioned as sources of her interest in psychology. The social environment around her offered contradictory suggestions regarding her choice of a profession. Accompanied by hesitations, Par began and finished studying psychology.

After obtaining a bachelor's degree, Par did not continue studies or work in the field of psychology. Par's relationship with the field has remained somewhat ambiguous over the years. She had doubts when she entered the university: "Is psychology for me? I can learn something useful." Forty-five months later, she is not sure whether she would make the same choice again. However, she still deals with others' expectations of her as if she were a psychologist. Once a psychologist, forever a psychologist (in everyday life)?

> *I came to study psychology because I became interested in that in high school. But I had doubts. In school, there were so many situations when I didn't understand why people behave and do things in a certain way. I wanted to become aware, and maybe I was also a little bit egoistic— I wanted to know more than others. I also wanted to understand myself: How can I help myself, maybe even change my behavior and thinking style? My mother always supported me; she has always been interested in psychology. But my grandparent didn't want me to go to study psychology, thinking that I cannot find a job in the future and that psychologists work only with very sick people like schizophrenics. My grandparent agreed only after my family members explained that psychologists can do very different work. When I applied for psychology, I was not sure that psychology was something for me or that I wanted to become a psychologist. My studies have not changed my life too much, but I feel that I am changed—I am now calmer, smarter. I am not so nervous anymore; I am more confident. If I had to decide again for or against psychology studies, I am not sure that I would study psychology. Maybe yes.*

In Year 4, Par's retrospective revealed that she had withdrawn from the field.

> *I don't know ... if it came from my studies, but I became calmer ... and in the workplace, when clients were screaming at me ... I didn't get upset. ... In my personal life, I don't apply psychological knowledge, I just don't*

want to, I want to be mad and not to understand people ... I think that in the workplace, people expect more from you because you are a psychologist ... Same in personal life ... they say that 'You are a psychologist,' and they think that I don't make mistakes ... But I also have emotions and I want to express those.

In Par's reflection, we can observe tension that is elicited by perceived social expectations. She reports that others expect her to never get angry, believe that she should understand other people because she is a psychologist, and believe that she does not make mistakes (implication: psychologists do not make mistakes; they understand people and do not feel anger). In other words, there are many voices in her inner dialogues that fuel negotiation of identity and suggest "You are a psychologist."

In general, it can be observed that one's perception of being a psychologist does not presume working as a psychologist.

Solutions to the items from DDTC

Theme 1 Providing confidential information to third parties

"When a psychologist has a dilemma whether to give out information on his/her patient, then he feels ____ because ____."

Year 1 ... confused, because it should not affect that person's life

Year 2 ... self-confident, because s/he must follow rules

Year 3 ... confused, because it is a great responsibility to give information out or not

---

When solving the dilemma of providing confidential information to third parties, Par's perspective remains professional over the three years. However, some variation can be noticed in the feelings Par reported, which seem to relate to the way the solution was interpreted. For instance, when in the first year, the psychologist is claimed to feel confused due to the requirements of professional conduct (i.e., the patient's life should not be affected), the second year sees the professional requirements as basis for self-confidence. The feelings turn negative again in the last year (confused self-confident, confused).

> **Theme 2   Disliked client**
>
> "When a psychologist does not like his/her client s/he feels ____ because ____."
>
> > Year 1 ... nervous, because s/he knows that s/he must help her/him, but s/he doesn't want to interact with her/him
> >
> > Year 2 ... calm, because s/he is his/her client and personal dislike doesn't play a role
> >
> > Year 3 ... constrained, because personal feelings should not disturb work

Here, we can observe a movement from the fluctuation of perspectives (must help, doesn't want to interact with client) to a professional approach. In fact, the emergence of professional perspective in the second year appears to eliminate the negative tension that was present in the solution the year before. The psychologist is now claimed to feel calm, instead of being nervous.

Nevertheless, the semiotic devices used in the third year manage to regenerate negative tension (should not).

> **Theme 3   An attractive patient**
>
> "When an attractive person of the opposite sex comes to a session at a psychologist's, then s/he feels ____ because ____."
>
> > Year 1 ... interested, because s/he is my patient
> >
> > Year 2 ... calmly, because s/he is his/her patient
> >
> > Year 3 ... [no reply]

The case of working with an attractive patient appears to evoke non-negative feelings in Par (feeling interested, calmly).

The potential negative tension is defused by underlining the fact that the other person is still "a patient" indicating to professional perspective.

> **Theme 4   Unable to help**
>
> "When a psychologist understands that he is unable to help his client, s/he feels ____ because ____."
>
> Year 1 ... disappointed, because s/he is incompetent (at solving) this problem
>
> Year 2 ... depressed, because s/he needs advice from another psychologist
>
> Year 3 ... like a winner, because the hardest thing is to admit to yourself that you don't know how to do it and to direct the patient to someone else

From negative tension (disappointed) in the first year to a positive feeling (winner) by the last, the dynamics of Par's role internalization can be observed. In the third year, the prevalence of professional perspective in solving this situation is replaced by a flux of personal and professional I-positions. More specifically, the psychologist is reported to feel like a winner, because of managing to exceed oneself through the act of admitting to shortcomings in one's professional competencies. In this case, the professional approach of referring a patient to another specialist is seen as a result of personal growth.

> **Theme 5   Close relations ("When a psychologist is to consult a person he has a close connection with, s/he feels ____ because ____."**
>
> Year 1 ... proud, because people close to her/him ask help from you, this means that for them you are a competent psychologist
>
> Year 2 ... insecure, because s/he cannot be objective
>
> Year 3 ... unjust, because s/he cannot objectively council a person who is close to her/him

When having to consult a person that the psychologist has a close relationship with, the perspective of "I as a person" seems to dominate Par's response pattern in all three years, whereas the reporting of accompanying feelings appears to vary.

In the first year, a positive feeling (proud) is created on the basis of compliments a psychologist receives for their (perceived) competence. Close people seeking advice become rewarding for Par in the beginning of the studies. However, as time passes, we can observe a change in the personal perspective which is highlighted by the realization that personal bond threatens the objectivity of a specialist. In Year 2 and 3 semiotic regulators generate negatively oriented tension.

Hence, the reference "a psychologist cannot be objective" indicates that the personal aspect of identity overrules professional.

Theme 6   Common acquaintances

"When a person whose problems involve people close to the psychologist comes in for an appointment, the psychologist feels ____ because ____."

Year 1 ... disturbed, because s/he knows people I am close with

Year 2 ... depressed, because form one side, s/he is his/her client, from another side—it concerns people who are close to him/her

Year 3 ... defenseless, because s/he knows about the story, cannot be objective

---

The issue of informal relations within professional settings tends to cause negative tension for Par over the three years. It is the perspective of "I as a person," constituted from the personal history and experiences, that began to guide Par's responses. In the second year, Par brings into the inner dialogue both of perspectives (i.e., flux).

Par's third year response admits that having informal connections with the patient outside the working environment does jeopardize psychologist's objectivity.

Theme 7   Inability to keep distance

"When a psychologist feels that s/he cannot distance oneself from the patient's problems, s/he feels ____ because ____"

Year 1 ... that s/he must refer the patient further to another psychologist, because s/he cannot think adequately and independently anymore, and cannot help in ways that are needed

Year 2 ... that it evoked a problematic situation, because s/he must be objective and independent

Year 3 ... not professional, because this is important part, that the psychologist stays within the boarder and won't overstep it

Par approaches the situation of being unable to keep the distance from a patient from a professional perspective throughout the three years by finding support, for instance, in the alternative that comes with the role—i.e., the possibility of referring patients to other colleagues. The grounds for deciding to opt out seem to stem from a concern about one's objectivity.

Hence, the external professional role regulations appear to operate as semiotic devices leading the negotiation between role demands and "the person in the role."

Theme 8 Different values

"When a person whose values differ greatly from those of the psychologist comes to a session, then s/he feels ____ because ____"

Year 1 ... that s/he is his patient, because everyone has his/her own opinion

Year 2 ... that everything is OK, because every person has his/her own worldview

Year 3 ... indifference, because there are as many opinions as there are people.

Concerning the theme of psychologist and patient having different value sets, Par approaches this situation from a third position (in line with DST).

Theme 9 Encountering a person in crisis after working hours

"When a psychologist meets a person in crisis outside working hours, s/he feels ____ because ____"

Year 1 ... bad, because in many situation people don't want to admit that they have a problem

Year 2 ... if it is possible to help s/he will do so, because s/he is a psychologist, but s/he cannot intervene, before the person asks for it

Year 3 ... helpful, because s/he is not only a psychologist but also a person

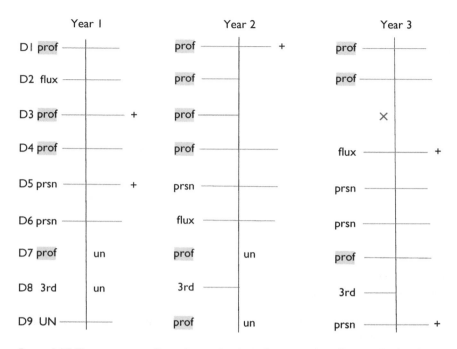

Figure 6.17 Temporary profiles of coordination of perspectives (i.e., professional, personal, 3rd position) and handling tension (i.e., positive and negative affectivity, neutral) in solutions to nine (9) dilemmas.

Note: Prof—the professional approach; Prsn—the personal approach; 3rd—the third I-position; Flux—the fluctuation of perspectives; UN —unknown; X—no answer provided.

Regarding the situation of encountering a person in crisis after working hours Par's first year response leaves the perspective unclear. The second year, however, brings forward a professional perspective where the role-specific regulations appear to direct Par's behavior even in informal settings: it is stated that a psychologist is not allowed ("cannot") to help if the person experiencing the crisis, has not asked for assistance. This restriction has disappeared in the third year. Par's response in the last year indicates to the domination of a personal perspective—it is because the psychologist is a person that leads to generation of feeling helpful (Figures 6.17 and 6.18).

Summary of case Par

The pattern of applying I-positions across the years allow to categorize Par as a self-personalizing case, since by the last year of study, the number of dominating professional I-positions utilized when solving the dilemmas drops from 6 in the second year to 3 by the third year. However, regardless of the direction of

154 Becoming a psychologist

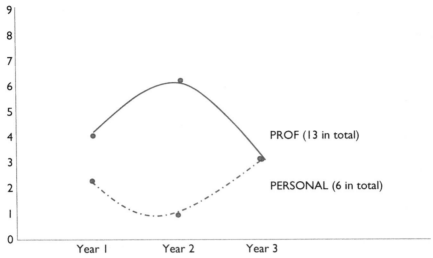

Figure 6.18 Trajectories of coordination of different sub-systems (i.e., professional, personal) in the self across the years.

Note: Occurrences of domination of professional and personal I-positions in the solutions to the dilemmas.

trajectory characterizing Par's entry into the professional role, proportionally, the utilization of professional perspective predominates Par's responses throughout the years. The same can be noticed in the cases of Gar who belongs to the same group with Par. Furthermore, in terms of tension regulation, like others, Par also applied semiotic tools that mostly led to the emergence of negative affectivity when solving professional role related dilemmas.

Nevertheless, when several participants (e.g., Gar, Ele, and Eri) interpreted having different value systems with the client as a source of negative feelings, the meaning that Par gave to this situation did not appear evoke negative tension. However, when it regards affective relating with the client (i.e., in the cases of working with a patient one dislikes/finds attractive), it seems that negatively oriented tensions are interpreted as a stronger threat to one's professional conduct than positive feelings. For instance, in Par's case, attraction does not appear to have power over professional relations; instead, the acknowledgment of "s/he is a patient" evokes interest and calmness.

Moreover, Par's responses allow to depict one's entry into the professional role of psychologist as a multilinear development encompassing the dynamic linking of professional role expectations, meaning that an internalized role expectation can be involved in one's psychological functioning in X time, but can lose its guiding position in the inner dynamics of the self later. For example, in Year 2, when encountering a person in crisis after working hours, Par appears to extend professional relations to informal settings by stating that *"if it is possible to help, s/he will do so because s/he is a psychologist,"* however it is also acknowledged that unless the person in crisis asks for help, the professional cannot intervene. A year later, the emphasis is placed on being human (i.e., *"s/he is not only a psychologist but also a person,"* Year 3).

156 Becoming a psychologist

Self-maintaining cases

Respondent 6j—Ele

I became interested in psychology a long time ago and wanted to know more about it because it helps in a life a lot. I also like to interact with people, and with young children, and I thought that studies of psychology will help me to get a kind of job that is satisfying and interesting. Some people don't understand my choice, like my partner, but my friends and my mother supported me a lot, and they think that it fits me.

2008—exited study

Solutions to the items from DDTC

Theme 1   Providing confidential information to third parties

"When a psychologist has a dilemma whether to give out information on his/her patient, then he feels ____ because ____."

Year 1 ... confused, because s/he has difficulties to decide what could be more right, maybe s/he needs someone's help

Year 2 ... disturbed, because s/he does not know how to behave and what could be right in this situation

Year 3 ... unconfident, it is difficult to make right choice

Over the three years of study, the presence of negative tension can be observed in Ele's responses to this dilemma through the application of semiotic regulators like right and wrong, referring to the ethical basis of one's professional conduct. Ele's approach to this issue remains professional in every response.

Theme 2   Disliked client

"When a psychologist does not like his/her client s/he feels ____ because ____."

Year 1 ... uncomfortable, because it is more difficult to establish contact with the patient that is necessary

> Year 2 ... unconfident, because s/he doesn't have the desire to interact with that patient
>
> Year 3 ... neutral (I think), s/he understands that everyone has a right to ask for help, no matter whether s/he likes that person or not

In Ele's case, experiencing negative feelings regarding the formal relations between a psychologist and a patient resulted from the application of personal perspective on this issue during the first two years of study.

Disliking a patient as a subjective affective-cognitive response is interpreted by Ele as disruptive for achieving one's professional aims in the role of a psychologist.

Nevertheless, the third year of study brings about a change in Ele's interpretation when the approach to this issue becomes professional. The utilization of a semiotic regulator stating that everyone has a right to find help, regardless of psychologist's feelings about the patient, provides Ele with a certain affective neutrality.

Theme 3 Attractive patient

"When an attractive person of the opposite sex comes to a session at a psychologist's, then s/he feels ____ because ____"

> Year 1 ... free, because contact will be created quickly, s/he likes to talk to that person, to help him/her
>
> Year 2 ... insecure, because s/he likes to interact with that person
>
> Year 3 ... good, because it is a pleasure to talk to an attractive patient

In the first year, Ele reports a positively oriented tension when solving this dilemma as a result of applying semiotic regulators that refer to the personal perspective (one likes to talk to that attractive patient and help him/her).

One year later, however, the ambivalence of being a person in a professional role is acknowledged, accompanied by the presence of a negatively oriented tension—the professional feels insecure in one's conduct because of the patient's attractiveness. However, the focus remains unclear.

Nevertheless, in the third year, Ele returns to the personal perspective when solving this situation, once again bringing about positively oriented tension.

Theme 4 Unable to help

"When a psychologist understands that he is unable to help his client, s/he feels ____ because ____."

Year 1 ... guilty, because s/he is not able to fulfill one's obligation

Year 2 ... [unfilled]

Year 3 ... sad, because s/he wants to help, but realizes that s/he cannot. But s/he also can feel neutral, because s/he knows that s/he can send the person to somebody more competent

When solving the dilemma of being unable to help a patient, Ele's first year response focuses on the professional perspective (references to role-related obligations) that is accompanied by a negatively oriented tension.

In the second year, Ele did not give a response for this dilemma, however, in the last year, the continuous utilization of professional perspective appears to eliminate the negative tension through the application of a semiotic regulator "can direct the patient to someone else"—an option available to Ele in her/his professional role as a psychologist. However, together with the application of personal perspective (wants to help > feeling sad) this approach is coded as fluctuation of perspectives.

Theme 5 Close relations

"When a psychologist is to consult a person he has a close connection with, s/he feels ____ because ____."

Year 1 ... helpful, because people close to him/her are important to him/her, s/he is very intent on helping, on solving problems

Year 2 ... incompetent, because s/he has the desire to help, but s/he is not able to do so

Year 3 ... good, because s/he has great desire to help people close to her/him, here is that chance

When solving the situation of having to consult a person that the psychologist has a close relationship with, Ele's responses in the first and the third year reveal the dominance of a personal perspective where a wish to help and support close people appear to elicit positive feelings (helpful, good). Here, it can be observed how the professional role is put in the service of one's personal needs.

The perspective of Ele's second year response, however, remains unknown.

Theme 6 Common acquaintance

"When a person whose problems are linked with the people who are close to a psychologist comes for an appointment, then s/he feels ____ because ____"

Year 1 ... obligated to help them, because the problems are related to the people who are important to him/her, their lives are not unimportant to her/him

Year 2 ... obligated to help her/him, because s/he cares about people who are close to her/him

Year 3 ... worried, because peoples' lives who are close to her/him are important to her/him, s/he worries about them

---

When dealing with the situation of working with a patient whose problems involve people close to the psychologist, Ele's responses tend to emphasize the importance of close relations and thus focus on the personal perspective.

Interestingly, Ele indicates that in this situation the psychologist is obligated to help not due to the professional role, but because of the informal relations (s)he has on the background. It can also be observed that the obligations and worries Ele expresses regard the people close to the psychologist and not the patient turning to the professional for help and support.

Finally, when during the two first years, the feelings Ele reported to experience in this situation were coded as neutral, the last year turns the orientation of tension negative due to the concerns that the psychologist expresses regarding the close people.

Theme 7 Inability to keep distance

"When a psychologist feels that s/he cannot distance oneself from the patient's problems, s/he feels ____ because ____"

160 Becoming a psychologist

> Year 1 ... disturbed, because s/he is thinking about the patient's problems and is not able to think about other things
>
> Year 2 ... disturbed, because s/he feels the patient's problems
>
> Year 3 ... anxious, because s/he is often thinking about the patient's problems, s/he emphasizes with the patient

When recognizing one's inability to keep the distance from the patient's problems, Ele's responses over the three years maintain a personal perspective and the utilization of semiotic regulators "unable to think about other things" and "living into the patient's problems" appear to generate negatively oriented tensions.

Theme 8 Different values

"When a person whose values differ greatly from those of the psychologist comes to a session, then s/he feels ____ because ____"

> Year 1 ... respect, because s/he realizes that all people differ in values, opinions, one should take disaccord into account
>
> Year 2 ... unpleasant, because it is probably uneasy to find a "common language" (contact), and step outside of one's own values
>
> Year 3 ... unpleasant, because it is quite difficult to make contact with that person (probably)

Although, it is difficult to identify feelings of "respect" (therefore, it remains unknown), Ele seems to utilize the third position (in line with DST) in the first year.

However, during the next two years, Ele approaches this dilemma from the personal perspective, applying semiotic regulators like "hard to establish contact" and "having to step over one's own values" which in turn appear to generate negatively oriented tensions (feeling unpleasant).

Theme 9 Encountering a person in crisis after working hours

"When a psychologist meets a person in crisis outside working hours, s/he feels ____ because ____"

> Year 1 ... obligated to help him/her, because a psychologist must be ready to help in all situations
>
> Year 2 ... as a supporter, because s/he tries to help that person, to help him/her out of the crisis
>
> Year 3 ... as a person who should help him/her, because it hurts to look at him/her, a huge desire to help her/him in this situation, and then is satisfaction, when s/he had succeeded in doing so.

When encountering a person in crisis after working hours, the presence of professional perspective is visible in Ele's response in the first year, when the moral imperative "must" is accompanied by a reference to the obligations of a psychologist.

Although, Ele's approach to this situation in the second year remains unknown, by the third year his/her strategy for solving this dilemma becomes person-centered.

Hence, a certain development can be observed here: when in the first year, it is the psychologist who is obligated to help ("a psychologist must ... "), then in the last year, it is the person (in the professional role) that senses to have the obligation to help ("feels as a person who should help").

Lastly, the tension in the first year is coded as neutral, whereas in the years 2 and 3, it remains unknown (Figures 6.19 and 6.20).

Summary of case Ele

Drawing on the choice of perspective when solving professional dilemmas, Ele's path of entry into the professional role has a self-maintaining inclination with a prevalence of personal perspective. In total, Ele utilized personal perspective in 15 cases throughout the years of study, while professional I-position was applied in 6 cases. The semiotic regulation in Ele's responses tended to generate prevailingly negatively oriented tension (i.e., 14 negatively and 8 non-negatively oriented affectivity identified during the three years of study). Thus, as was the case for many other students in this cohort, Ele's entry into the professional role was also rather challenging regarding their affective relating to ambivalent professional problems.

Moreover, despite the domination of personal perspective in Ele's responses, there was also one dilemma that was solved solely from a professional I-position —i.e., providing confidential information to third parties. Regarding the former situation, negative tension was reported throughout the years because of perceived pressure to make the right decision. Hence, the ambiguity of the task and lack of clarity regarding the "right" response generated negative affectivity in Ele.

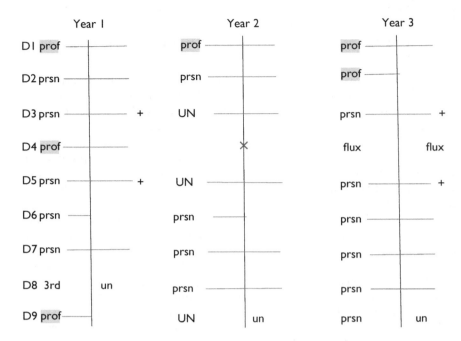

Figure 6.19 Temporary profiles of coordination of perspectives (i.e., professional, personal, 3rd position) and handling tension (i.e., positive and negative affectivity, neutral) in solutions to nine (9) dilemmas.

Note: Prof—the professional approach; Prsn—the personal approach; 3rd—the third I-position; Flux—the fluctuation of perspectives; UN —unknown; X—no answer provided.

Furthermore, there were two dilemmas that Ele solved solely from a personal perspective: i.e., (1) having a common acquaintance with and (2) being unable to keep the distance from patient's problems.

What is more, regarding the semiotic regulation of different sub-systems within the self in case of affective relating with the client (disliked and attractive person), the dynamic of utilizing I-positions across the years and the accompanying regulation of tension revealed opposite tendencies. For instance, according to Ele, working with a client one dislikes makes the psychologist feel uncomfortable (Year 1) and unconfident (Year 2). Only the recognition of everybody's right to get help allows the psychologist to put aside personal preferences and generate a neutral state (Year 3). In contrast, counselling a patient one finds attractive makes the psychologist feel *free* and *good*, with the exception of Year 2, when positive affectivity turns negative (i.e., feeling *insecure*). Apart from Year 2, the first and last year of study show Ele's tendency not to consider attraction as a source of risk in professional relations; instead, Ele outlines the benefits of liking the client. However, disliking a patient one must work with is regarded as an obstacle in

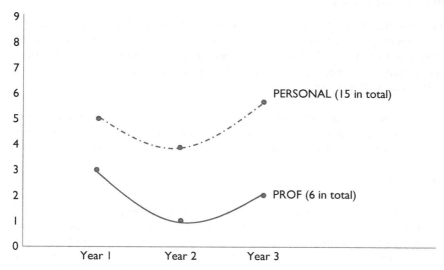

Figure 6.20 Trajectories of coordination of different sub-systems (i.e., professional, personal) in the self across the years.

Note: Occurrences of domination of professional and personal I-positions in the solutions to the dilemmas.

professional settings, since it complicates the establishment of contact between the psychologist and the client. Hence, like several other students from this cohort, Ele also demonstrated a general tendency to view negative affectivity toward a client as an obstacle in the counselling context, whereas no risk was acknowledged to one's professional conduct (e.g., to objectivity) in the case of positive affectivity.

Lastly, encountering a person in crisis after working hours was the case that illustrates the gradual linking and internalization/externalization of role expectations. More specifically, it shows that assuming professional role may have fluctuating directions: for example, a professional perspective (*obligated to help, because a psychologist must be ready to help*) can become personal (*as a person, the psychologist should help, the psychologist has a huge desire to help*).

Respondent 6k—Pai

The practicality of psychological knowledge is highlighted in Pai's report. Pai's journey of becoming a psychologist manifests from time to time in attempts to test herself: "And sometimes I have tested myself while interacting with other people to prove that I can handle them."

In Year 1, Pai wrote:

> *I decided to study psychology because I was just interested. In particular, my parents supported that idea. I am satisfied with my choice. I would make the same decision again to come to study psychology.*

In Year 4:

> *I work with young people; at least, I think that due to psychology studies, I know how to motivate them, make contact with them . ... I have used different motivational techniques . ... Also, I ask them questions—it supports their development . ... Thanks to my studies, I understand that sometimes I do or say something wrong ... .In my personal life, I don't pay attention to that anymore. I became critical toward what happens in society. And sometimes I have tested myself while interacting with other people to prove that I can handle them.*

Solutions to the items from DDTC

Theme 1 Providing confidential information to third parties

"When a psychologist has a dilemma whether to give out information on his/her patient, then he feels ____ because ____."

Year 1 ... little bit bad, because s/he doesn't want to do it, but when someone is in danger then s/he feels that s/he should do it

Year 2 ..bad, because in spite of everything s/he doesn't want to do it, but if not providing this information does harm to the patient then s/he should do it

Year 3 ... bad, because on the one hand s/he wants to be loyal to the patient, but because this information must be reported, then s/he must do so

---

Throughout the years of solving this dilemma, Pai utilizes the moral imperative "should" and "must," thus indicating the professional "voice" in his/her inner dialogue. However, Pai also applies the personal perspective suggesting the fluctuation of perspectives.

The orientation of tensions reported stayed negative throughout the three years of study.

Theme 2   Disliked client

"When a psychologist does not like his/her client s/he feels ____ because ____"

>   Year 1 ... normal, this is the job of a psychologist and it is forbidden to make distinctions between people
>
>   Year 2 ... as usual, because one doesn't have to like every single person
>
>   Year 3 ... uncomfortable, because s/he must constantly control and analyze him/herself

---

Over the years, Pai's responses to this situation reveal the dynamics in the reporting of tension orientation. Namely, when in the first two years, Pai manages to achieve neutrality (i.e., feeling normal and as usual, respectively), then in the third year, negatively oriented tension (i.e., feeling uncomfortable) is recognized.

The choice of perspective in the second year, however, remains unclear.

Theme 3   Attractive patient

"When an attractive person (of the opposite sex) comes to a session at a psychologist's, then s/he feels ____ because ____"

>   Year 1 ... as usual, because s/he is a patient like any other
>
>   Year 2 ... normal, because s/he feels very good when helping the patient
>
>   Year 3 ... good, because it is nice to counsel a pleasant person

---

When it regards counselling a patient whom the psychologist finds attractive, Pai's choice of perspective shifts from professional in the first to unknown in the second and personal in the third year.

Although the perspectives are changing, the semiotic regulators Pai utilizes when coordinating different sub-systems of the self still manage to generate positive affectivity and neutral state throughout the three years of study.

Theme 4   Unable to help

"When a psychologist understands that he is unable to help his client, s/he feels ____ because ____."

Year 1 ... unsure, because s/he is not confident about the professional skills s/he has

Year 2 ... sad, because s/he must send her/him to somebody else

Year 3 ... bad, because s/he wishes to help, and has given from him/herself everything, and now must send the patient to somebody else

---

Acknowledging one's inability to help the patient generated negative feelings (e.g., unsure, sad, and bad) for Pai during the entire study period. The respondent's choice of perspective remains professional over the two years. In the third year, the solution consists of both of perspectives (i.e., fluctuation).

Theme 5   Close relations

"When a psychologist is to consult a person he has a close connection with, s/he feels ____ because ____."

Year 1 ... confident, because s/he feels good that a person who is close to her/him dares to talk about his/her problems to her/him

Year 2 ... flattered, because a person who is close to her considers/thinks that s/he is competent and trustworthy

Year 3 ... a little bit uncomfortable, because s/he must be able to stay neutral and fair, and at the same time to council a close person in a way that they would still be able to talk in their free time

---

Here, the utilization of personal perspective generates positively oriented feelings for Pai in the first two years of study, when the respondent interprets personal relations as a resource supporting one's professional conduct.

However, by the third year, Pai's choice of perspective as well as the orientation of tension reported shift—we cannotice fluctuation of perspectives.

> **Theme 6 Common acquaintance**
>
> "When a person whose problems are linked with the people who are close to a psychologist comes for an appointment, then s/he feels ____ because ____"
>
> > Year 1 ... uncomfortable, because it is difficult to hear a stranger say bad things about people who are close to you
> >
> > Year 2 ... a bit bad, because s/he has to take pains to stay objective
> >
> > Year 3 ... anxious, because s/he must be able to set aside personal interest and approach the problem objectively

When it concerns consulting a patient whose problems are linked to the people close to the psychologist, Pai's solutions over the three years illustrate a gradual socialization into the professional role through a shift of perspective from personal (Year 1) to professional (Year 2 and 3).

Nevertheless, regardless of Pai's choice of perspective, the orientation of tensions expressed remains negative throughout the study (i.e., feeling uncomfortable, a bit bad, and anxious).

When in the first year, feeling uncomfortable stems from the difficulty Pai senses in having to hear bad things about the people dear to him/her, then in the next two years, negative feelings arise from the recognition that one must consciously make an effort to maintain objectivity in the professional role.

> **Theme 7 Inability to keep distance**
>
> "When a psychologist feels that s/he cannot distance oneself from the patient's problems, s/he feels ____ because ____"
>
> > Year 1 ... bothered, because the patient's problems are disturbing
> >
> > Year 2 ... burdened, because the patient's problems are burdening him
> >
> > Year 3 ... confused, because s/he is not able to relate adequately to the problem

Pai's choice of perspective as well as the orientation of tensions expressed when realizing the psychologist's inability to keep a distance from the patient's problems remain the same throughout the study—i.e., personal approach accompanied by the reporting of negative feelings.

Theme 8   Different values

"When a person whose values differ greatly from those of the psychologist comes to a session, then s/he feels ____ because ____"

Year 1 ... calm, because every person is different and everyone has his/her different system of values

Year 2 ... as usual, a patient's values don't have to fit with those of the psychologist

Year 3 ... as usual, because s/he accepts different values and doesn't disapprove of anyone based on that

---

Unlike some other respondents, Pai managed to eliminate negative tension from his/her responses to this situation in all three years. Pai's choice of perspective, however, refers to application of the 3rd position in the first and last year and to professional position in the second year. Apparently, the perceived neutrality (i.e., as usual) results from the acknowledgment of people's right to their values and the acceptance of differences. In the second year, Pai's focus tends to dominate by the professional perspective when describing the professional logic—a patient's and psychologist's values do not have to overlap.

Theme 9   Encountering a person-in-crisis when workday is over

"When a psychologist meets a person in crisis outside working hours, s/he feels ____ because ____"

Year 1 ... obligated to help him/her, because it is hard to watch how a person "suffers," and the psychologist knows that she could help him/her

Year 2 ... a little bit obligated to help him/her, because s/he has the knowledge and skills to help, and through that to make the person a bit happier

> Year 3 ... somehow obligated to help him/her, yet, because it is no longer a workday and the person hasn't turned to her/him directly, s/he would hesitate to intervene

Professional perspective takes the leading position in Pai's solutions to this dilemma throughout the three years, as Pai reports feeling obligated to provide assistance because of having the appropriate professional skillset for it (Figures 6.21 and 6.22).

Summary of case Pai

Pai's choice of perspective when solving ambivalent professional situations throughout the years reveals a rather self-maintaining trajectory with the domination of professional approach (in 11 cases) over personal (7 cases)

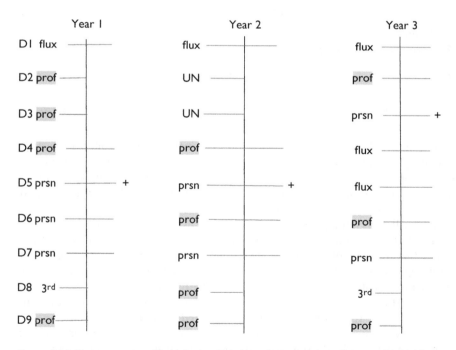

Figure 6.21 Temporary profiles of coordination of perspectives (i.e., professional, personal, 3rd position) and handling tension (i.e., positive and negative affectivity, neutral) in solutions to nine (9) dilemmas.

Note: Prof—the professional approach; Prsn—the personal approach; 3rd—the third I-position; Flux—the fluctuation of perspectives; UN —unknown; X—no answer provided.

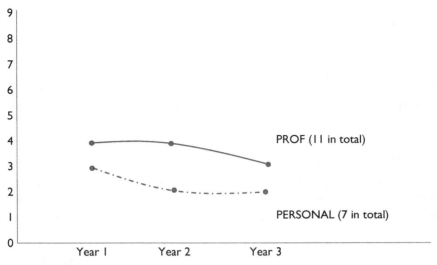

Prof – the professional approach
Personal – the personal approach

Figure 6.22 Trajectories of coordination of different sub-systems (i.e., professional, personal) in the self across the years.

Note: Occurrences of domination of professional and personal I-positions in the solutions to the dilemmas.

and with the slight tendency toward self-personalizing direction. Specifically, when by the 2nd year the utilization of professional I-position showed stabilization and a slight decline by the last year, then the dynamics of application of the personal position was exactly opposite (decline by the second year followed by stabilization).

Regarding assuming the professional role in terms of tension regulation, similarly to Hei, and Mes, Pai's profile of reported feelings is in rather balanced with a total of 14 cases of negatively oriented tensions and 13 cases of non-negatively oriented affectivity (i.e., positive, neutral). However, unlike Hei whose profile reveals an increase in positive affectivity in Year 3 compared to the year before, Pai's dynamic was the opposite—there appeared an increase in the reporting of negatively oriented tension by Year 3.

There was one dilemma (i.e., encountering a person in crisis after working hours) that Pai solved exclusively from a professional perspective, and one situation (inability to keep the distance) that was approached solely from a personal I-position.

Furthermore, providing confidential information to third parties, being unable to help a client and keep the distance from the client's problems, as well as having (a) common acquaintance(s) with a client, and inability to keep distance were the dilemmas that evoked only negative affectivity in Pai, even if the perspective is taken to solve these issues changed in time.

Moreover, there were also a few dilemmas that evoked mainly non-negative (i.e., neutral, positive) affectivity in Pai: these included working with a patient one finds attractive, having different value systems with the client, and encountering a person in crisis after working hours. When comparing Pai's solutions to counselling a person one dislikes versus an attractive person, certain similarities appear. For instance, during the first two years of study, both dilemmas were solved through the use of semiotic regulators that generated a neutral state (i.e., feeling *normal, as usual*). The difference emerges only in Year 3, when working with a disliked patient makes the psychologist feel *uncomfortable* because of the obligation to constantly control and analyze him/herself (i.e., to take the professional position). Yet, in the same year attraction was not interpreted as a factor that would require self-control in professional settings (i.e., it is nice to counsel a pleasant person).

Lastly, contrary to the tendency among participants to apply semiotic regulators that led to the reporting of negative affectivity when having different value systems with a client, Pai's reference to the dialogue between different I-positions within the self allowed the psychologist to maintain a non-negative affective state.

Respondent 61—Ain

Ain's professional journey began with doubting her initial plan to study law. She was also interested in math. However, she ended up studying psychology. Ain, like other participants, found that psychological knowledge is useful in her life. Also, like others, the beginning of her professional path unfolded under the influence of the others' opinions about her professional choice. We can see that relatives' choices affected her plans for the future. However, after her studies in the bachelor's program, Ain exited the field of psychology. Yet, she does not exclude the possibility of returning to the field: "I don't exclude the possibility that one day I may continue studies of psychology in a master's program."

> *After I finished high school, I was sure that I would go to study law. But then I suddenly started to doubt. There was a period when I wanted to study math, and I was attracted a little bit by psychology, too. At the end of the summer, I was convinced that I want to study psychology, and so I did. I began to like psychology because I knew that it is useful in the future, in every sphere of life ... it is like the base for everything. I heard that some of my friends who studied psychology had never regretted their decision. And so, I made my choice. I thought that if it is not for me, then I can quit and make a new choice. My mother supported me a lot; she was delighted. My grandmother and father weren't so happy at the beginning because they thought that I would go to study economics or math. Most of our relatives have studied economics. So, 'and how do you now go to study psychology?' For now, they have come to terms with it and like that I like what I do. But I think that, deep inside, they still hope that in the future I will study some additional specialty. At the beginning, it was difficult, but studying psychology has made me happy, and it is easier to me to understand things. I haven't regretted my choice.*

In Year 4, Ain had withdrawn from the field of psychology and reported:

> *My studies have helped me a lot in the workplace. I want to say that psychology is a profession that is not useless in life. For me, it is easier to interact now; I know what to say and when. ... My studies have also helped me in my personal life. I noticed that a few years ago, I was afraid to express my thoughts, but in that sense, I am much more open now. I try to take problems more neutrally and pay attention to many aspects. Also, my friends have said that my advice to them is more elaborate. But sometimes, when I have problems and don't know how to solve them, I think, how it can it happen? I have studied psychology. ... I don't exclude the possibility that, one day, I will continue studies of psychology in a master's program.*

Solutions to the items from DDTC

> **Theme 1** "Providing confidential information to third parties ("When a psychologist has a dilemma whether to give out information on his/her patient, then s/he feels ____ because ____"
>
> Year 1 ... suspicious, because s/he cannot be sure what is right and what is wrong. It may depend on the situation
>
> Year 2 ... confused, his/her profession doesn't allow it, but at the same time, it could be necessary
>
> Year 3 ... unconfident, because it is like the confusion that appears when facing a dilemma

When it regards deciding whether or not to provide confidential information to third parties, Ain refers to the semiotic regulators that derive from the ethical code coordinating the professional conduct of a psychologist (i.e., what is right and wrong). In fact, Ain utilizes the perspective of "I as a professional" during the first two years of studies.

In the third year, however, Ain's choice of perspective remains unclear and is therefore coded as "unknown."

Nevertheless, the semiotic regulators Ain utilized throughout the three years of study did appear to bring about negatively oriented tension.

> **Theme 2** "Disliked client" ("When a psychologist does not like his/her client s/he feels ____ because ____"
>
> Year 1 ... a little bit uncomfortable, because s/he must help to solve the client's problem, and to do it with a person who is not pleasant is not the most pleasant experience for any of us. And is not known how long s/he will have to deal with that person
>
> Year 2 ... uncomfortable, because s/he should still treat all equally, but if a person is unpleasant, then not showing it may cause problems
>
> Year 3 ... uncomfortable, because s/he may think too much about and observe too closely his/her own behavior and what s/he says. May feel tension.

Regarding solving the situation where a psychologist dislikes a patient, a certain dynamics can be observed in Ain's choice of perspective: namely, the initial preference of professional I-position in the first year of study shifts toward the utilization of a flux position (i.e., a mixture of personal and professional perspective within the same response) in the second, and back to the professional position in the last year.

For instance, in the second year, Ain's response includes a reference to a professional role prescription ("[a psychologist] should regard everyone as equal") which is followed by a personal perspective revealing difficulties one can experience when having to cover up their subjective feelings (e.g., disliking someone) in formal relations.

In the last year, however, negative tension seems to arise from following the rules that govern professional conduct ("a psychologist observes his/her own behaviour").

All in all, the presence of negatively oriented affectivity can be observed in Ain's responses to this dilemma throughout the three years and it appears to be the result of applying semiotic regulators (i.e., must and should) pertained to the professional role.

> **Theme 3 "Attractive patient"** ("When an attractive person of the opposite sex comes to a session at a psychologist's, then s/he feels ____ because ____"
>
> Year 1 ... constrained, because it can be risky, that the psychologist starts to like that person, and they tend to miss the topic
>
> Year 2 ... constrained, because maybe s/he will selectively choose the words that s/he says and maybe s/he will not be able to think very clearly
>
> Year 3 ... anxious, because maybe one cannot behave in an adequate manner, observes her/himself too much and is too pleasant toward the patient

When working with an attractive patient, Ain's responses throughout the three years acknowledged the potentially destructive impact that attraction may have on patient-psychologist relations.

In the first year, the perspective of "I as a person" appeared to lead the inner dialogue within Ain's self. Here, the possibility of attraction interfering the formal relations between a patient and a psychologist is already underlined.

Although, the same possibility is also indicated in the second year, it is now followed by a reference to professional role regulations (a psychologist pays more attention to communication). Role-related regulations and position "I as a person" are also present in Ain's response in the last year (i.e., the fluctuation of perspectives).

Theme 4 "Unable to help" ("When a psychologist understands that s/he is unable to help his client, s/he feels ____ because ____"

Year 1 ... helpless, because his/her obligation would still be to know how to do so and to be able to help patient with the problem

Year 2 ... helpless, because s/he wants to help him/her but it seems that s/he doesn't know how to do so, is not able to do it and it shows that the psychologist himself/herself needs someone's helping hand

Year 3 ... bad, because s/he is thinking that s/he does not know how to do his/her work and that is disappointing a patient to some extent.

Regarding Ain's responses to this dilemma, the dynamics of shifting perspectives can once again be observed from professional to personal I-position. In the first year, references to the obligations regarding one's professional conduct as a psychologist indicate the domination of role-centered focus to the issue. The failure to fulfil one's professional role in turn brings about negatively oriented tension (i.e., feeling helpless).

In the second year, however, Ain's professional perspective appears to become secondary to the personal position—in this case, the psychologist him-/herself is seen to need assistance for failing to provide help for the patient. In the last year, negatively oriented tension seems to be generated by focussing on not having performed the work tasks correctly.

Theme 5 "Close relations" ("When a psychologist is to consult a person s/he has a close connection with, s/he feels ____ because ____"

Year 1 ... free, because s/he can interact with him/her freely, the psychologist knows about her/him more, and maybe they can tell the psychologist his/her thoughts straightforward

Year 2 ... more free, because s/he knows the close person's problems and maybe s/he has even already given advice and can do so now too—more freely and skillfully and s/he doesn't have to feel that s/he is not able to do so

> Year 3 ... confident, because s/he knows better what might fit the person, and how the person might react. Yet, the psychologist should stay within a formal framework for sure

When having to consult a person the psychologist has a close relationship with, Ain's choice of semiotic regulators over the years appeared to generate mostly non-negative affectivity.

Personal perspective can be observed to dominate over the professional one during the first two years of study. Here, the reporting of positively oriented tensions (i.e., feeling "free" in year 1 and "more free" in year 2) seem to stem from the impact that the informal (personal) relations are perceived to have on one's professional conduct.

By the last year of studies, Ain solves this dilemma by bringing in the person-centered approach and role-related regulations (recognizing the restriction of the professional role).

Generally, Ain views close relations are as an additional source of knowledge that can contribute into achieving one's goals in a professional setting.

> **Theme 6 "Common acquaintance" "When a person whose problems involve people close to the psychologist comes in for an appointment, the psychologist feels ____ because ____."**
>
> Year 1 ... touched, because s/he is looking at that problem not only through the patient's eyes, but is also thinking about people who are close to her/him, takes both parts into consideration—and that may be confusing
>
> Year 2 ... more free, because s/he knows that person better and is more knowledgeable about his/her life and can better advise him/her
>
> Year 3 ... like s/he is in the same situation as a person, because s/he knows what can happen next, s/he might not be able to help, s/he might be afraid of all of that, cannot face the problems of the acquaintance

When having to consult a patient whose problems involve people close to the psychologist, a domination of personal perspective over professional can be observed in Ain's responses in the second and last year.

In the first year, Ain reports feeling confused when the people close to him/her —whose needs have to be taken into account—are involved, yet, as a psychologist one is taking into consideration a patient's perspective (i.e., the fluctuation of perspectives).

In the second year, however, close relations are considered as a factor that contributes to the achievement of one's professional goals, generating a positively oriented tension.

Nevertheless, in the last year, close relations are once again depicted having a negative influence on one's professional conduct by hindering the realization of work aims.

Theme 7 "**Inability to keep distance**" ("When a psychologist feels that s/he cannot distance oneself from the patient's problems, s/he feels ____ because ____"

Year 1 ... helpless, because s/he cannot find the proper distance that is needed

Year 2 ... incompetent, because s/he is not as skilled as s/he should be

Year 3 ... inapt, because s/he doesn't know how to solve the patient's problems, cannot begin from unraveling any of the problems

---

Throughout the three years of study, Ain approaches the situation of being unable to maintain a distance from the patient's problems from a professional perspective. The leading I-position in this professional perspective in turn appears to generate negative tension in Ain's self system due to the realization of lacking professional skills.

Theme 8 "**Different values**" ("When a person whose values differ greatly from those of the psychologist comes to a session, then s/he feels ____ because ____"

Year 1 ... confused, because the value systems do not coincide and its more difficult to give advice that could be proper

Year 2 ... intense, because s/he must take into account the other's value system too, proceed from that and maybe to some extent to change it

178   Becoming a psychologist

> Year 3 ... unpleasantness, because s/he doesn't try to find a common language with the patient and maybe the psychologist even doesn't want that

Regarding the situation where a psychologist is to work with a patient whose values differ greatly from his/her own, a certain dynamics can be observed in Ain's choice of perspective whereas the tension reported remains negative throughout the three years of study.

In the first year, Ain takes a personal focus on the situation, admitting to feeling confused about giving proper advice when the value systems do not coincide. Hence, recognizing the difficulty of functioning efficiently in the professional role as a result of sensing the mismatch between his/her own personal values and those of the patient.

Then, in the second year, negatively oriented tension is reported together with the application of professional role regulations ("a psychologist must").

In year 3, Ain's focus on this issue becomes personal once again.

However, there is a difference between the two personal approaches applied in the first and last year. Namely, when in the first year, the person in the professional role tries to give advice, then in the final year, the person in the professional role no longer wants to find a common language with the patient.

Theme 9 "Encountering a person in crisis after working hours" ("When a psychologist meets a person in crisis outside working hours, s/he feels ____ because ____"

> Year 1 ... like a helper, because I believe, that s/he would still help the person who is in crisis
>
> Year 2 ... compassionate, because s/he feels sorry for the person, but s/he also could help him/her more because of his/her work
>
> Year 3 ... like a helper, because the psychologist should actually help him/her, to invite him/her to an appointment

When in the first year, Ain's approach remains unclear, the second year adds a hint to the personal position and to the professional role (feeling sorry for the person, meanwhile acknowledging one's ability to provide assistance because of one's profession)—i.e., the fluctuation of perspectives.

In the last year, Ain's perspective becomes entirely professional when helping a person in crisis is considered as explicitly linking to the role ("a

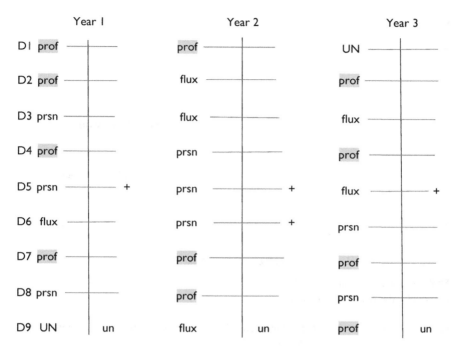

Figure 6.23 Temporary profiles of coordination of perspectives (i.e., professional, personal, 3rd position) and handling tension (i.e., positive and negative affectivity, neutral) in solutions to nine (9) dilemmas.

Note: Prof—the professional approach; Prsn—the personal approach; 3rd—the third I-position; Flux—the fluctuation of perspectives; UN —unknown; X—no answer provided.

psychologist should help"), thus, viewing one's professional affiliation as an option to help someone (to make an appointment) (Figures 6.23 and 6.24).

Summary of case Ain

Regarding the general dynamics of the choice of perspective across the years, Ain classifies as a self-maintaining case. More specifically, in the first year, four (4) dilemmas out of nine (9) were solved through professional perspective, whereas three (3) were approached from a personal perspective. In the second year, three (3) dilemmas were solved utilizing a professional position and 3 were approached from a personal perspective. In Year 3 dominating professional positions increased back to four (4) and the use of dominating personal positions dropped to two (2). In total, 6 occurrences of fluctuations of perspectives was identified in Ain's approaches to the

180 Becoming a psychologist

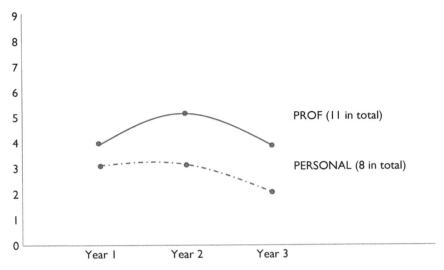

Prof – the professional approach
Personal – the personal approach

Figure 6.24 Trajectories of coordination of different sub-systems (i.e., professional, personal) in the self across the years.

Note: Occurrences of domination of professional and personal I-positions in the solutions to the dilemmas.

dilemmas during three years. Regarding Ain's choice of perspective across the years of study, there occurred a shift in 7 cases out of 9.

Furthermore, despite the externalization of role-related regulations (e.g., the application of moral imperatives *must, should, not allowed*), negatively oriented tension dominated Ain's responses to dilemmas across the years. In total, 20 responses from Ain contained signs of negative affectivity, whereas only four (4) answers included references to a non-negative affectivity (i.e., a positive feeling). Additionally, 6 dilemmas out of 9—i.e., (1) providing confidential information to third parties, (2) working with a patient one dislikes or (3) finds attractive, (4) being unable to help the client, (5) being unable to keep the distance from client's problems, and (6) having different values from the client—were solved by using semiotic regulators that appeared to evoke only negatively oriented tensions throughout the years of study.

Similarly to other participants in this study, being aware of role-related regulations (e.g., in the case of sharing confidential information) did not equip Ain with semiotic tools that would eliminate negative tension. Like others, Ain appeared to acknowledge the difficulties that the ambivalent situation—i.e., being a person in a social role—evokes. For instance, in cases of working with a client one dislikes or finds attractive, Ain seemed to understand the risk that affective relating to the client could propose on one's functioning in a professional setting.

Moreover, when it concerns the influence one's personal life and history may have on one's professional conduct in various settings (e.g., in the cases of close relations and common acquaintances), the perspective of "I as a person" may be perceived as an extra resource that can support one's functioning in a professional role, and the achievement of desired outcomes. For example, according to Ain, having personal relations with the client enables the professional to feel more comfortable (i.e., making the psychologist feel *"free"*) as it provides them with information about the client that would otherwise remain unknown.

However, when it regards coping with interpersonal differences in value systems, Ain reports feeling negative tension, since those differences may hinder the cooperation between the client and the professional, and thereby make the situation emotionally difficult to the psychologist. Contrary to Ain, when solving this dilemma, Vik and Snap (see above) applied semiotic regulators that evoked positive or neutral feelings. For instance, in Vik's case, the psychologist's adjustment to differences in value systems was achieved by recognizing inter-individual differences as something natural.

To sum up, Ain's entry into the professional role was characterized rather by a dominance of the externalization of professional perspective. Nevertheless, the semiotic regulators that Ain used tended to generate mainly negative affectivity.

Respondent 6m—Eri

Eri's choice to study psychology seemed to be shaped by the practicality of psychological knowledge and by personal contacts with experts in the field. Again, we can identify the pattern—an initially unexpected decision turns into a life changing experience ("I think that I have found a place for myself.") Becoming a psychologist was not Eri's first preference.

> *My decision to study psychology was unexpected. Actually, it was not my first preference. It was made at the spur of the moment. I was influenced by two persons—by our psychologist in school and by one psychiatrist. The reasons why I started to study psychology were probably my wish to better understand myself and others. Plus, it seems that psychological knowledge is useful everywhere. Studies have made my life a little bit more interesting . ... Now I look at people and at life differently. I try to understand what is behind their behavior ... .I think that I have found a place for myself.*

Eri's report in Year 4:

> *I got that job thanks to my education. I can be in the role of a psychologist and use different techniques. I can help people to cope. I also have other work tasks that are not linked with psychology. But I feel in my soul that I am a psychologist. The studies have not helped me in my personal life. I still behave as a person (not constructively) [implication: psychologists behave constructively], but regardless of that, I try to analyze people and understand why they behave like they do. I am often in the role of a listener. Maybe because I am tolerant, people like to talk to me. Still, sometimes I feel at work that I don't have enough (psychological) knowledge, regardless of my years in the university.*

Solutions to the items from DDTC

Theme I   Providing information

"When a psychologist has a dilemma whether to give out information on his/her patient, then he feels ____ because ____."

Year 1 ... like a liar, because s/he doesn't want to betray the patient and his/her trust

> Year 2 ... responsible, because either giving out information or not giving it out can affect how things are going
>
> Year 3 ... hesitation, while one part of him/her wants to keep the information confidential, and other part forces her/him to give out the information

In the first year, Eri approaches this situation from a personal perspective, utilizing a semiotic regulator of "betrayal," and reports negatively oriented tension (feeling like a liar).

A year later, however, the respondent's focus has shifted toward a professional perspective which becomes explicit in the professional reasoning/ logic present in Eri's response.

Lastly, in the third year, Eri's choice of perspective remains professional with references to the demand of confidentiality pertained to the role of a psychologist.

> **Theme 2   Disliked client**
>
> "When a psychologist does not like his/her client s/he feels ____ because ____"
>
> Year 1 ... guilty, because s/he should leave his/her opinion aside and treat all equally
>
> Year 2 ... incompetent, because as a good psychologist s/he should be able not to have prejudices against anyone
>
> Year 3 ... like a bad human being, because a psychologist should be tolerant and respect people

When having to work with a patient one dislikes, Eri's choice of perspective stays professional during the first two years and turns flux in the third year. However, the accompanying feelings reported remain negative throughout the three years of study.

Moreover, when in the first two years, it is the application of professional perspective along with the use of the moral imperative "a psychologist should" that generates negative tension in Eri, then by the last year, it is the mixture of personal and professional I-positions within Eri's inner dialogue that brings about negatively oriented tension.

Theme 3   Attractive patient

"When an attractive person (of the opposite sex) comes to a session at a psychologist's, then s/he feels _____ because _____."

> Year 1 ... excited, because the patient attracts him/her in an unprofessional way
>
> Year 2 ... like s/he is doing wrong, because intimate relations with patients are not ethical
>
> Year 3 ... flattered, because a "beautiful person" is also seeking her/his help

In the first and third year, Eri solves this dilemma through a personal perspective, expressing positively oriented tensions (e.g., feeling excited and flattered) that seem arise from a perceived attraction toward the patient (Year 1) as well as the realization of an attractive person seeking assistance from this particular psychologist (Year 3).

Moreover, in the second year, Eri's focus turns professional when (s)he deems attraction toward and intimate relations with a patient as unethical in a professional setting.

Theme 4   Unable to help

"When a psychologist understands that he is unable to help his client, s/he feels _____ because _____."

> Year 1 ... useless, because s/he wasn't competent enough to deal with, or solve, the problem
>
> Year 2 ... unhappy, because s/he feels sorry for the patient
>
> Year 3 ... unprofessional, because it is his job and he/she is skilled enough to help the patient

When it regards the psychologist's inability to help a patient, negatively oriented tension appears in Eri's responses every year, regardless of his/her choice of perspective.

Furthermore, in the first and third year, Eri's solutions hold references to professional competencies along with the moral imperative "a psychologist should," which emphasizes the perceived mismatch between what is expected from a professional (to be competent and skilled enough).

Unlike in the first and third years, Eri's second year response focuses on the patient instead of the psychologist, indicating feeling sorry for the patient for not being able to provide the assistance needed.

Theme 5   Close relations

"When a psychologist is to consult a person he has a close connection with, s/he feels ____ because ____"

Year 1 ... at a loss, because s/he isn't behaving professionally and at the same time s/he is not able to be objective

Year 2 ... incompetent, because s/he is not able to see the behavior of a close person in an unbiased way

Year 3 ... unethical, because s/he perceives that maybe s/he is not objective in this situation

---

When a psychologist is to consult a person (s)he has close relation with, Eri continues to express negatively oriented tensions throughout the three years of study. The reason for this appears to stem from Eri's realization of the effect that one's personal life can have on one's professional functioning.

More specifically, in the first two years, the negatively oriented tensions arise from the acknowledgment of one's inability to maintain objectivity in a professional role due to the interference of one's personal relations (i.e., personal approach), then in the last year, Eri's choice of perspective is coded as "unknown."

Theme 6   Common acquaintance

"When a person whose problems are linked with the people who are close to a psychologist comes for an appointment, then s/he feels ____ because ____"

Year 1 ... incompetent, because s/he cannot be totally objective in this case

Year 2 ... partial, because deep inside s/he wants to protect people close to him or her, and not the patient

Year 3 ... not objective, because probably s/he already has his/her opinion about people close to him/her

Similarly to the previous dilemma, Eri also tends to view this situation from a personal perspective, this time throughout the three years of study, describing how his/her personal connection to the case can influence his/her professional conduct.

The orientation of tensions reported in the second and third year (i.e., feeling partial and not objective, respectively) remains unclear, whereas in the first year, feeling "incompetent" carries a negative undertone as it arises from one's inability to maintain objectivity due to the personal connection.

Theme 7   Inability to keep distance

"When a psychologist feels that s/he cannot distance oneself from the patient's problems, s/he feels ____ because ____."

> Year 1 ... burdened, because s/he is not able to keep her/his private life and professional life apart

> Year 2 ... disturbed, because the patient's problems are always on her/his mind and are mixing with her/his private life

> Year 3 ... tired, because thoughts keep bothering her/him and s/he cannot switch out from the work

---

When it regards the psychologist's inability to keep the distance from the patient's problems, Eri's choice of perspective remains personal throughout the study, generating negatively oriented tension for the respondent. The main point of concern becomes the influence that the inability to maintain the distance is perceived to have on Eri's personal life.

Theme 8   Different values

"When a person whose values differ greatly from those of the psychologist comes to a session, then s/he feels ____ because ____."

> Year 1 ... a block against the person, because s/he is unable to put her/himself into patient's position

> Year 2 ... interested, because maybe s/he can even learn something from the other person's view

> Year 3 ... anger, because a person [the patient] doesn't realize what the actual truth is

When having to work with a person whose values differ significantly from the psychologist's, Eri's responses in the first and third year are dominated by personal perspective and accompanied by the reporting of negatively oriented tensions (i.e., feeling a block against the person and feeling anger, respectively).

Those negatively oriented tensions appear to stem firstly from Eri's realization of the hindering influence that difference in values has on the psychologist's professional performance (i.e., being unable to put oneself to the patient's position), and secondly from the understanding that his/her own values are somehow sublime to those of the patient—hence, the reference of the patient not comprehending what the "actual truth" is.

Nevertheless, in the second year, Eri manages to eliminate the negative tension when solving this situation by displaying openness and curiosity toward the patient's views, stating that one may learn something from the other's perspective. Eri's choice of I-position here, however, remains unclear.

> **Theme 9 Encountering a person in crisis after working hours**
>
> "When a psychologist meets a person in crisis outside working hours, s/he feels ____because ____"
>
> Year 1 ... touched, because as an empathetic person, s/he wants to help another person
>
> Year 2 ... that s/he is obligated to help, because s/he has specific skills and the possibility to do so
>
> Year 3 ... obligated to help, because inside him/her is something that enables her/him to give psychological help to another person

When encountering a person in crisis after working hours, a shift in Eri's choice of perspective can be observed to take place in the second year.

When in the first year, Eri highlights his/her wish to help to stem from the kind of person he/she is (i.e., empathetic)—thus, taking the personal approach—then in the second and third year, the person becomes secondary to the profession, as the former wish turns into a perceived obligation to provide help due to the competencies one has obtained through their professional role.

The orientation of tension reported in the first year remains unclear, whereas in the second and third year, the respondent manages to generate neutral state (Figures 6.25 and 6.26).

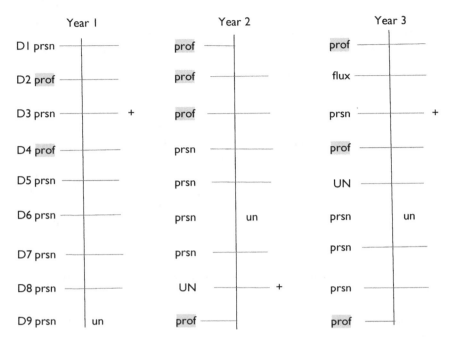

Figure 6.25 Temporary profiles of coordination of perspectives (i.e., professional, personal, 3rd position) and handling tension (i.e., positive and negative affectivity, neutral) in solutions to nine (9) dilemmas.

Note: Prof—the professional approach; Prsn—the personal approach; 3rd—the third I-position; Flux—the fluctuation of perspectives; UN —unknown; X—no answer provided.

Summary of case Eri

Eri's dynamics of dominating I-positions in solutions throughout the years reveal rather a self-maintaining trajectory of entry into the role of psychologist. If in Year 1, there were two (2) dominating professional and seven (7) leading personal I-positions used to solve the dilemmas, then in Year 3, the number of solutions entailing professional I-position had increased to three (3) and the utilization of personal I-position had dropped to four (4). In the second year, four (4) cases were solved from the professional and four (4) from the personal position.

Across the years of study, Eri, similarly to Ele, Ris, Uur, and Aet, tended to solve role-related tasks predominantly from a personal perspective (in total, 15 leading personal and 9 dominating professional I-positions were identified in Eri's solutions).

Regarding the regulation of tension when solving ambivalent professional situations, Eri, like several other students in this cohort, tended to report

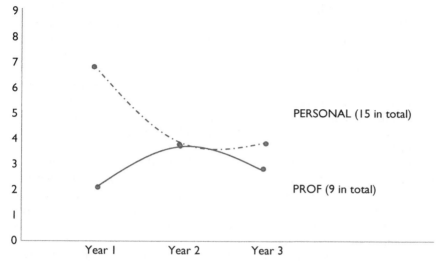

Prof – the professional approach
Personal – the personal approach

Figure 6.26 Trajectories of coordination of different sub-systems (i.e., professional, personal) in the self across the years.

Note: Occurrences of domination of professional and personal I-positions in the solutions to the dilemmas.

mostly negatively oriented tensions (18) whereas non-negative feelings (i.e., neutral, positive) were conveyed in only six (6) cases.

Moreover, Eri's choice of perspective throughout the years of study reveals a dynamic entry into the role with several shifts from personal to professional perspective when solving dilemmas like providing confidential information to third parties, working with an attractive patient, unable to help, and encountering a person in crisis after working hours. In the latter case, a gradual internalization of professional role expectations can be observed over the years as the description of a psychologist as an empathetic person who wants to help (Year 1) is replaced by an obligation to help (Year 2 and 3). In fact, feeling obligated to help does not stem from one's inclination to want to help others, but is instead placed upon the psychologist because of the specific (professional) skillset s/he possesses.

Furthermore, there was one dilemma where Eri's shift of focus took an opposite direction—from professional to personal. This was the situation of working with a client one finds attractive. When following Eri's responses to this dilemma, the acknowledgment of professional role expectations can be observed in Year 2 (i.e., feeling *like s/he is doing wrong*), but not in Year 1 or Year 3.

What is more, regarding the case of disliking a patient, Eri, similarly to several other respondents, displayed an awareness of professional regulations. However, the internalization/externalization of professional role related rules did not manage to eliminate negative affectivity in Eri. In comparison, working with a patient one finds attractive did not lead to negatively oriented tension (except in year 2).

In addition, there were three dilemmas Eri solved exclusively from a personal perspective: these were (1) having (a) common acquaintance(s) with a client, and (2) being unable to keep the distance from the client's problems. In all these cases, the semiotic regulators applied generated negative affectivity in Eri.

Moreover, like several other respondents, Eri tended to interpret having a different value system from the client as a potential obstacle hindering the effectiveness of one's professional conduct and causing negative affectivity in the psychologist (Year 1 and 3; in both years, the approach to the problem was personal). The only exception occurred in Year 2, when Eri was able to eliminate negative tension (reported feeling *interest*) by valuing interpersonal differences as a source of knowledge, indicating that the psychologist may be able to learn something from the other person (Eri's approach to this issue was coded as unknown).

Another dilemma that was mainly accompanied by positive affectivity for Eri was working with an attractive patient. In this case, Eri's choice of perspective was personal in Year 1 and 3, and professional in Year 2. The character of tensions reported shifted from positive (feeling *excited*, Year 1) to negative (feeling *like s/he is doing wrong*, Year 2) and back to positive (feeling *flattered*, Year 3), respectively.

Lastly, regarding the psychologist's ability to provide professional services and keep the distance from patient's problems, the semiotic regulators that Eri applied generated only negative affectivity. For instance, according to Eri, being unable to help a client makes the psychologist feel *useless* (Year 1) and *unprofessional* (Year 3) as it highlights the lack of competencies necessary to succeed in the professional role.

Summary of the general findings

The various reasons behind the emergence of professional trajectory

Students enroll in a university for various reasons that have their "roots" in the pre-period of studies, a significant phase in professional socialization. This period is the departure point of trajectories of becoming a psychologist, and from where these trajectories arrive at the equifinality point—a university—to diverge again after the studies are over. Even though two or more individuals may share the same main direction of their professional socialization paths (e.g., studies of psychology) the socio-cultural-psychological conditions behind the emergence of those paths are unique. Not everyone wants to become a professional psychologist, and some choose to study psychology to obtain practical knowledge. The same directions take shape, but the subjective meanings of studies of psychology are and remain different. The beginning of the path of becoming a psychologist is co-constructed and negotiated in informal settings. In the essays, we can also see the involvement of multiple agreeing and disagreeing I-positions in shaping the professional trajectory by bringing the stereotypical understanding of psychology into the student's inner dialogues and incorporating critical and encouraging voices of others. When the students reflected on their initial conditions, the triggers and motivations behind the professional choices mentioned in the essays were different. Some emphasized the practicality of psychological knowledge in life (that it is applicable in interpersonal relations as well as in understanding oneself). Others referred to psychology courses in high school as relevant to their professional choice. Some got inspiration from role models (e.g., a school psychologist) who made the profession of psychologist attractive to them.

In addition to the reported events and experiences that the students linked to their decision to study psychology (e.g., friends' comments, students' experiences in high school, students' wish to comprehend principles of human behavior), attention was paid to their reported interest in the field of psychology. Among the participants were students whose choice to study psychology did not originate from a long-lasting commitment to the field of psychology, according to their own words. Rather, their decision to study psychology was more like a "last minute" decision that shifted their developmental trajectory (in the cases of Snap, Eri, Uur, and Hei). They did not know exactly what they wanted to study, based on their reports. However, making "a last-minute" decision about the course of studies does not hinder a student's efforts to pursue a career as a psychologist after obtaining a bachelor's degree, as we can see in the findings. Vik, Gar, Par, Aet, and Ele's entries to the field were described as "long and smooth"—they tended to describe their interest in psychology as long-lasting, and they did not report "unexpected" enrollment in a university. However, Vik exited the field, and did not plan to work as a professional psychologist. Thus, not everyone who claims to have a long-term interest in psychology continues working as a psychologist, and those who do not have a long-lasting preference for the field of psychology in the beginning nevertheless may find their calling in psychology.

However, the process of becoming a psychologist was not "finished" or "completed" for those participants who continued working as psychologists after their undergraduate studies were over, nor for those who exited the field. Drawing on Par's experiences, even if one exits the field, one may still experience aspects of being a psychologist (or being expected to be one) in everyday life and may be guided to re-negotiate one's professional identity as a psychologist.

The main generic developmental directions

The DDTC method enabled exploration of microgenetic dynamics at the intra-psychological level and the temporary dominance of sub-systems of the self (i.e., professional, personal) over the course of three years. The students' solutions to nine (9) dilemmas over the years allowed detailed insight into the intra-psychological dynamics of applying different I-positions (i.e., professional, personal, and the 3rd position) Additionally, the findings introduce the affective side of entry into the professional role, and the semiotic regulators that the psychology students applied when constructing reality revealed different affective orientations.

Dynamics in applying different approaches to the dilemmas

In general, three major generic developmental directions (i.e., self-professionalizing, self-personalizing, and self-maintaining) were found across the 13 case studies. These thirteen cases were described in terms of their general directions when unfolding over the years: self-professionalizing (N = 7), self-personalizing (N = 2), and self-maintaining (N = 4) cases.

However, the directions of trajectories should be considered as general tendencies of the internalization and externalization of professional role expectations. Importantly, as the analysis outlines, every student's profile and its dynamics in respect to the utilization of I-positions in the self remained unique. For instance, Vik and Uur, despite having shared experiences as psychology students who enrolled in the university in the same year and were guided by the same academic-institutional representations in their professional socialization and who both belong to the self-professionalizing group of cases, represent two different ways of becoming a psychologist in terms of the dynamics of applying the I-position I as a psychologist in their inner dialogues when solving a dilemma. For example, Vik is characterized by stable dominance of the professional perspective over the personal perspective through the years, while Uur "switched" to the "professional mode" only in the last year of studies (i.e., two (2) occurrences of professional position and seven (7) occurrences of personal position were recorded in Year 1, and in the last year, nine (9) occurrences and zero (0) occurrences, respectively). Uur's transition to a qualitatively different approach was abrupt and total—all personal voices within the self were silenced at once.

Generally, participants' profiles of becoming a psychologist did not only differed in terms of general tendencies of utilization of I-positions (i.e., the domination of professional or personal positions, use of the third I-position, fluctuation of perspectives) but also in respect to how they handled tension (i.e., generation of negative and non-negative affectivity).

As the analysis of the temporary profiles of coordinating sub-systems in the self reveals, there were also cases that, in contrast, represent a tendency toward internalization/externalization in the direction of non-professionalization (i.e., self-professionalizing, self-maintaining) of socialization through the professional role. In other words, becoming a psychologist may not manifest only in growing or more extensive application of professional role expectations. Gar, for instance, was one of two psychology students with a tendency to silence the professional voice by the last year of studies when socializing through the professional role. However, even though Gar applied an increasingly personal I-position and decreasingly professional I-position over the years, the voice of the professional I-position dominated in solutions to the dilemmas. Namely, Gar, together with Par, represents cases with overall dominance of the professional position in solutions but with an inclination toward self-personalizing socialization through the role.

Additionally, there were cases of becoming a psychologist that displayed tendency to maintain the general pattern of utilization of both of perspectives throughout the years not revealing a clear direction toward professionalizing or personalizing direction—the self-maintaining direction (Pai, Eri, Ele, and Ain) (for more information in Chapter 3).

In general, in parallel to the unfolding direction of the trajectory by the last year of studies (increasing or decreasing utilization of a specific type of perspective), it is possible to identify the overall dominance of the use of particular I-positions: I as a psychologist or I as a person (i.e., dominance of the professional I-position, the prevailing use of personal positions, or balanced distribution of personal and professional perspectives) across all three years. For example, these can be seen in cases of dominance of the professional position (i.e., Par, Gar, Vik, Snap, Hei, Ain, Pai) and dominance of the personal position in the solutions (i.e., Ris, Uur, Aet, Ele, Eri) in total. Mes' utilization of personal and professional perspectives was balanced (12 occurrences of professional position and 11 uses of personal position).

Utilization of a professional approach in solutions to professional dilemmas

Taking into consideration the total number of self-professionalizing cases in the same cohort of psychology students (7) and the total number of applications of the leading professional and personal I-positions (i.e., 155 and 129, respectively) in solutions across all the study years in total, we can find that being guided by the frame of regulations of the professional role when solving role-related dilemmas tended to dominate. Further, the general tendency over the years concerning the application of I-positions was toward decreasing utilization of the personal perspective (i.e., 52 occurrences of the leading personal position were recorded in Year 1, 45 in Year 2, and 32 in Year 3) in parallel with increasing appearance of role-orientation in the solutions (i.e., 46 occurrences of the professional position were recorded in Year 1, 50 in Year 2 and 59 in Year 3). (Table 6.1 below) However, additionally to the above presented occurrences of dominating/leading perspectives in solutions, 29 fluctuations of perspectives—the cases of non-leading perspective in solving the ambivalent condition—were identified, meaning that the actual total number of the use of both of perspectives in solutions is higher. Additionally, it can be observed in Table 6.1 that 21 responses were marked as unknown, 11 positions were coded as 3rd I-position, and six (6) times the answer was not provided by the participants.

Table 6.1 The application of I-positions in solutions to dilemmas from DDTC

	Year 1	Year 2	Year 3	Total		3rd	Flux	UN	NA
D1 Prof	10	12	11	33		0	3	2	
Person	1	0	0	1					
D2 Prof	6	6	9	21		0	6	2	
Person	4	4	2	10					
D3 Prof	4	7	4	15		0	4	3	3
Person	8	1	5	14					
D4 Prof	11	7	8	26		0	4	3	1
Person	0	4	1	5					
D5 Prof	1	1	4	6		0	4	2	1
Person	11	11	4	26					
D6 Prof	2	4	3	9		0	4	1	
Person	9	8	8	25					
D7 Prof	3	2	8	13		0	1	0	
Person	10	10	5	25					
D8 Prof	2	4	4	10		11	2	2	1
Person	6	3	4	13					
D9 Prof	7	7	8	22		0	1	6	
Person	3	4	3	10					
Total PROF				155	Total	11	29	21	6
Total PERSON				129					

Note. D—Dilemma, Prof—the professional perspective, Person—the personal perspective, 3rd—the third position, Flux—the fluctuation of perspectives, UN—unknown, NA—no answer provided.

Dilemma 1. Providing confidential information to third parties
Dilemma 2. Disliked client
Dilemma 3. An attractive patient
Dilemma 4. Unable to help
Dilemma 5. Close relations
Dilemma 6. Common acquaintance
Dilemma 7. Inability to keep the distance
Dilemma 8. Different values
Dilemma 9. Encountering a person in crisis after working hours

Solutions to dilemmas according to the approach

Specific dilemmas and the application of I-positions

There were differences in terms of the perspectives from which the dilemmas were solved. Application of the professional position appeared most often in solutions to four (4) dilemmas: *providing information, disliked client, unable to help*, and *a person in crisis*.

Three (3) dilemmas were most frequently solved from the personal position throughout the study years: *close relations, common acquaintance*, and *inability to keep distance*.

The dilemmas of *different values* and *attractive person* were distinct in terms of the distribution of the I-positions in solutions to the dilemmas compared to other cases: the personal and professional perspectives were almost balanced regarding their use in solutions across the study years in total. The *different values* was also the only dilemma with such a high frequency of utilizing of the 3rd position (8 times in three years).

The dilemma of *providing information* is also distinct from the other dilemmas, with only one (1) personal perspectives in total (and 33 occurrences of applying the professional I-position).

Dynamics in the use of the I-positions in solutions to dilemmas

Decreasing use of the personal position in solutions, together with the increasing application of the professional position by the last year of studies was identified in three (3) dilemmas: *disliked patient, close relations*, and *inability to keep distance*. However, decreasing use of the professional position, together with the increasing utilization of personal position by the last year of studies was identified in one (1) dilemma: attractive patient (Table 6.1).

Handling tensions: Regulating affective relations with the professional role

The semiotic regulators the students applied to construct the meaning of a situation primarily generated negatively oriented affectivity: in total, 185 responses were coded as negatively oriented compared to 102 with non-negatively oriented affectivity.

The dynamics of tension in the specific dilemmas

When the dilemmas were compared on the basis of frequency of occurrence of non-negative forms of affectivity (i.e., positively oriented tension or a neutral) and negative tension in the solutions, it appeared that three (3) dilemmas were "non-negative" dilemmas in which non-negative affectivity dominated overall in the solutions. These were *attractive person* (25 responses were coded as non-negatively oriented tension and nine (9) as negatively oriented tension), *different values* (17 responses were coded as non-negatively oriented feelings and 12 as negatively oriented feelings), and *a person in crisis after the working hours are over* (15 responses were coded as non-negatively oriented affectivity and five (5) as negatively oriented tension). In solutions to the other six (6) dilemmas, negatively oriented tension prevailed compared to the other three (3) dilemmas.

The dilemma of *attractive person* had the highest number of reported non-negative affectivity (25 occurrences in total), and the dilemma of *inability to keep distance* had the lowest number of responses with non-negative affectivity (0 occurrences in total). The same dilemma was also the "most negative" dilemma (30 occurrences of negative tension in total) (Table 6.2).

Regulation of tension among the thirteen cases

When analyzing the 13 cases, we can find that, compared to other students in this cohort, one of the respondents more frequently reported non-negative af-

Table 6.2 The regulation of tension in solutions to dilemmas across the years

	Non-negative affectivity				Negative affectivity				UN	Flux	NA
	Year 1	Year 2	Year 3	Total	Year 1	Year2	Year 3	Total			
D1	4	5	3	12	8	7	8	23	4	0	0
D2	2	3	3	8	10	10	10	30	1	0	0
D3	9	7	9	25	2	5	2	9	2	0	3
D4	2	1	4	7	10	11	6	27	3	1	1
D5	5	4	3	12	6	8	8	22	5	0	0
D6	3	3	0	6	8	9	10	27	4	1	1
D7	0	0	0	0	11	10	9	30	8	1	0
D8	4	7	6	17	5	3	4	12	7	0	3
D9	5	3	7	15	3	2	0	5	19	0	0
Total	34	33	35	102	63	65	57	185	53	3	8

Note. D—Dilemma, Non-negative affectivity (i.e., positive, neutral), UN—unknown, Flux—the fluctuation of tension, NA—no answer provided

Dilemma 1. Providing confidential information to third parties
Dilemma 2. Disliked client
Dilemma 3. An attractive patient
Dilemma 4. Unable to help
Dilemma 5. Close relations
Dilemma 6. Common acquaintance
Dilemma 7. Inability to keep the distance
Dilemma 8. Different values
Dilemma 9. Encountering a person in crisis after working hours

Table 6.3 Regulation of tension among the 13 cases across the years

	Negative affectivity				Non-negative affectivity (i.e., positive affectivity, neutral state)			
	Year 1	Year 2	Year 3	Total	Year 1	Year 2	Year 1	Total
Par	5	3	5	13	2	4	3	9
Ain	7	6	7	20	1	2	1	4
Hei	4	5	2	11	4	2	6	12
Snap	2	5	2	9	6	4	2	12
Mes	6	4	2	12	2	3	5	10
Eri	7	5	6	18	1	3	2	6
Ele	4	6	4	14	4	1	3	8
Pai	4	4	6	14	5	5	3	13
Gar	4	5	5	14	2	4	3	9
Uur	5	6	6	17	0	0	0	0
Ris	3	5	3	11	2	0	1	3
Aet	8	6	5	19	1	2	3	6
Vik	4	5	4	13	4	3	3	10

fectivity. This "most positive or neutral" student, based on the identified affective orientation, was Snap (with 9 negative and 12 non-negative occurrences in total). Regarding the dominance of negative affectivity in total, Uur seemed to be the "most negative" among the participants—only negative affectivity was identified in Uur's solutions to the dilemmas (with 17 occurrences of negative tension in total) together with nine (9) unknown types of tension. Like Uur, Ain also was inclined to handle tension by generating mostly negative affectivity (with 20 negative occurrences compared to four (4) non-negative occurrences, in total). Eri may also be called "negative" due to the dominance of negative tension in the solutions (with 18 occurrences of negative tension and six (6) occurrences of non-negative affectivity).

However, although Uur inclined toward generation of negative affectivity and Snap seemed to most frequently generate positive affectivity in the solutions, they both belonged to the self-professionalized cases. Ain was a case with a self-maintaining trajectory.

Additionally, some students had more balanced profiles of orientation of affectivity. They include Pai, with 13 non-negative and 14 negative occurrences, Mes, with 10 non-negative and 12 negative occurrences, Hei, with 11 negative and 12 non-negative occurrences, and Vik with 13 negative and 10 non-negative occurrences (Table 6.3).

Conclusion

This study found 13 cases with different initial conditions of developmental trajectories, thirteen unique profiles of the coordination of sub-systems and ways of handling tension during the equifinality period, and thirteen different professional paths after the studies of psychology concluded. The coordination of sub-systems in the self when solving dilemmas and handling tension in the solutions reveals unique patterns of the dynamics of becoming a psychologist during studies in a bachelor's program. Similarly, every student had unique triggers that affected their professional choice before enrollment in a university and after obtaining the bachelor's degree.

The findings reveal how the emerging professional identity gradually unfolds through a non-linear developmental process. Observing the dynamics in the profiles of utilization of the I-positions (i.e., as a person or psychologist), we can conclude that establishing self- or role-centeredness as a general tendency is a temporary state of an ongoing developmental process of identity, rather than a fixed state. All thirteen cases were characterized by the dynamics of dominant positions in the solutions to the dilemmas. The same pattern applies to how tensions were handled through the use of semiotic mediators, which fluctuated over the years and across the dilemmas.

Regarding general tendencies across the longitudinal study, the dilemmas from DDTC were solved in seven (7) cases with overall domination of professional position in solutions, five (5) cases were characterized rather by prevailing use of personal perspective across the years in total.

Additionally, based on the findings, we can see that handling tension and the coordination of I-positions are context sensitive matters. For instance, some dilemmas had more consistent dominance of non-negative affectivity in their solutions (e.g., *attractive person*) and others had more frequent dominance of negative affectivity (e.g., *common acquaintances*).

Furthermore, the findings also suggest that being aware of regulations and guidelines does not eliminate the negative tension that the ambivalent conditions PERSON in a ROLE elicit. This became explicit, for instance, when solving the dilemma concerning providing information to third parties. It seems that, regardless of the role-related guidelines of professional practice, professional situations remain ambiguous to various extents. In general, we can observe the effect of the boundary of the psychologist's role—making a PERSON feel X, but it actually has to elicit feeling Y (e.g., "I MUST stay objective, BUT I cannot, and that makes me feel sad."). To sum, these findings should be interpreted as intermediate results or a "snapshot" of the students in the process of professional socialization. The directions of the students' professional trajectories will be continuously shaped going forward.

Reference

Kullasepp, K. (2008). *Dialogical Becoming. Professional Identity Construction of Psychology Students*. Tallinna Ülikooli Kirjastus.

Conclusion to Part III

This study found 13 cases with different initial conditions of developmental trajectories, 13 unique profiles of the coordination of sub-systems and ways of handling tension during the equifinality period, and 13 different professional paths after the studies of psychology concluded. The coordination of sub-systems in the self when solving dilemmas and handling tension in the solutions reveals unique patterns of the dynamics of becoming a psychologist during studies in a bachelor's program. Similarly, every student had unique triggers that affected their professional choice before enrollment in a university and after obtaining the bachelor's degree.

The findings reveal how the emerging professional identity gradually unfolds through a non-linear developmental process. Observing the dynamics in the profiles of the utilization of the I-positions (i.e., as a person or psychologist), we can conclude that establishing self- or role-centeredness as a general tendency is a temporary state of an ongoing developmental process of identity, rather than a fixed state. All 13 cases were characterized by the dynamics of dominant positions in the solutions to the dilemmas. The same pattern applies to how tensions were handled through the use of semiotic mediators, which fluctuated over the years and across the dilemmas.

Regarding general tendencies across the longitudinal study, the dilemmas from DDTC were solved in seven (7) cases with overall domination of professional position in solutions, five (5) cases were characterized rather by prevailing use of personal perspective across the years in total.

Additionally, based on the findings, we can see that handling tension and the coordination of I-positions are context-sensitive matters. For instance, some dilemmas had more consistent dominance of non-negative affectivity in their solutions (e.g., *attractive person*) and others had more frequent dominance of negative affectivity (e.g., *common acquaintances*)

Furthermore, the findings also suggest that being aware of regulations and guidelines does not eliminate the negative tension that the ambivalent conditions PERSON in a ROLE elicit. This became explicit, for instance, when solving the dilemma concerning providing information to third parties. It seems that, regardless of the role-related guidelines of professional practice, professional situations remain ambiguous to various extents. In general, we can observe the effect of the boundary of the psychologist's role—making a PERSON feel X, but it actually has to elicit feeling Y (e.g., "I MUST stay objective, BUT I cannot, and that makes me feel sad."). To sum, these findings should be interpreted as intermediate results or a "snapshot" of the students in the process of professional socialization. The directions of the students' professional trajectories will be continuously shaped going forward.

Part IV

General implications: Basic principles of the socio-cultural construction of professional identity

Chapter 7

The construction of professional identity through the lens of cultural psychology

Psychologists are not alone as professional identity makers, and the issues covered in this book are relevant for any profession. The unique aspect of psychologists—being human minds themselves who handle the issues of other human minds—adds a special flavor to their identity as human services specialists. Similar phenomena could be explored in the professional identity construction of teachers, nurses, and financial consultants, in contrast to other professions like bus drivers and forest rangers.

The role of the psychologist is a social invention that expresses "modern societies' efforts to regulate human life-worlds through their social institutions" (Salvatore & Valsiner, 2006, p. 129) and that is one of the numerous professions that can be chosen. The societal invitation to become a psychologist may be rejected or ignored. However, some do accept it and will expand their selves to account for the accompanying professional role expectations. Their identities change: some begin to see themselves as more tolerant, others define themselves through their improved interaction skills and pay more attention to listening when socializing "because I am becoming a psychologist," and some may encounter dilemmas in everyday life regarding how to respond—as a friend or as a psychologist. All these responses belong to the gradual internalization of this professional role.

This book has attempted to contribute to the field by investigating how professional identity is constructed during students' preparation period in a university. Specifically, how different parts of the self—professional and personal—are coordinated when an individual internalizes the professional identity of being a psychologist, the issue that is still not widely understood.

By applying the perspective of cultural psychology, this book has highlighted the *process* of constructing trajectories of entry into the professional role.

Before moving on, the ideas presented in this chapter must first be put into perspective. Specifically, the underlying study investigated the experiences of undergraduate psychology students who had limited experiences in professional settings—their first short-term professional internships took place in the last semester of the last year of studies. That means that the

DOI: 10.4324/9781315519616-14

students constructed their professional identity when attending lectures and seminars, conducting practical work, and socializing in non-professional settings. Specialization in the field (e.g., in areas like counseling psychology, school psychology, or organizational psychology) and internship would take place in the next phase of studies for those who went on to enter a master's degree program. Thus, the three years of studies in the bachelor's program provided limited experiences in which to form the I-position "I as a psychologist" in *professional* settings where the guidelines for professional practice form the framework for professional conduct.

The general principles of assuming a professional role

Unique non-linear trajectories of entry into the role

Viewing their development through the lens of cultural psychology, every student's becoming is regarded in this book as a unique path. The findings illustrate this point: a cohort of students completed the same curriculum, but each student had a distinct way of relating with the professional role. In Part 3, this is especially explicit in the exhaustive overview of interindividually different developmental trajectories of handling tension and coordinating different sub-systems of the self. Additionally, the same findings reveal that there is no shortcut to becoming a psychologist. The process of relating with the professional role was revealed to be non-linear by the changes in the coordination of different sub-systems in the self and the individual's affective orientation in solving professional dilemmas. Once established, relations with the professional role can change over time and are continuously re-shaped.

Regulation of the discrepancy: Moving toward "what should be"

At the very core of accepting the professional role is the process of regulating the gap between "what is" and "what should be." Reducing the discrepancy between "what is" and "what should be" can be considered central to becoming a professional, as one is expected to follow the guidelines of professional practice and meet role-related criteria (e.g., the role requires X > "I should change to be able to do X or be X"). In institutionally organized professional socialization, psychology students are expected to act upon the world in an institutionally prescribed "psychologist's way" (whatever that means) in correspondence with professional role expectations. Thus, "the self is subjected to social expectations and role-prescriptions" (Hermans & Hermans-Konopka, 2010, p. 76). That, in turn, entails the transitional task that individuals encounter when assuming the professional role—to be X while being Y.

Part 2 provides an overview of how the psychology students in the study regulated the gap between their present and future (desired) selves. In general, the students believed that they went through changes. Additionally, the students' reflections pointed to improvements in skills and knowledge (e.g., interaction skills, the ability to understand another person, a changed worldview). They constructed a self-understanding that more closely matched the role expectations.

It can be assumed that these were personally selected features that were, according to each student's personal understanding, considered to be useful, needed transformations that they should undergo. Also, to construct the desired self, the students implemented personal transfer strategies that enabled them to experience the transition inherent in becoming a psychologist. That is, being engaged in certain activities feeds into the impression of development (e.g., listening carefully to other people, improving interaction skills). In general, these activities allowed experiences of advancement, improvement, or development toward the desired state by supporting the formation of (desired) image of the self.

However, if we compare how the students described themselves during the interviews with their responses to the themes from DDTC, we can observe differences. Students' reflections on their changes depict them, in general, as becoming more tolerant, empathetic, interpersonally more competent, yet, the solutions to the dilemmas (in Part 3) reveal that the regulation of different aspects in the self—personal and professional—is a complex, ambivalent condition that elicits tension in the self-system. The dominance of negative tension in solving professional role-related dilemmas indicates that becoming a professional can be an emotionally challenging developmental task.

I-positions are considered to be contextual and are used to deal with any concrete task. The DDTC method offered professional tasks to solve, and thus, it offered concrete professional contexts that made the I-position, I-as-a-professional-in-the-present-moment-of-time, visible. The students' self-descriptions of becoming a psychologist and their regulation of sub-systems in the self in professional situations mostly refer to different versions of "being a psychologist" and to different experiences of internalizing professional identity.

Role-centered and person-centered ways of being a psychologist

The process of internalizing institutional social suggestions—the role expectations of a psychologist—goes through complex pathways to integrate the features of such suggestions into individuals' personal cultures (Valsiner, 2001). Part 3 introduces three general directions of the internalization of the professional role: self-professionalization, self-personalization, and self-maintenance. An analysis revealed that, in seven of the cases, there was a dominance of an increased tendency toward using professional I-position I as professional in the imagined professional context. At the same time, we can also find self-personalizing forms of movement into the profession in which the individual's approach to issues. All these findings lead to a general conclusion—a professional role needs to be accepted personally as part of the complex process of changes in the students' personal cultures.

Others in the self

The principle of dynamic open systems states that psychological phenomena develop through interactions with other systems (Valsiner, 2017; 2021). Professional identity construction is not a solo effort or an achievement accomplished in isolation but is co-constructed in interpersonal interactions (Vygotsky, 1978). In line with the concept of the dialogical self (Hermans, 2001), according to which the self is extended in the sense that it entails others' ideas and thoughts, becoming a psychologist is a process that brings new I-positions and perspectives into inner dialogues that demand, request, suggest new approaches to the events occurring in one's life-world. Regarding others' voices in the self, together with "academic voices" (e.g., academic staff, fellow students), "non-academic voices" frame the formation of professional identity. As can usually be assumed, psychologists are prepared for their professional future in an academic-educational context, but this book reveals that informal relations have a more substantial role in becoming a psychologist than might be expected at first glance. Becoming a psychologist is also rooted in informal relations outside of the formal environment of university studies. Psychologists emerge through informal relations in their everyday lives. As the findings in this book suggest, the directing, suggesting, and controlling voices of friends, family members, and colleagues from various microsystems had parts in the students' inner dialogues. Interactions in informal relations in everyday life were the arenas in which professional identity was negotiated. Others recommended that the students should change (e.g., "You are a psychologist; you should do X"), confirmed their forming I-position (e.g., "You are a psychologist; tell me what to do"), and contested their identity (e.g., "You don't behave like a psychologist > you are not a psychologist or not a 'real' one.") Informal microsystems had a guiding influence on the students' entry into the professional role by organizing their socialization. After arriving at a university, each student's unfolding developmental trajectories are further shaped in academic-educational microsystems in parallel with the continuous impact of informal relations.

It was also found that academic and non-academic environments provide different socialization practices. For the most part, academic communities (e.g., faculty members, fellow students) formed students' self-understanding (e.g., "I am a psychologist") through the feeling of being a member of the same professional group. This was accompanied by defining the "other" (van der Zwet, 2015): "A process of identity formation includes a process of 'othering' by which is meant the establishment of mental boundaries between in- and out-group" (p. 62). It was through the feeling of belonging that the academic settings fostered the I-position I as a psychologist. However, as became explicit in this book, non-academic settings turned into playgrounds in which the acquired professional skills and knowledge were put into practice. The students defined themselves as psychologists in everyday settings, but non-academic others also offered them the position of being experts on human issues. The initial societal invitations to become a psychologist thus appeared in the regulation of inter-individual relations.

Navigating a plurality of meanings

This book posits that one's image of psychologists is central to the context of becoming a psychologist. Representations of psychologists become the basis of the expectations that the students hold about their professional development. For instance, Chapters 4 and 5 both deal in-depth with this issue. The analysis of the case of Gar in Chapter 5 introduces intentional attempts to construct self-understanding that draws from how the student understands what is needed to be a psychologist.

In terms of constructing representations, enrollment in a university is the turning point for students, "the moment of truth," after which they are exposed to social-institutional representations of the institutional concept of the psychologist. At this point, the preconceptions about psychologists that had previously affected the students' choices are about to change. For the students, this is probably their first broad-based exposure to the field, and it can turn into a catalytic event—as a consequence, students' professional choices are reviewed. Some may exit the field, while others may, conversely, discover their passion and calling.

Involvement in multiple microsystems opens access to various cultural meanings attached to psychologists. Due to their membership in multiple communities, the students encounter different, possibly also controversial, images that affect their experiences and their knowledge about psychologists. Educational-institutional representations feed into the formation the of I-position I as a psychologist as "students negotiate their images of themselves as professionals with the images reflected to them by their programs" (Ronfeldt & Grossman, 2008, p. 41). At the same time, their common-sense understanding also has an impact on the students' professional socialization. Falgares, Venza, and Guarnaccia (2017) claim that the "shared images that exist in one social group or society about psychology and the psychologist profession can have significant effects on attitudes toward learning and the interests of learners" (p. 235). They found that inadequate representations and expectations for studying psychology can lead to disappointment, similarly to Lopukhova (2014) who found that "disappointment of the chosen profession and complexity of professional identity" (p. 124) can result in an inadequate psychologist's image.

In general, the process of assuming a professional role is guided by heterogeneous representations.

References

Falgares, G., Venza, G., & Guarnaccia, C. (2017). Learning psychology and becoming psychologists: Developing professional identity through group experiential learning. *Psychology Learning & Teaching*, *16*(2), 232–247. 10.1177/1475725717695148

Hermans, H. J. M. (2001). The dialogical self: Toward a theory of personal and cultural positioning. *Culture Psychology*, *7*(3), 243–281. 10.1177/1354067X0173001

Hermans, H. J. M., & Hermans-Konopka, A. (2010). *Dialogical Self Theory: Positioning and Counter-Positioning in a Globalizing Society*. New York, NY: Cambridge University Press. doi.org/10.1075/ld.2.3.10vit

Lopukhova, G. O. (2014). Dynamics of psychology students' "image of a psychologist" conception during education. *Procedia – Social and Behavioral Sciences*, *159*, 120–124.

Ronfeldt, M., & Grossman, P. (2008). Becoming a professional: Experimenting with possible selves in professional preparation. *Teacher Education Quarterly*, *35*(3), 41–60.

Salvatore, S., & Valsiner, J. (2006). Editorial introduction. "Am I really a psychologist?". *European Journal of School Psychology*, *4*(2), 127–149.

Valsiner, J. (2001). *Comparative Study of Human Cultural Development*. Madrid, Spain: Fund. Infancia y Aprendizaje.

Valsiner, J. (2017). Focus of cultural psychology: Culture within persons. In M. Raudsepp (Ed.), *Between Self and Societies: Creating Psychology in a New Key*.Tallinn, Estonia: Tallinn University Press.

Valsiner J. (2021). *Phenomenology of the Psyche and Semiotic Foundations for Human Psychology. General Human Psychology*. Denmark: Springer Cham. https://doi.org/10.1007/978-3-030-75851-6

van der Zwet, A. (2015). Operationalising national identity: The cases of the Scottish National Party and Frisian National Party. *Nations and Nationalism*, *21*(1), 62–82. 10.1111/nana.12091 https://onlinelibrary.wiley.com/doi/full/10.1111/nana.12091

Vygotsky, L. S. (1978). The development of higher psychological processes. In M. Cole, V. John-Steiner, S. Scribner, & E. Souberman (Eds.), *Mind in Society*. US: Harvard University Press.

Concluding thoughts:
The future in construction

The relevant question to pose at the end of this endeavor is "What next?" This book examines the period of undergraduate studies of psychology—what can be inferred about this period of professional preparation? As to the implications of this research for educational activities, providing specific recommendations for students' entry into a professional role would be a heroic project to carry out. Making recommendations is difficult because institutional-educational settings are distinct in respect to local sub-cultures and the requirements and regulations for organizing learning activities in each university. Instead, some of the general and preliminary ideas will be highlighted below for further elaboration and testing in different contexts.

The findings presented in this book support the idea that training programs may benefit from a structure that, in general terms, facilitates and supports the students' professional transition by enabling activities that guide students' attention to the possible impact of interpersonal relations in academic and non-academic settings. These programs would additionally illuminate the involvement of heterogenous environments of representations in internalizing the professional role and increase awareness about the complex coordination of different I-positions in the self. As this book reveals, it may be challenging to navigate the multiplicity of voices in the self, the students may hold unrealistic and contradictory images of psychologists and receive feedback from (non-academic) others regarding the role of a psychologist that has an impact on how students construe their professional development.

Identity is a social phenomenon built through interactions with others (Wenger, 1998) and is shaped and re-shaped in various social encounters in different communities (Ibarra, 1999). As we have seen throughout this book, interactions in academic contexts enable a feeling of belonging, and socializing with fellow students seems to be a crucial factor in articulating professional identity. I take a position that by supporting the formation of environments where sharing experiences with the professional community is

DOI: 10.4324/9781315519616-15

made available to students the educational institutions can scaffold students' professional transition. The topic is especially interesting to reflect upon in the context of the increasing trend of providing online learning programs that may lessen substantial contact or socialization with other fellow students and faculty members.

Another relevant theme I would like to reflect on concerns the students' personal representations of psychologists. This book reveals that the students' depictions of psychologists shape their professional choices, guide their professional identity construction, and regulate their relations with the role. Their involvement in dynamics of professional socialization is quite evident; students' understandings about the profession are the factors that cannot be disregarded. Unrealistic representations can lead to inadequate expectations for personal development and their professional future in general. The question is especially relevant in the beginning of studies when students have limited knowledge about their field. Their pre-concepts of the profession are likely to be influenced by stereotypes and a common understanding represented in everyday discourse and in the media. Considering this, increasing the students' awareness of the impact of personal representations to their professional development, and the contradictions of personal images of psychologists with academic-educational representations enables them an additional perspective to their development when they assume the role.

Further, psychologists are humans, a declaration that may sound trivial. They are not a special kind of people; they are simply individuals with their own unique personal culture who navigate institutionally established expectations according to which they regulate different aspects of the self. Thus, contradictions in the self are unavoidable. Broadly translated, it can become a challenge to coordinate different parts in the self, the issue to be addressed during the formal studies through different developing activities. However, it has been suggested (Hermans & Hermans-Konopka, 2010) that facilitating dialogue between the different self-systems that would lead to the construction of new positions can reconcile conflicting I-positions and enable the synthesis of new perspectives to solve the conflict between the personal I-position and professional expectations.

As noted above, specific guidelines on how to address these issues in particular educational contexts are not introduced in this book. Instead, this book invites readers to think beyond these findings. However, raising awareness of the challenges of a highly complex developmental process is the first necessary step toward providing an environment for professionals-to-be in their professional journeys. Future (longitudinal) studies might enrich our understanding by exploring in-depth coordination of different sub-systems in the self when professionals-to-be have the initial experiences in operating in the professional settings. Furthermore, exploration of the regulation of tension between role expectations and pleromatic, and schematic side of identity can provide an additional insight into the complexity of professional socialization. Our horizon in the field can be also widened by examining the construction of professional identity along the inter-personal and societal dimensions. Becoming a professional unfolds through various socio-cultural surroundings and studies on how specific microsystems shape the meaning-making are fruitful sources for gaining complementing knowledge about the topic. In regard to the macrolevel events and processes, societies are institutionally coordinated systems that guide persons' development by setting up frames like the internalization of social roles, which feeds into the differentiation of the self. In terms of this, one of the avenues for future research is the topic of social-collective representations of professions circulating in society. Common-sense understanding about a psychologist, images of them shared in everyday interactions are in dialogue with students' personal representations of the profession and with their personal culture guiding professionals-to-be through the ambiguity of professional roles.

To conclude, although this book illuminates many aspects of the process of becoming a professional, we still have a limited understanding of professional identity construction, and there are pending issues to be solved. This is understandable, as the construction of identity is a multilayered developmental phenomenon that can be analyzed at different levels of functioning. Although this book centers on microlevel processes, interpersonal dynamics and macrolevel processes form an inherent part of becoming a psychologist or any other professional, and together with intra-psychological events, compose an interrelated system that organizes individuals' socialization. How interactions between the different levels coordinate the persons' development is continuously the research subject to be explored in the future.

Finally, there are numerous ways to approach the internalization of a professional role, and different conceptual frameworks are available to investigate this complex process. This book has introduced cultural psychology as a fruitful theoretical framework that invites one to reflect on becoming as a semiotic and dialogical process. With a strong focus on developmental processes, cultural psychology provides a theoretical tool to explore the emergence of psychological transformation resulting from transactions between individuals and their surroundings.

References

Hermans, H., & Hermans-Konopka, A. (2010). *Dialogical self theory: Positioning and counter-positioning in a globalizing society*. New York: Cambridge University Press.

Ibarra, H. (1999). Provisional selves: Experimenting with image and identity in professional adaptation. *Administrative Science Quarterly*, *44*(4), 764–791. 10.2307/2667055

Wenger, E. (1998). *Communities of Practice: Learning, Meaning, and Identity*. Cambridge University Press. 10.1017/CBO9780511803932

Appendix

The dilemmas from DDTC

Dilemma 1. Providing confidential information to third parties. "When a psychologist has a dilemma whether to give out information on his/her patient, then s/he feels _____ because _____."

Dilemma 2. Disliked client. "When a psychologist does not like his/her client (s)he feels _____ because _____."

Dilemma 3. An attractive patient. "When an attractive person (of the opposite sex) comes in for a session, then psychologist feels _____ because _____."

Dilemma 4. Unable to help. "When a psychologist understands that s/he is unable to help his/her client, s/he feels _____ because _____."

Dilemma 5. Close relations. "When a psychologist is to consult a person s/he has a close connection with, s/he feels _____ because _____."

Dilemma 6. Common acquaintance. "When a person whose problems involve people close to the psychologist comes in for an appointment, the psychologist feels _____ because _____."

Dilemma 7. Inability to keep the distance. "When the psychologist feels that s/he cannot distance him-/herself from the patient's problems, s/he feels _____ because _____."

Dilemma 8. Different values. "When a person whose values differ greatly from those of the psychologist comes in for an appointment, the psychologist feels _____ because _____."

Dilemma 9. Encountering a person in crisis after working hours. "When a psychologist meets a person in crisis outside of working hours, s/he feels _____ because _____."

Index

abductive interference 32
academic environment 49, 52, 54–9
affective orientations 42, 73, 192, 197, 204
ambivalence 19, 25, 37–40

becoming a psychologist 3, 4, 5, 7, 8, 9, 10, 15–6, 18, 20, 27, 45, 53, 59, 71–2, 193, 204–07
borders 52, 53, 55, 56, 58, 63
Bronfenbrenner's ecological theory 49

chronosystem 49–50
co-genetic logic 53
construction of professional identity 8, 10, 20, 24, 28, 62, 203
constructivist perspective 45
cultural material 14–5, 20, 50, 61, 65
cultural psychology 4, 14, 31–3, 43, 61, 211

developmental direction 72, 192
developmental trajectories 72–3, 197
dialogical self 4, 22–3, 27, 45, 206
dilemmas 40–2
Double Direction Theme Completion (DDTC) 35, 37–40, 72–3, 192

ecological perspective 49
equifinality 32; equifinality point 190
essays 36
exosystem 49–50
externalization 4, 16, 62, 193

fluctuation of perspectives 40

hierarchy of signs 19, 66
historically structured sampling 32–3

hypergeneralized affective semiotic fields 18

I-position 4, 22, 23, 24, 40, 41, 42
I-position I as a person 40, 54–9
I-position I as a psychologist 40, 53, 54–9
identity 8, 45, 59, 210
idiographic paradigm 32
image of psychologist 36–7, 63–4, 207, 209, 210
internalization 4, 16, 20, 26, 28, 62, 192
interview 35
intra-psychological level 22

laminal model 4, 16–7

macrosystem 49–50
meaning complexes 15, 66
meaning system 16
meaning-making 14, 18, 19, 22, 32, 62, 63, 211
mesosystem 49–50
microgenetic processes 24, 26, 28
microsystem 49–50, 58–9
multiple case-study 32

non-academic environment 49, 51, 55–6
non-academic voice 50–1
non-linear process 28; trajectory 28; transition 26

obligatory passage points 32
orientation of tension 42; positively and negatively oriented affectivity 42; neutral state 42

personal culture 15–6

personal meaning 16, 36, 40, 65
personal perspective 40, 75, 76, 85, 86, 89, 90, 91, 94
personal representations 4, 35, 61, 66
pleromatic side of identity 19–22
pleromatization 16, 18, 19
pleromatization of identity 20
professional approach 40, 76, 79, 94, 113, 144, 146, 149–50, 193
professional identity 3–5, 8–10, 14–5, 18, 22, 25, 32, 45, 59, 203, 205–06, 210–11
professional role 4–7, 10, 15, 19, 20–2, 25–6, 28, 32, 50–1, 53, 55, 59, 71, 192–93, 196
professional socialization 8, 10, 20, 22, 50, 205, 207, 210–1
psychologist 6, 8, 204–06, 208, 209, 211

questionnaire 35

rating scales 36
role expectations 6, 20, 21, 28, 37, 38, 71, 192, 193, 203, 204, 205, 210

sample 33
schematic side of identity 19–21
schematization of identity 21
schematization 16, 18–9
self-maintaining case 41–2, 72–3, 156
self-personalizing case 41, 72–3, 137
self-professionalizing case 41, 73–4
semiosis 18–9, 27
semiotic autoregulation 18
semiotic border 53
semiotic control system 27
semiotic devices 15
semiotic mediating system 14
Semiotic mediation 14, 18
semiotic regulation 19
Semiotic-dialogical approach 45, 71
Semiotic–dialogical perspective 14, 23
sign 14–6, 18–9, 45, 59, 66; field like signs 18; pleromatic sign 18; point like signs 18
social representations 4, 15, 20, 27, 37, 45, 61, 66
sub-systems of the self 4, 23, 25

tension 21, 23, 24, 26, 27, 38, 40, 42
trajectories 190
Trajectory and Equifinality Model 32
transfer strategies 64